Democratic Disunity

Lexington Studies in Political Communication

Series Editor: Robert E. Denton, Jr., Virginia Tech University

This series encourages focused work examining the role and function of communication in the realm of politics including campaigns and elections, media, and political institutions.

Recent Titles in This Series

Democratic Disunity: Rhetorical Tribalism in 2020 by Colleen Elizabeth Kelley

Third Parties, Outsiders, and Renegades: Modern Challenges to the Two-Party System in Presidential Elections by Melissa M. Smith

Studies of Communication in the 2020 Presidential Campaign edited by Robert E. Denton, Jr.

Horror Framing and the General Election: Ghosts and Ghouls in Twenty-First Century Presidential Campaign Advertisements by Fielding Montgomery

Political Rhetoric, Social Media, and American Presidential Campaigns: Presidential Candidates' Use of New Media by Janet Johnson

The Rhetoric of the American Political Party Conventions, 1948–2016 by Theodore F. Sheckels

President Trump and the News Media: Moral Foundations, Framing, and the Nature of Press Bias in America by Jim A. Kuypers

Media Relations and the Modern First Lady: From Jacqueline Kennedy to Melania Trump edited by Lisa M. Burns

Alternative Media Meets Mainstream Politics: Activist Nation Rising edited by Joshua D. Atkinson and Linda Kenix

Political Humor in a Changing Media Landscape: A New Generation of Research edited by Jody C Baumgartner and Amy Becker

Democratic Disunity

Rhetorical Tribalism in 2020

Colleen Elizabeth Kelley

LEXINGTON BOOKS
Lanham • Boulder • New York • London

Published by Lexington Books
An imprint of The Rowman & Littlefield Publishing Group, Inc.
4501 Forbes Boulevard, Suite 200, Lanham, Maryland 20706
www.rowman.com

86-90 Paul Street, London EC2A 4NE

Copyright © 2022 by The Rowman & Littlefield Publishing Group, Inc.

All rights reserved. No part of this book may be reproduced in any form or by any electronic or mechanical means, including information storage and retrieval systems, without written permission from the publisher, except by a reviewer who may quote passages in a review.

British Library Cataloguing in Publication Information Available

Library of Congress Cataloging-in-Publication Data

Names: Kelley, Colleen Elizabeth, author.
  Title: Democratic disunity : rhetorical tribalism in 2020 / Colleen
    Elizabeth Kelley.
  Description: Lanham : Lexington Books, [2022] | Series: Lexington studies
    in political communication | Includes bibliographical references and
    index.
  Identifiers: LCCN 2021042673 (print) | LCCN 2021042674 (ebook) | ISBN
    9781793639851 (cloth) | ISBN 9781793639868 (ebook)
  Subjects: LCSH: Democratic Party (U.S.)--History--21st century. |
    Rhetoric--Political aspects--United States--History--21st century. |
    Communication in politics--United States--History--21st century. |
    Political parties--United States--History--21st century. | United
    States--Politics and government--21st century.
  Classification: LCC JK2316 .K38 2021 (print) | LCC
    JK2316 (ebook) | DDC
    324.2736--dc23
  LC record available at https://lccn.loc.gov/2021042673
  LC ebook record available at https://lccn.loc.gov/2021042674

∞™ The paper used in this publication meets the minimum requirements of American National Standard for Information Sciences—Permanence of Paper for Printed Library Materials, ANSI/NISO Z39.48-1992.

To my brother and sister-in-law
John Marvin Kelley and Janet Fager Kelley

Contents

Preface	ix
Introduction	1
Chapter 1: Democratic Intraparty Tribalism	7
Chapter 2: Rhetorical Tribalism	21
Chapter 3: American Rhetorical Tribes	35
Chapter 4: Congressional Tribalism	51
Chapter 5: Mediated Tribalism	67
Chapter 6: Caucuses, Primaries, and Convention	83
Chapter 7: The Election	105
Chapter 8: The Legacy of Intraparty Tribalism	121
Chapter 9: Tribalism as a Rhetorical Form	137
Conclusion	155
Bibliography	165
Index	217
About the Author	227

Preface

My Dad was a life-long Republican, my Mom a life-long Democrat. Each stood comfortably within their respective political parties while standing together through a sixty-year marriage. Perhaps not surprisingly, I knocked on doors in support of my first presidential candidate at 18, three years before I could legally vote. By the time I voted in my second presidential election, I was well into my graduate studies and by the time I voted in my third, I had begun my academic life in rhetorical theory and criticism. It has been suggested that since certain moral tenets have long been constitutive elements of the discipline, those imperatives become a rhetorical scholar's responsibility as well. Foremost among these is the pragmatic and necessary relationship between rhetoric, civility, power, and politics. Accordingly, *Democratic Disunity: Rhetorical Tribalism in 2020* emerges from the confluence of my life as an engaged and curious participant in the longest democratic experiment in the world, as well as a dedicated and curious academic studying one of the world's oldest disciplines, upon which the well-being of that experiment depends.

Collaborative support has always been instrumental in my writing and research, rather pen to paper or hand to keyboard. Such encouragement has also been essential at all stages of this project, from momentary and occasionally lengthy conversations to perception checking of ideas or constructs or writing style to spontaneous moments of simple and appreciated words of encouragement. In particular, I wish to acknowledge four individuals. First, colleagues Rod Troester and Eric Corty have unconditionally supported this project from its inception. Dr. Troester, who joined the communication faculty only a year after I did, has been steadfast in his friendship, exceptional in his scholarship, and, to my point, championed my research then and now. Dr. Corty has acted on my behalf as well, as an administrator, when possible, in decidedly lean times and, more importantly, also as a friend. In addition, former colleague and forever friend Miriam McMullen-Pastrick continues to share empathy and enthusiasm, attributes which endeared her to students. I consider myself most fortunate to be in Dr. Miriam's orbit. Lastly, I wish to acknowledge Michael J. Miller's professional expertise and unwavering patience in reading first drafts and indexing of *Democratic Division: Rhetorical Tribalism in 2020*. Again, Professor Miller's enduring friendship informed my writing throughout.

Finally, I wish to acknowledge my son John-Daniel Kelley, who even as a small child rarely hesitated to ask, "How's the book going Mom?" Even now, as an adult embarking on his own career track, J-D still asks the same question. In sum, I am indebted to friends and colleagues and family for collectively sharing their time, expertise, and ethos of caring.

Introduction

The intratribal hostility, which by 2020 was impacting both major American political parties, albeit in different ways and with different outcomes, was anticipated four years earlier. During the 2016 presidential campaign, Bernie Sanders and Donald Trump each became the others' rhetorical reflection, albeit from opposite extremes of the American political continuum. Both rhetorically mirrored an anti-establishment, populist ethos that drove a juggernaut of voter anger toward an "elite" political mainstream (Madden 2015; Le Miere 2017; Epstein and Karni 2020). Lepore (2016) configured both the Trump and Sanders campaigns as populist intertribal assaults, unique at the time, in that the attacks were against their own parties (see also Gutmann and Thompson 2010; Tuttle 2017).

A central premise of *Democratic Disunity: Rhetorical Tribalism in 2020* is that while considerable attention has recently and rightly been paid to the tribal bifurcation of the GOP, the Democratic Party is similarly divided. An additional theme is that, because Americans live in a democratic republic rather than a direct democracy, governing concerns are chiefly configured through communicative action. In this view, "making a democracy work" is contingent on "how it is lived," a challenge best met by pragmatically deconstructing the communication practices that inform an electorate's understanding and choosing the "messy business of a democracy's rhetoric" (Hauser 2004, 3). These choices include those made between and within American political parties. Accordingly, the final premise of *Democratic Disunity* is that, without rhetorical mediation and intervention, toxic partisan tribalism within the two major American political parties is likely to destabilize the nation's federalist system of government. While not an immediate threat, systems similar to that of the United States have recently flipped from liberal to illiberal democracies, in part due to the weight of hyper-partisan tribalism (Pedersen 2012; see also Zakaria 1997).

METHOD

Symbolic Interaction

For the purpose of this study, reality is considered a construct of communication; what one knows and thinks and speaks is shaped and framed by symbolic interaction (Pedersen 2012; Schutz 1970; and Watzlawik 1967). Rhetoric is understood through Kenneth Burke's perspective of language as a symbolic means of "inducing cooperation in beings that by nature respond to symbols" (1969, 43). A framework is suggested within which reality is represented through as well as constructed by symbolic interaction, the paradigm example being discourse or language-in-action.

Burke emphasized that humans respond to the events of life through language, with which they also coordinate and construct their own lives as well as their interactions with others. Rhetorical discourse, then, creates and sustains the common arguments and narratives with which societies organize into cooperative action. An essential component of this framework is that such cooperation (persuasion) occurs when one individual identifies with another through "talking their language by speech, gesture, tonality, order, image, attitude [and] idea" (1969, 5). Specifically, this standpoint configures symbols as simultaneously reflecting and creating the realities of both source and receiver (Cooper 1989).

The Rhetorical Situation

Bitzer (1968) suggests rhetoric is pragmatic and "comes into existence for the sake of something beyond itself" ultimately to "produce action or change the world." Accordingly:

> Rhetoric is a mode of altering reality, not by the direct application of energy to objects, but by the creation of discourse which changes reality through the mediation of thought and action. The rhetor alters reality by bringing into existence a discourse of such a character that the audience, in thought and action, is so engaged that it becomes mediator of change. (3–4)

Rhetorical discourse, then, exists as a response to a situation, often a question or problem. Bitzer contends there are three constituents of a rhetorical situation that, together, provoke or call forth rhetorical discourse. The first is an exigence, "an imperfection marked by urgency," something that is "other than it should be," the management of which "requires discourse or can be assisted by discourse." The second required constituent of Bitzer's rhetorical situation is the audience, "persons who function as mediators of change" and "are capable of being influenced by discourse and of being mediators of change" even when an individual engages "self or 'ideal mind'" as audience. "Constraints," the final component, are situational elements that regulate the actions needed to address the exigence, including beliefs, facts, traditions and motives" (Bitzer 1968, 7–8).

Consequently, rhetorical exigences emerge naturally in a world in which humans communicatively interact. Most are addressed, some more mindfully than others. In brief, just as scientific inquiry is "called forth" by a physical world that presents "objects to be known" and "complexities to be understood" (Bitzer 1968, 13–14), within that same physical space and in similar fashion, problems consistently emerge as rhetorical situations, the result of humans interacting with other humans, the majority of which necessitate interventions in the form of strategic discourse. Clearly, some of these situations are rhetorically addressed more efficaciously than others. This premise informs the discussion of intraparty tribalism within the major American political parties, specifically with regard to distinct rhetorical responses to such discourse as it emerged in both.

RHETORIC AND DEMOCRACY

Contemporary democratic public discourse is differentiated from messages addressed to a general audience. As such, it is a meaningful symbolic exchange that brackets its subject matter as a shared concern of a discrete community, specifically a pluralistic representative democracy (Reid and Klumpp 2005; see also Sillars and Gronbeck 2001; and Zompetti 2018).

Delivery System of Democracy

Democracy originated twenty-five centuries ago as system of self-governance in which all who were recognized as citizens were equal and participated by directly casting votes according to decisions based on well-constructed arguments. Historically, the practice and study of rhetoric had "never known a more friendly environment," since a lack of unitary authority within Greek city-states at the time mandated decision making through consensus, resulting in the invention of democracy. Significantly, rhetoric flourished as essential for enacting, validating, and administering this unprecedented system, vested in citizens and performed by them directly or through freely elected representatives (Bilansky 1999). In Hauser's (2004) view, this original form of democracy was, and to some extent still remains, a "utopian ideal" of a state governed by deliberation in which an electorate is guided by reason and the "better angels of the human spirit." It follows that neither democracy nor the "delivery" system for that form of government, rhetoric, are "entirely rational" nor do humans always follow the advice of their "better angels." From this perspective, twenty-first century rhetorical democracies, including that of the United States, are as vulnerable to manipulation for personal gain "under the guise of the common good" as any of their Athenian predecessors.

Democracy—then and now—is "at best, a reflection of the culture in which it is situated, and still carries the price of permitting the wise and the foolish their say" (Hauser 2004, 1). While acknowledging the "legitimating force" of an electorate's voice "expresses the fundamental principle of a democracy," it nonetheless also delineates what constitutes political power. It follows that rhetorical analysis examines how symbols are combined to achieve identification between a source and receiver. As the case in point, ideologies internal to discrete American political parties become coherent worldviews through which events are interpreted, power is justified, and actions managed.

Ideologies as Rhetorical Constructs

A particular ideology, itself a rhetorical creation, provides criteria for assessing "good," "bad," "right," and "wrong" for those sharing in and so persuaded by its substance. Such an ideology also functions as a discursive defense to shield and bolster the attitudes, beliefs, values, and mythologies internalized by members of the rhetorical community or faction sharing its vision. It follows that such rhetorical inventions, are pertinent to understanding the different etiologies and enactments of democratic intraparty tribalism. Those united by sharing in the substance of such ideologies will invariably and with varying levels of commitment accept them as accurate representations of the "way the world works," as rhetorically configured by the source (Cooper 1989). More important for this study, those not identifying with the vision will generally find fault with its substance and so also respond accordingly, rhetorically taking issue and pushing back. The degree to which this occurs depends on a community's (or political party's) degree of commitment to the fundamental arguments and conclusions as discursively created by the source (or leadership). Within a rhetorical democracy then, such symbolic behavior could be anticipated and expected and, preferably if not idealistically, responded to in kind: through civic, civil, and effective deliberative dialogue, a signature rhetorical behavior.

Kenneth Burke centered rhetoric as the primary mechanism of organizing citizens into cooperative action, including that of democratic party politics. In addition, the study of rhetorical discourse was configured as foregrounding humans' language use an "equipment for living" as well as mechanism for identification and its antithesis division (1969, 43; see also Reid and Klumpp 2005, 2–3). Such rhetorical behavior is an innate attribute and so the chief means of provoking and reinforcing as well as disintegrating tribal alliances, albeit to different ends. This text situates American intraparty tribalism as rhetorical in invention, content, delivery, and intervention.

SCOPE

Democratic Disunity: Rhetorical Tribalism in 2020 initially positions intraparty tribalism, in particular its variation as extreme polarization, as an emerging and disruptive discourse within the contemporary Democratic Party. The Republican Party's "eradication by capitulation" response to their own version of such dysfunctional tribalism is also discussed. The next segment of the text investigates language-in-use speech acts that inform tribalism. Rhetorical constructs including identification and division as well as feminist principles such as equality, immanent value, and self-determination are also considered. Ideological fractures specific to the Democratic Party are then reviewed. Identity politics and the United States as a distinctly politically tribalized nation are also considered. Specifically, disputes over the nation's global persona and, notably, over the meaning of being American are spotlighted as paradigms of this polarization. The latter is considered as a defining exigence for the United States.

Then, conflict between congressional members within the same party, including "primarying" are considered as antecedents to tribalism. The rise of the Tea Party Republicans in 2010 as well as the emergence of progressive Democrats in 2016 are suggested as contributing factors to tribalistic division as it has essentially embedded within American political culture. The influence of mass media on foundational principles of democracy, including trust, informed dialogue, and a shared sense of reality, is next assessed. Technologically driven social media, because of attributes including time and space compression and the monetizing of public attention, is examined as the primary source of disinformation and so a significant contributing factor to the rise of dysfunctional tribalism within American political parties.

Unique Democratic intraparty divisions that appeared or accelerated during the 2020 election cycle are deconstructed within the next segment of the text. In addition, entrenched tribalism within the Republican Party, which had fully presented by the end of that election cycle, is suggested as an allegory for the future of the Democratic Party. Then the initial division between moderate and progressive Democrats is examined as a chasm which, by 2020, had widened exponentially into a partisan tribal binary. The elevation of Joe Biden and Kamala Harris to the top of the 2020 Democratic ticket is then reviewed. Although both survived to win the presidency, by January 2021, intraparty tribalism was organic within both the Republican and Democratic parties, mutating into a monolithic structure in the former and presenting as divisively viral in the other.

In sum, *Democratic Disunity: Rhetorical Tribalism in 2020* recognizes that intraparty tribalism poisons public life and consumes public space within which electoral politics, including discussion, deliberation, and compromise, should be thriving. Principally, toxic intratribal partisanship undermines if not entirely eradicates the potential for such crucial communication events to occur between American political parties. Without intervention, the rhetorical elements organic to and essential for representative democratic governing to exist, let alone function, wither to partisan and unproductive and quite possibly undemocratic governing systems. The book concludes speculatively, suggesting the consideration of intraparty tribalism as a rhetorical form, uniquely positioned within the twenty-first century. To that end, *Democratic Disunity: Rhetorical Tribalism in 2020* details pragmatic language-in-use strategies with which to rhetorically disrupt intraparty tribalism. In so doing, a shared community agency may emerge that empowers American political actors, electorate and elected, to redirect or, at a minimum, slant their public discourse in the direction of democracy rather than intimidation-into-silence.

Chapter 1

Democratic Intraparty Tribalism

The emergence of strong populist insurgencies in 2016 in both the Democratic and Republican Parties suggested that constituencies might be joined to create a genuine cross-party populist alliance. Common attributes included that Bernie Sanders and Donald Trump identified with Americans at the middle and bottom of the economic ladder, rejected super PACS, and insisted politicians "inside the Beltway" had "sold out" to corporate interests. At one point, during an interview, when Donald Trump was asked to identify what candidate fit the description of a "populist outsider" who was "tapping into the anger of voters" and drew "thousands of people at his rallies," he responded, "you're describing Donald Trump." The MSNBC reporter responded that the comments were about Bernie Sanders (Goins-Phillips 2016).

TRANSFORMATIONAL POLITICAL PARTIES

The Consent of the Governed

The Constitution was initially configured as a national government system within which parties could not easily develop. Embedded in this plan was the possibility that polarized populist-driven factions within each cohort could develop egregious breaches which became unmanageable for future governments (Horger 2013). This was a major concern of James Madison, articulated in Federalist #10, when he wrote:

> Among the numerous advantages promised by a well-constructed Union, none deserves to be more accurately developed than its tendency to break and control the violence of faction. (cited in Hamilton et al. 1787, 2014, 41)

Madison and his eighteenth-century colleagues were anchored in the notion that if a partisan majority ever controlled the federal government of the United States, it could wield power to assume control of that government.

In such circumstances, the consent of the governed would likely fragment with a real likelihood that authoritarianism could replace the already compromised democracy. Madison referred to impetuous mobs as factions, which he defined in Federalist #10 as a group "united and actuated by some common impulse of passion, or of interest, adversed to the rights of other citizens, or to the permanent and aggregate interests of the community." He envisioned a government enacted by a select group of enlightened citizens, so that the nation matured as a constitutionally driven representative republic rather than a direct democracy. As a result, elected and select leaders would be well versed in such concerns and so the essentials required for a healthy democracy would necessarily prevail. Such a system was further encouraged by a series of strategic stop-gap measures embedded within the Constitution, both to inhibit the formulation of mob majority rule and, conversely, to ensure that reasonable majorities would prevail in the emerging American system of government (Hamilton et al. 1787; 2014, 41–47; Rosen 2018a).

Eighteenth century founders including George Washington and John Adams as well as Madison were well aware of past failed republics that collapsed into civil wars. As such, they were mindful that the new republic as they imagined it must not follow such trajectories. In so doing, from this standpoint, the combination of "a large diverse republic with a separation of powers" as well as the hyper-partisanship that felled earlier republics would likely be averted. Or not.

Modern Mass Democracy

Less than a century later, political parties had coalesced in response to "modern mass democracy" to such an extent that the institutional constraints in which Madison and others had faith collapsed what remained of the republic's diversity into "just two camps" (Drutman 2020). The Democratic Party and the Republican Party have won every presidential election in the United States since 1852 and have controlled Congress since at least 1856. Furthermore, since the mid-twentieth century, Democrats have moved center-left as the "liberal party" while Republicans reciprocated by moving center-right into the "conservative party," both solidifying around central ideological beliefs while jointly rejecting the idea of consensus.

To illustrate, by the 1960s, conservatives argued against expanded government while liberals protested against what they viewed as "hegemonic liberalism." Within the next decade, the "left" and "right" had begun to function as rhetorical devices through which to express disagreement with others on what previously might have seemed to be "their own side of things." By the 2000s, a binary-dominant American political party system had crystallized into polarized opposites, rigidly defined as "right" and "left," united against each other through a perverse shared ideology that the "middle—the establishment, the powers that be"—was "messing things up and not doing a good job" (Carlisle 2019). As a result, both parties ironically and jointly agreed to reject "compromise" as a reasoning conduit to joint governing.

Since the 2010 "Tea Party midterms," both Republican and Democratic constituencies have overlapped enough to yet sustain the sort of "bargaining and coalition building natural to multiparty democracy." However, such an outcome seems unlikely and, probably unsustainable as the nation's two-party system, while centuries old, is "breaking the system of government the Founders put in place in the Constitution." In brief, there are "just two parties and that's it" (Drutman 2020).

By the 2020 election cycle, both American political parties had essentially gone to ground, tracking laws, norms, and customs not delineated in the Constitution. Voter-centric, populist-driven campaigns have become discursively prioritized so that "winning" is the raison d'état for running, often at the expense of historical election protocols and precedents put in place with the Constitution. It is this exigence to which tribalism has responded in American politics, particularly its manifestation as virulent polarization or illiberal partisanship, both between and within the dominant parties.

CROSS-PARTY AFFILIATION

Both Bernie Sanders and Donald Trump mastered tapping into an anti-elite political mindset. Constituents in the bases of both shared anti-establishment attitudes that in turn motivated them to fully embrace an "outside the Beltway" ethos of their respective candidates. Intraparty division, compounded by the animosity of emergent populist wings toward their respective establishments, undermined the underlying premise of the presidential nomination process: that internal factions compete in caucuses and primaries until a winner emerges, at which time losers, after a period of reflection, would return to their parties.

There was speculation in 2016 about what might happen if either Sanders or Trump failed to win their respective nominations and whether or not their supporters would fall in line, stay home, or even vote for the opposition (Kelley 2018). Such levels of intraparty polarization had not been seen since Barry Goldwater's challenge to Nelson Rockefeller in 1964 or George McGovern's to Hubert Humphrey in 1972. Large defeats for both Goldwater and McGovern resulted in profound changes in both party's ideological appeals and geographic bases of support. Republicans realigned to emerge based in the South with dominant narratives targeting civil, women's, gay, and reproductive rights movements as adversaries. Conversely, Democrats moved to the left until mainstream Americans assimilated their rhetorically compelling narratives (Edsall 2019b).

Parallel Rhetorical Styles of Political Rhetoric

Mason (2018) configures this shared discursive frame and the presidency situated within in as so compelling that it became the catalyst for a contemporary and fully entrenched polarization shared between American political parties dominated by voters mobilized at ideological poles against the center (Teles and Saldin 2021). McClosky and Chong (1995) suggest that, while the conventional view holds that the "radical left and the radical right" belong at opposite ends of the American liberal-to-conservative continuum, they resemble each other so closely that it is misleading to classify them at opposite poles. While some argue that authoritarianism is characteristic only of the right and not the left, there are parallels in each cohort's style of political engagement. As a case in point, while both adhere to different strategies through which to persuade their constituents, both are "estranged from certain features of American society" and "highly critical of what they perceive as the spiritual and moral degeneration of American institutions" (329–30).

To that end, each faction configures American society as dominated by "conspiratorial forces" that work to defeat their respective ideologies. This mutual alienation is further intensified by the "zealous and unyielding" manner in which each enact their respective beliefs. Both factions also demonstrate inflexible psychological and political styles informed by a joint vision of social political life as a distinct conflict between "us" and "them," a "struggle between good and evil "played out on a [shared] battleground where compromise amounts to capitulation and the goal is total victory" (McClosky and Chong 61; Thiessen 2019).

Each rely on parallel rhetorical strategies to achieve their political goals. These include censoring opponents, dealing harshly with "enemies," and sacrificing the well-being of "even the innocent in order to serve" their group's "higher purpose." Both will also, on occasion, support or oppose civil liberties in a "highly partisan and self-serving" manner "supporting freedom for themselves and for the groups and causes they favor while seeking to withhold it from enemies and advocates of causes they dislike" (McClosky and Chon 1995, 361). The 2016 presidential campaign revealed two distinct political tribes that found common ground by uniting against the center. The campaign also foreshadowed the splitting of each political party into distinct, mutually antagonistic factions. Within a "permanent campaign" environment, these divisions were rapidly internalized, their rhetoric of intraparty discord normalized through partisan isolation. By 2020, suppression of dissent rather than cooperation and compromise necessary to sustain American democracy had become default responses to disagreements between and within American political parties (Mason 2018; Masket 2016). As a case in point, the Republican Party ruptured so severely that one faction absorbed the other into invisibility. The Democratic Party remains vulnerable to a similar outcome at some point if conflict within their ranks remains configured as something to oppress rather than about which to deliberate.

THE POST-2016 DEMOCRATIC PARTY

By 2019 about half of Democratic and Democratic-leaning registered voters (47 percent) described their own political views as liberal, including 15 percent who reported their views as very liberal, according to an average of Pew Research Center political surveys. The share of Democratic voters who describe their political views as liberal has changed little over the past few years after increasing steadily between 2000 and 2016. While liberals outnumber moderates (38 percent) and conservatives (14 percent) as a share of Democratic voters, when combined, conservatives and moderates continue to make up about half of Democratic voters (51 percent) (Daniller and Gilberstadt 2020). This contingent of Democrats who successfully consolidated as spoilers for their own party's candidate in 2016 has rhetorically and dramatically evolved into the post-2016 Democratic "progressive left."

In doing so, they also strategically united in their division from other Democrats, particularly those configured as "moderates" (see Scott 2019a; Lerer 2019; Wagner 2019b). Essentially a closed culture, this cohort includes a portion of Democrats, who in the Bill Clinton or Barack Obama eras, might have endorsed a campaign platform of compromise or moderation as integral to American political well-being. However, in its current incarnation this political culture manifests a distinctly different message. Typical headlines representing this political personality include "Stop Trying to Be 'Responsible' on the Budget, Democrats" (Waldman 2018b) and "Yes, Democrats Are the Party of Fiscal Responsibility, But That Will (and Should) Change" (Schmitt 2018).

At its most extreme, the group is represented by the so-called "Bernie Bros"—a term coined in 2016 to describe privileged white males with allegiance to Bernie Sanders. This faction, while not indicative of the Democratic left in its entirety, obscures its complexities as a subculture that flourishes primarily on social media. The group has organized around liberal-leaning media outlets and engage in online attacks, often through crass jokes in podcast episodes and on Twitter. Sanders's political ally Elizabeth Warren has expressed anger at this segment of Sanders's base for tweeting snake emojis at Warren and online harassment of Warren's female supporters during the 2020 presidential campaign (Beauchamp 2000; Bowles 2020).

Migration from "Mainstream" to "Moderate and Conservative"

By the beginning of the 2020 campaign cycle, a well-defined and oppositional moderate Democratic identity began to cohere into its own culture in response to the exigence posed by the liberal left party contingent. Such discourse suggests an intraparty tension wherein the adversaries emerge from moderate and liberal blocs within their own party rather than Republicans. As a result, ideological silos, initially configured as symptomatic of post-partisanship othering and division primarily between parties, have developed within them ("Political Polarization" 2014; Davis 2019b; Ember et al. 2019; Olsen 2019; Bump 2019; and Brick and van der Linden 2018). And the stage has been set for the emergence of intraparty tribalism.

TRIBALISM

It has been suggested that Americans "live in a time of tribes," an elemental concept "not of ideologies, parties, groups, or beliefs" but "badges of identity, not of thought" (Packer 2018; Stalder 2018; Anderson and Hoekstra 2019; Buchanan 2020). Chua (2018) maintains all humans are tribal, driven by primal motives to belong to specific groups while excluding others from those same groups. Furthermore, individuals' discrete identities are simultaneously dependent on and constitutive of the same groups. As such, tribalism reaches beyond partisanship, the manifestation of an instinctual tendency of humans to associate around shared norms, values, histories, customs, and traditions (Mendenhall 2018; Fukuyama 2018; Davis 2019a).

Partisanship as the Antecedent to Tribalism

Hobfoll (2018) argues from an evolutionary biology perspective to attribute instinctual tribalism as universal to all human brains, which are "biologically built, emotionally primed and cognitively programmed." The key mismatch that creates this brain "flaw' is the timing differential between societal progress and brain evolution. According to this perspective, society evolved very rapidly, over "no more than perhaps 20,000 years," while human grey matter "had over 2 million years of time to develop." As a result, "fight and flight" have become reflexive responses, situated in primitive brain structures developed for survival. Responses to threats against the tribes to which they belong alert the brain and body to concentrate, act without thought, and ignore reasoned arguments as well as complex rhetorical interventions of productive (rather than destructive) discourses to address such exigences as they emerge within American political parties as (Hobfoll 1–3; Mounk 2018a).

Traditionally, polarization between political parties, and likely within them as well, was understood to primarily be the result of issue-based conflict. As an example, such a situation would be when, without any other information, one individual voices dislike of another because they support a universal health care program, and the first individual does not. However, recently, "affective polarization," has been spotlighted as a distinct and pervasive type of animosity between parties, with origins in the power of partisanship as a social identity (Iyengar et al. 2019). In brief, regardless of party affiliation, Americans frequently describe the other party's members as hypocritical and closed-minded. Republicans and Democrats both refuse to cross party lines to socialize for inherently any cooperative activity. Significantly, consensus building is rarely, if at all, "on the table" for discussion between members of the different parties and, increasingly, within each political organization.

Mason (2018) considers the election of Donald Trump to be the culmination of a process through which the American electorate became deeply involved politically and socially along such heavily drawn polarized partisan lines that the resulting breach between Republicans and Democrats generated a unique conformation of identity politics. The resulting discursive forms have not only broken along clearly demarcated lines to shatter political, public, and electoral norms, but done so with few if any consequences. This in turn has created a distrust of "the other" to such an extent that candidates who rhetorically embrace polarizing binaries such as "us versus them" and "winning versus losing" retreat even further into such discursive safety zones when the targets of their divisive talk respond in kind (Masket 2016; Davis 2019b).

Identity Tribalism: The "Other" as Enemy

When considering tribalism, a central focus is the pull of race, religion, or ethnicity. Contemporary Americans on both the left and the right generally view their political opponents not as fellow Americans with differing views, but as enemies to be vanquished. They often imagine the Constitution not as an aspirational statement of shared principles and a bulwark against tribalism, but as a cudgel with which to attack those enemies. Such hyper-partisan political loyalties can themselves become tribal. American post-2016 cross-party public discourse is dominated by fundamental organic disagreements, grounded in acute forms of identity politics, most of which constitute what it means to be American as well as what the United States should stand for at the global level.

These narratives emerge to such extremes that "even neighborly conversations can quickly turn adversarial" and situated as tribalism (Shapiro 2019). The resulting schism in political discourse has widened to the point that political tribes modify essentially every political debate into a clash over national identity, moral judgment, or partisan identity, including that which occurs within the Democratic Party.

THE LIBERAL LEFT

In 2016, according to Adam Bozzi of the group End Citizens United, only three of the 41 Democratic challengers in the nation's most competitive House races rejected money from corporate PACs. By 2018, 45 of the 73 most competitive challengers did. Most of the Democratic senators who sought the presidency in 2020 also pledged to do the same (Beinart 2018). Notably, the American left has become increasingly influenced by identity politics, a major factor in constructing progressives' view of the Constitution. For some, the document is irredeemably flawed because of its eighteenth-century origins. Shortly after the 2016 election, the president of the University of Virginia quoted Thomas Jefferson, the school's founder, in an email to students. In response, hundreds of students and faculty signed an open letter declaring that they were "deeply offended" at the use of Jefferson as a "moral compass." Speaking to students at the University of Missouri in 2016, a Black Lives Matter co-founder went further, interpreting vows to protect the Constitution as endorsements of "white supremacy and genocide" (Chua and Rubenfeld 2018; Olsen 2019).

It's Not Just About Trump

By the 2020 election cycle, a dichotomy appeared to dominate the vision of left-leaning Democrats (Rubin, 2019a). While Bernie Sanders's supporters generally expressed disapproval of Donald Trump, a portion nonetheless suggested that they would not support the Democratic nominee unless it was their candidate. Some appeared willing to coerce the party to push the party to adopt his ideas. This progressive bloc of Democrats tended to configure their politics in absolutes, as a binary tribal struggle between a wealthy ruling class and ordinary workers who are being exploited. It also framed moderate Democrats as part of the problem. Such members of the progressive-liberal constituency were also unmoved by party loyalty arguments that mandated voting for "any Democrat"—including centrists or moderates—over Trump as counterproductive, maintaining that removing Donald Trump was not their only goal (Kapur 2019; Harris and Tarchak 2019; Peoples and Fram 2020).

The February 3 Iowa caucus race between Pete Buttigieg, a moderate Democrat, and Sanders reflected party divisions that broke along ideological polarities and foreshadowed tensions in the New Hampshire primary (Burns and Goldmacher 2020). The extent to which Sanders's base initially tribalized is indicated by the decisions of all but Joe Biden to avoid making an issue of Sanders's switch on the issue of gun control during the February 2020 New Hampshire debate. The other Democratic nominees believed the wiser path to the nomination was to form a coalition of voters apart from Sanders's constituents, and so avoid angering his portion of the party's base (Epstein and Goldmacher 2020).

Leaning Toward the Radical Right

It has been argued that the end game of left-leaning Democrats is closer to the Republican right that galvanized in 2016 than the moderates in their own party in 2020. To illustrate, *New York Times* reporter Bret Stephens described Elizabeth Warren as the "left-wing answer to Trump, minus the ethnic bigotry and sophomoric narcissism: railing against a 'rigged' system and making promises she can't deliver" (Collins and Stephens 2019a). *Washington Post* columnist Dana Milbank positioned Bernie Sanders as the "Donald Trump of the Left," suggesting that in the 2020 election cycle it was "not difficult to picture a scenario in which Bernie captures the Democratic presidential nomination with the same formula that worked for Trump with Republicans in 2016" (2019a).

During the March 2020 primaries, the hashtag #DemExit began trending on Twitter across the United States as supporters of Bernie Sanders threatened to leave the Democratic party entirely if Joe Biden secured the nomination (Zhao 2020). Others suggested sitting out the general election or voting for Donald Trump or a third-party candidate should Sanders lose in 2020 (Tavernese and Cohn 2019). After the results revealed that Sanders lost Michigan, a state he had won in 2016, some moderate Democratic senators suggested Sanders consider ending his campaign and help unify the party (Martina and Whitesides 2020). However, they did so carefully, mindful of repeating 2016, when a segment of Sanders's base "revenge voted" for Trump or skipped the general election entirely in protest against the party that they believed had tipped the scales unfairly against their candidate (Reston 2020; Wilson 2020).

THE MODERATES

A former centrist Democratic mayor worried that some Democratic candidates, as evidenced in the July 2019 debates, were moving too far to the left on key policy issues, damaging the party's chances of defeating Trump (Roarty 2019). This view was common among contemporary moderate or centrist Democrats, many of whom reported deep concerns that such shifts to the left on issues including border crossings or health insurance might alienate swing voters in battleground states like Pennsylvania, Michigan, and Wisconsin, with majority voters who wanted a more moderate party (Black 2019; Edsall 2019c, 2019b; Yglesias 2019).

Primaries traditionally encourage candidates to back policy proposals that appeal more to the party's ideologically passionate base than moderates. In most cases, whoever emerges as the eventual nominee inevitably pivots back toward the center for the general election. However, centrist Democrats expressed concerns that Democratic candidates generally were fixated on subjects that either didn't interest or outright repelled voters in the middle of the political spectrum (Roarty 2019).

Alienation of Moderate Democrats

Beinart (2018) suggests that who wins an election is often less important than who sets the agenda. According to this view, the Democratic Party has veered so sharply away from any consideration of moderation and compromise that even "establishment" Democrats frequently supported larger expansions of government, and more vehemently scorned Big Business and Big Finance, than more liberal Democrats (Burns and Martin 2019; Rendell and Platt 2019).

Democratic moderates also expressed worry that the sweeping proposals and "hardball tactics" of liberal Democrats could alienate centrist voters in the 2020 election, even as they held out hope that Democratic primary voters, focused on defeating Donald Trump, would check the party's move to the left (Peters and Karni 2019; Scherer and DeBonis 2019). The former, represented by many then new to national politics at the time including "The Squad" (Alexandria Ocasio-Cortez, Ilhan Omar, Rashida Tlaib, and Ayanna Pressley), argued that the party has been too timid, caving to Republican pressure and Democrats' failing to inspire voters with calls for sweeping change (Kampf-Lassin 2019).

Speaker of the House Nancy Pelosi voiced her concern that infighting among Democrats—specifically between the four new women and older, more-centrist Democrats—could jeopardize the House majority and chance at winning the Senate as well as the White House in 2020 (Scott 2019a). Embraced by the progressive cohort, "The Squad" joined Congress to merge with the most diverse freshman class in American history, and "quickly emerged as a proxy for the debate over the future of the Democratic Party, exposing its ideological and generational divisions" (Alberta 2019). *Guardian* reporter Arwa Mahdawi (2019) criticized Ocasio-Cortez in particular for not supporting Pelosi and warned that the New York representative needed to realize "her place" and not get ideas "above" her station.

Emerging Intraparty Divisions: Rhetorical Aggression

Some House liberals, including Ocasio-Cortez, were not pleased when the Speaker negotiated with Republicans and Democratic moderates to pass a bill to send more funding to the border, rather than demanding protections for migrant children in border shelters. Such conciliatory strategies on the part of Pelosi provoked Ocasio-Cortez to describe "The Mighty Moderates" as "the new Tea Party" and their behavior as "just horrifying." The accusations of another liberal, Representative Mark Pocan of Wisconsin, that moderate colleagues were enabling child abuse, provoked moderate accusations that Pocan was only "chasing followers on social media." For her part, Pelosi referred to the "Squad's" opposition to the funding bill by observing:

> All these people have their public whatever and their Twitter world, but they didn't have any following. . . . They're four people and that's how many votes they got. (Dowd, 2019; Davis 2019b)

Ocasio-Cortez, commenting on tension between House Speaker Nancy Pelosi's responses to "offensive tweets" from liberal Democrats that Pelosi was only "keeping the progressive flank at more arm's distance in order to protect more-moderate members," insisted that Pelosi was "outright disrespectful" (Chua and Rubenfeld 2018). Other Democratic moderates suggested the left needed to rethink its "scorched-earth" approach to American history and ideals. In this view, while exposing injustice is important, "there's a world of difference" between insisting that the United States has failed to live up to its constitutional principles and asserting that those principles are "lies or smoke screens for oppression":

> Washington and Jefferson were slave owners. They were also political visionaries who helped give birth to what would become the most inclusive form of governance in world history. (Chua and Rubenfeld 2018)

Moderate Democrats warned that imposing ideological "purity tests" on the party could provoke a Democratic version of the conservative revolt that transformed the post-2010 Republican Party. The freshman Representatives countered that the surge of new voters in the midterm elections reflected the excitement and support generated by such proposals (Scott 2019a). However, it may be telling that, while four years earlier such a Republican surge also brought new energy as well as a presidency into their ranks, it also cost them dearly in congressional races and legislative victories (Scherer and DeBonis 2019; Davis 2019a).

THE RIFT

Early indications of tension within the Democratic party during the 2020 campaign cycle "reads like a microcosm of a much larger rift." Older establishment white liberals and younger people of color from activist backgrounds struggled to find common ground from which to defeat the incumbents. Party leaders had clearly indicated they could not win the presidency without the support of the entire Democratic base, including that represented by "The Squad," people of color, women, and working-class voters. However, public comments from the younger representatives—including Ayanna Pressley who criticized Nancy Pelosi's comments as "demoralizing"—emphasized questions about these groups' confidence in their party leaders' interest in advocating for people of color (Scott 2019a).

The Largest Cohort and a Former Governor

Beinart (2018) observes that the left has historically rarely wielded much influence inside the Democratic Party. Only twice before has it secured enough power to compel Democrats to co-opt their organization's core ideas. In both cases—in the mid-1930s and the mid-1960s—progressives gained that power through mass movements that threatened public order. To maintain that order, and forestall more radical alternatives, Democrats passed laws that made America markedly more equal. But the very threat of radicalism and chaos that empowered progressives eventually provoked a backlash enthusiasm that produced a historically large and diverse field of 2020 Democratic presidential candidates.

While former Republican Governor William Weld, the only Republican challenger to Donald Trump's try for a second term, failed to add to the single delegate he won in Iowa, the March 3 "Super Tuesday" results—a "landslide loss in all"—were still enough for him to justify continuing his crusade against Donald Trump. If Bill Weld was generally alone at the beginning of the primaries, he was invisible at the end. It is likely the former governor never had the slightest chance within the Republican Party. Three years earlier, on January 20, 2017, the day of his presidential inauguration, Donald Trump officially filed for re-election with the Federal Election Commission. Accordingly, Weld's challenge aside, Trump was firmly established as the Republican nominee in all but name, and likely had been so for some time (Rogers and Haberman 2018).

Tribal Unification for the Win

By contrast, the 2020 Democratic primary field was occupied by more than twenty candidates at one point, making it the largest and most diverse in modern history (Burns, Flegenheimer et al. 2020). After the "Super Tuesday" primaries, the field narrowed to three Democrats: former Vice President Joe Biden, Senator Bernie Sanders, and Representative Tulsi Gabbard. With Representative Gabbard considered to have "virtually no chance" of winning the nomination, having won only two delegates and consistently finishing last in the polls, Sanders and Biden emerged as the Democratic front-runners (Touchberry 2020).

Biden became not only Sanders's main competition but also the standard bearer for moderate Democrats, gathering multiple endorsements from fellow moderates Kamala Harris, Michael Bloomberg, Amy Klobuchar, Pete Buttigieg, Beto O'Rourke, John Delaney, Deval Patrick, Cory Booker, Tim Ryan, and Andrew Yang (Perrett 2020; Verhovek 2020). Finally, on April 13, 2020, the Democratic intratribal leaders compromised in order to be competitive in the national election when Bernie Sanders contacted Joe Biden to say he was "asking all Americans to come together in this campaign to support your candidacy, which I endorse" (Swasey 2020).

Intertribal Divisions: Throwing Down the Gauntlet

By the time President Joe Biden signed his first bill into law in January 2021, more than 40 percent of Americans were already thinking the "other side's" policies were a threat to the nation. In addition, both national political parties described the other as "closed-minded, unpatriotic and immoral." Levendusky and Stecula (2021b) maintain that such extreme polarization "poisons" American politics. Moreover, the toxic discourse undermines support for core democratic principles to such an extent that violence against the "other side" is justified. Political compromise is difficult and, increasingly, rarely attainable in modern American democracy, although few doubt its necessity. Such a resistance is integral to the democratic process itself, particularly as enacted in the United States. While the classic end state ideal of decision by consensus may be the preferred form of participatory democracy, it is difficult to realize. Crucially, consensus building requires time, commitment, citizen-to-citizen contact, and, in particular, skilled deliberative discussion.

Taking those constraints into consideration, individuals who mindfully attempt such "talk" tend to get better at it over time. Focused (if not enthusiastic) efforts to purposely engage others' ideas through dialogic interaction ameliorates rhetorical skills and empowers agency for the discussants (Bilansky 1999; Pateman 1970; Searing et al. 2007). As an example, destructive conflict may convert into "creative argumentation," driven by a general agreement (consensus) that such dissension is to be mediated through deliberative civil discourse, situated within a viable rhetorical culture. In lieu of defaulting to coercion, intimidation, and other deleterious behaviors counterintuitive to a constitutional representative democracy, this configuration mandates citizens' (voters, elected leaders, political party members) mutual commitment to the means of resolving the disagreement, not the final solution. In sum deliberative discussion (with the specific conflicts to be determined), situated in and within a vigorous and resilient rhetorical culture, becomes the default method of making political decisions.

Embedded and Emerging Intraparty Tribalism

For the third time in a century, the Democratic left mobilized, and the Democratic center responded. And a Democratic president was inaugurated in January of 2021. Conversely, the likelihood of a coalition forming again, to address such the national exigence of winning a presidency within this century, is not necessarily a given. There is another option, while likely not as democracy-friendly, and not yet institutionally organized as such, for which the groundwork is already in place. The Democratic Party could disunite into discrete binaries of fully realized, adversarial and antagonistic, polarized political tribes. There is a precedent of sorts, as the Republican Party appears to have realized in the run-up to the 2020 election cycle and eradicated by 2021. How Democrats choose to respond to the nascent variation of intraparty divisive tribalism that appears to be emerging within their ranks is significant. Ultimately, their choice may itself be a binary: defaulting again to the progressive/moderate alliance (Judkis 2020; Stein 2017; Robinson 2017) or relying on a novel configuration of American party politics as populist partisanship in the twenty-first century.

Chapter 2

Rhetorical Tribalism

It would appear that human beings are tribal. In her book *Political Tribes,* Amy Chua argues that, historically and globally, loyalty to groups has often and powerfully outweighed ideological considerations. In addition, this fundamentally innate "tribal instinct" predisposes humans not only to "belong" but, more significantly, "to exclude" (2018b; see also Shermer 2012; and Nesse 2001).

Midway through Donald Trump's presidency, *The New Yorker* columnist George Packer observed that contemporary American politics had become entrenched in tribalism and, accelerated by the president, "winner-take-all" elections and dehumanizing mass mediated commentaries as well as "the people we choose to talk to and live among" (Hawkins et al. 2018). Tribalism becomes, in this view, identifying oneself with a nation or cohort, placing it beyond moral polarities, and prioritizing its interests. Significantly, tribal competition is enacted over political, mediated, and rhetorically established territories. This may intensify to such an extent, driven by public discourse, that amoral tribalism embeds within political parties. It follows that when politics becomes a perpetual tribal war, ends justify almost any means and individuals are absolved from the constraints of normal decency (2018).

TRIBAL TYPOLOGIES

More in Common, a research organization based in Europe and the United States, released a 2018 report called "Hidden Tribes: A Study of America's Polarized Landscape" (Hawkins et al. 2018). Grounded in the company's prior work in France, Germany, and Italy the study was part of their effort to understand and counteract rising populism and fragmentation in the Western democracies. Based on their beliefs and values, Americans were grouped into seven "tribes": Progressive Activists, Traditional Liberals, Passive Liberals,

Politically Disengaged, Moderate, Traditional Conservatives, and Devoted Conservatives.

Actively Progressive to Staunchly Conservative

Progressive Activists tended to be "younger, highly engaged, secular, cosmopolitan [and] angry" while the Politically Disengaged were "young, low income, distrustful, detached, patriotic [and]conspiratorial." Moderates were "engaged, civic-minded, middle-of-the-road, pessimistic [and] Protestant"; and Devoted Conservatives, "white, retired, highly engaged, uncompromising [and] patriotic" (Hawkins et al. 2018). The study revealed that "tribal membership" predicted differences in Americans' views on various political issues with more reliability than demographic, ideological, and partisan groupings. Further evidence of the relevance of core beliefs and their associated tribal identities revealed that tribal membership predicted differences in Americans' views on political issues better than demographic, ideological, and partisan groupings.

The seven tribes were considered "hidden" because, while Americans were used to "seeing" categories such as race, gender, region, and religion align with political preferences in "numbingly predictable ways," they were generally unaware of the values in which those categories were embedded (Hawkins et al. 2018, 5; and Packer 2018).

The most striking binary rupture occurred between Progressive Activists and Devoted Conservatives, the latter demanding that Americans be raised as "obedient, well behaved and hard-working." Furthermore, this faction took pride in and prioritized the Judeo-Christian faith to such an extent that its traditional values were configured as redemptive options through which flawed individuals could be transformed into people of "self-discipline, character and responsibility." Conversely, Progressive Activists, skeptical of traditional authority and norms, configured such values as selfishly enforced by socially dominant groups such as straight white men. As a result, Progressive Activists sought to "correct" the historical marginalization of groups based on their race, gender, sexuality, wealth, and other forms of privilege (Hawkins et al. 2018, 10).

A large segment of the population in this study included individuals whose voices were silenced by those of more strident tribes. These were individuals who believed that Americans had more in common than that which divided them. While they still differed on significant issues, they were exhausted by the discordant factions within the nation. Moreover, these individuals considered compromise integral to politics and wished to see the country coalesce to resolve its problems. Specifically, "Hidden Tribes" provided considerable evidence of deep, discourse-driven fissures and evolving tribalism within the United States. Even so, the report also revealed that while tribalism was organically situated in the nation's political culture, 77 percent of Americans believed their differences were "not so great" that they could not come together (Hawkins et al. 2018, 7). In particular, the report indicated that, among the seven tribes, the Exhausted Majority contained distinct groups of people with multiple and varying degrees of political understanding and activism. However, the members of this coalition all shared a sense of fatigue with the "polarized national conversation," as well as a "willingness to be flexible in their political viewpoints, and a lack of voice in the national conversation" (2018, 11).

Finally, when considering "extremism" as a singular attribute of American political inter- and intraparty tribalism, it is significant that members of the Exhausted Majority were considerably more ideologically flexible than members of other groups. In particular, members of both left and right leaning groups, which generally "dominate the national conversation," adhered to rigidly consistent and decidedly polarizing views across essentially all political issues while the Exhausted Majority tended to express more moderate and equitable assessments from issue to issue (Hawkins et al. 2018, 12).

POLITICAL TRIBES

While conflicting core values have fundamentally existed side-by-side in healthy societies, such differences in contemporary contexts are clearly more difficult to mitigate, with regular and increasingly intense manifestations between and within American political tribes. Deconstructing what rhetorically constitutes cohort differences could alleviate this polarization, perhaps preventing its escalation into an out-of-control spiral. Contemporary Americans suffer from deep injustices related to their ethnicity, race, sex, religion, sexuality, and other facets of their identities. However, constructive as well as productive rhetorical exchanges about these and other critical issues have reached a stalemate in large part because of substantial breaches between the major ideological and partisan perspectives (Hawkins et al. 2018, 15).

Specifically, partisan tribalism between Republicans and Democrats has steadily increased over the past three decades. Congressional voting patterns have accompanied this partisanship since the cessation of the Cold War. Kane and Yoran (2021) speculate that lack of a common external threat may be a contributing factor in such interparty conflict, with the 1990s characterized as more divisive than the previous eras. While Americans consolidated for a short period after 9/11, a backlash developed against the president and

Republicans to the extent that "Bush lied, people died" became a rallying cry for those who opposed the invasion of Iraq.

Accusations of criminality followed, intensifying the rupture between the two dominant political parties (Toner and Ruenberg 2006; see also Oliphant 2018; and Taibbi 2019).

During his administration, Barack Obama also disappointed centrists hoping for unity. To illustrate, some Republicans configured his approach to the economy and health care as "zero-sum partisan battles," without input from or compromise with their party. Laws were passed along straight party-line votes, despite "deep blue Massachusetts" electing a Republican senator who campaigned against it to succeed Democrat Ted Kennedy (Parsons and Mascaro 2017; Gao 2015). In addition, Obama's administration was a major player in culture wars that "ravaged" the nation in "new and aggressive ways as white, working-class Americans were scorned" as "clinging to guns or religion" (Kane and Yoran 2021; see also Gerson 2012).

Acceleration During the Trump Administration

Interparty tribalism accelerated during Donald Trump's presidency as Democrats refused to embrace major aspects of his platform (Wehner 2020; Packer 2018; and Seib 2017). Conversely, Trump enacted his leadership through an adversarial "pugilistic, no-apology" discourse grounded in instinctual ethos (see Gregory 2020; Theye and Melling 2018; and Batton, 2019). This rhetorical configuration exacerbated the animosity between Democrats and Republicans to such an extent that members of Congress as well as journalists openly abandoned any pretense of objective reporting (Kane and Yoran 2021).

The discord between parties became pathological to such an extent throughout 2020 that, by early 2021, the nation's "national psyche" was in crisis (Gregory 2020). Some Democratic governors blamed Donald Trump for the COVID-19 pandemic even as, in the views of their Republican critics, their states suffered from "self-inflicted disasters and lockdowns." In addition, Republicans argued violent rioting during the summer of 2020 was sanctioned by progressives and that "right-wing extremists adopted the same confrontational violence in the guise of protest." Consequently, while partisan political violence is rare, Americans' tolerance of and support for it has risen and continues to do so exponentially (Kane and Yaran 2021; see also Diamond et al. 2020; and Peter Coleman 2020).

RHETORICAL FRAMES

Gregory (2020) configures rhetoric as the "driving force fueling every persuasive, informative speech or message relayed by an individual or institution." As a result, rhetorical communication has influenced, represented, and, significantly, created world history as well as the "way that events of both positive and detrimental value have unfolded within the timeline of human existence." Within this perspective, rhetorical behavior strategically manages human symbolic interaction in all of its variations, setting particular agendas for particular "audiences." It is this "language-in-action" that ultimately determines a rhetors' success or failure. "Both positive and detrimental values have unfolded within the timeline of human existence" through such rhetorical invention (Gregory 2020; see also Barrett 1991).

Politics and Democracy: A Rhetorical Imperative

Rhetorical acts—specifically symbolic interaction—are integral to the function of politics. "Politics," in this sense, are configured within a pluralist theory of democracy as envisioned by political theorist Robert Dahl. In this view, democracy may be understood as literally "rule by the people" buttressed by specific mandates for democratic decision making (Dahl 1989, 108–14; see also Mayhew 2015; and Coglianese 1990). These include participation and equal access to voting for all adults, who subsequently must agree that the collective decisions made within their system are binding. It is also imperative that citizens be afforded opportunities to develop civic literacy in order to facilitate their own decision-making abilities. Dahl (1982) argues that within this context, political outcomes are enacted through the communicative interactions of competitive, if unequal, interest groups within pluralist-democracies. In this view, such democratic rhetorical processes constitute the democratic process itself, minimizing government coercion and so enacting political liberty.

It is possible that political parties may offer such opportunities to directly participate in robust and healthy democratic interactions within those organizational cultures. Yet, just as individuals within democracies, the independence or autonomy of organizations also creates opportunities to "do harm." As a result, political parties may increase or perpetuate injustices rather than reduce them and do so at the expense of the broader public good. Without intentional language-in-action behaviors, and so rhetorical interventions, the United States could backslide into illiberal democracy, severing the rule of law (including free and fair elections) from constitutional liberalism. Such governments produce centralized regimes, erosion of liberties, ethnic intolerance, and conflict (Zakaria 1997). Specifically, such an elected government could threaten human rights or deconstruct the mechanisms of a constitutional democratic government by silencing adversarial voices, essentially shutting down rather than dialogically engaging competition. As a case in point, Turkey's Recep Tayyip Erdogan, at different points in his presidency, fired judges who openly challenged his authoritarianism and supported the criminalization of "insults" to himself, once describing democracy as a train "you ride until you arrive at your destination, then you step off" (cited in Somin 2016).

Rhetoric therefore becomes essential to pluralistic democracy as a liaison between the "contingency" of politics as it is enacted and a desired outcome as it is "happening" (see Ballacci 2018). From this standpoint, rhetoric simultaneously embodies language-in-action, configuring and advocating different visions of tribal behaviors between and within American political parties.

Language in Thought and Action

Hayakawa and Hayakawa (1941; 1990) argue that widespread intraspecific cooperation through the use of language is the fundamental mechanism of human survival. A parallel assumption is that when the use of language results, which is often, in the creation or aggravation of disagreements and conflicts, there is something "linguistically wrong with the speaker, the listener, or both." Survival, then, depends on humans' ability to "talk, write, listen, and read in ways that increase the chances for you and fellow members of the species to survive together" (12):

> Instead of remaining helpless because of the limitations of their own experience and knowledge, instead of having to rediscover what others have already discovered, instead of exploring the false trails others have explored and repeating their errors [human beings] can go on from where the others left off. Language . . . makes progress possible. (16)

These formational rhetorical conventions and tactics of meaning and how such speech-acts affect human behavior inform rhetorical tribalism, as do practices that induce civility and cooperation rather than confrontation. Hauser (2004) argues that, while the "partisan impulse" is present in deliberative democracy and "not easily curbed" by criteria of rationality, "rhetorical democracy" expands civic participation from "the negotiating table to the myriad forms by which free people express their social, political, and personal aspirations and identities." While such relationships are the "defining characteristic" of a modern democracy, they also pose a "significant problem" for it: the invention of discursive practices as well as designing dedicated public spaces within which to pursue such civil communicative behaviors (Hauser 2004, 12; see also Smith 2003).

Rhetorical Mechanisms of Tribalism

When rhetoric functions in "real-life" language-in-use situations such as political interaction, specific speech-acts may purposely obstruct cooperation and facilitate division between and discord within groups. Three of these constructs inform tribalism in particular. First, "slanting" is a rhetorical strategy through which an individual deliberately creates a biased, subjective account of a perceived "reality." The described attributes are communicated in a precise manner that convinces the audience that certain conclusions are "inescapable." Next, "stereotyping" configures certain beliefs or assertions as "automatically projected onto a group of things or people" without considering unique attributes of individuals within a group. Finally, "two-valued orientation" is a rhetorical tactic that provokes discord within and between factions such as political parties. This discursive strategy involves generalized, misleading, and simplified language intentionally structured to symbolically create a reality in limited, binary terms such as "yes" or "wrong" or "right." Using language in this manner is generally more easily believed than complex or nuanced discourse. Rather than only being "heard" as merely two different or opposite opinions, such a strategy manifests "a thought system that leaves no alternative to a binary view of reality" ("S. I. Hayakawa" 2008).

Within the context of intraparty tribalism, a "two-valued orientation" could account for both the "blue versus red" binary of Republican and Democratic mutual hostility as well as its variation as intraparty tribalism. Notably, all three of these discursive behaviors are counterintuitive to the deliberative discourse necessary for healthy democratic systems.

Division and Identification

A historically significant and particularly salient rhetorical theory for an investigation of intraparty tribalism is Kenneth Burke's conceptualization of identification and division (1969). "Identification" is fundamental to rhetoric and an extension of the traditional term "persuasion." It is a communicative process fundamental to being a human and creating meaning as a human. From this perspective, because they are biologically separate from one another at birth and throughout their life cycle, humans are fundamentally and organically driven to identify with others in order to assuage the singularity of isolation. It follows that rhetorical techniques, both acquired and taught, may be developed with which interests, attitudes, values, experiences, and perceptions may be shared. In this way, people become "consubstantial" with one another; their "substances" or core aspects merge so that identification traverses interpersonal differences.

Language, the exchange of symbols through which meaning is created, becomes "symbolic action" that, in turn, creates the material from which discursive platforms are built and social cohesion is made possible. Accordingly, it is through this creation and exchange of symbols (words are the paradigm examples) that all humans—including those engaging in political symbolic behavior within and between their respective parties or organizations—connect with one another and build their realities about those connections. Within this frame, "reality" becomes "what things will do to us and for us" with "identification" and the concomitant term "substance" foregrounded as constituent elements in that perception:

> A is not identical with his colleague, B. But insofar as their interests are joined, A is identified with B. Or he may identify himself with B even when their interests are not joined, if he assumes that they are, or is persuaded to believe so. (Burke 1969, 562)

The primary states of identification include: (1) naming something or someone according to specific properties, (2) the process of associating with and disassociating from others, and (3) the ultimate outcome of identification: being consubstantial with others. Identification, in all of its forms, occurs through "speech, gesture, tonality, order, image, attitude, and idea." In this way, identification between a rhetor and an audience or group of listeners is both a process and an end, as well as a necessary response to the reality of shared perception that humans are distinct and divided from one another but must nonetheless, "come together." Ultimately, this action of "consubstantiality," or the sharing of "common attributes, values, needs and feelings" is imperative if individuals and groups are to create, experience, and enact together for their own survival (Burke 1969; 1984).

In so doing, A is "substantially one" with a person other than self. There is an additional impetus for this process that develops, in that identification essentially follows division. As Kenneth Burke suggests, an ambiguous combination of identification and division, when individuals are not certain where one ends and the other begins, is the "characteristic invitation to rhetoric" (1966, 7, see also 27–28; and Meadows 1957). Consequently, and not surprisingly, identification is instrumental to mitigating disagreements or public contention (division) between or within competing factions, including political parties.

Invitational Rhetoric

Foss and Griffin (1995) propose a rhetorical frame grounded in feminist principles of equality, immanent value, and self-determination. Strategic discourse is configured as a means to facilitate understanding between people while "its communicative modes are the offering of perspectives and the creation of the external conditions of safety, value, and freedom" (1; see also Tindale 2004, 51–55).

Invitational rhetoric does not advocate the correctness of one position regarding a complex problem or issue, such as taxes or border walls or election integrity. Rather, the outcome of this communication method is the creation of a rhetorical environment within which dialogue and understanding are prioritized instead of winning or victory over "the other." In this way, a metaphoric (or on occasion literal) safe space is rhetorically created within which dialogue and discussion of such complex public issues may be deconstructed. Also, flawed binaries, such as those often created within polarized tribes that simplify into dichotomous and often untenable positions, are reconstituted into more democracy-friendly "words-in-action." The interaction, or relationship between those involved ("the rhetors") in the exchange, is grounded in reciprocity and respect. In certain hostile situations, re-sourcement—a "response made by a rhetor according to a framework, assumptions, or principles other than those suggested in the precipitating message"—could be a productive behavior for managing tribal discord:

> In re-sourcement the rhetor deliberately draws energy from a new source, which involves disengaging from the framework offered by another rhetor, and makes a "swerve, a leap to the other side, which lets us . . . deploy another logic or system." (Foss and Griffin 1995, 9)

Invitational rhetoric is established through precepts including "principles of equality, immanent value, and self-determination" rather than attempts to control others through intimidation and coercion. Such communicative behaviors are "at work in the world" through contemporary public deliberations, promoting and establishing civility in a "variety of venues," specifically situations demanding "ethical exchanges in difficult situations" (Bone et al. 2008, 435). To that end, invitational rhetoric very likely also has a place, if not a "job to do," within the public spaces of American political discourse, including rhetorical space unique to and situated within the Democratic Party.

UNITED THROUGH DIVISION: POLITICAL TRIBALISM

The contentious 2020 presidential campaign laid bare these deep divisions in American society, exhibiting a tribal politics—when strict loyalty to a foundational identity (such as race, religion, clan, or region) is the organizing principle of political life within a country that "sets off alarm bells when seen abroad." This occurred to such an extent that the campaign "looked less like a contest of ideas and more like a battle between tribes, with voters racing to their partisan corners based on identity, not concerns about policy" (Brigety II 2021).

Contemporary Political Cohorts

American post-2016 politics have foregrounded disputes within the nation's two major political parties to such an extent that significant alignments are possible, if not likely. This dissent has been characterized by internal divisions and power-brokering to determine the future trajectory of each. Such conflict is not a modern phenomenon. As a case in point, parallels can be drawn with the Whig party, which devolved from majority status to extinction between 1848 and 1854 (see Wallach 2017; and Bibby 1996).

Although there have been other moments in US history when the country's governance failed to arbitrate tribalism—most notably during the Civil War—the current era ranks high among them. Contemporary Democratic and Republican tribes are the country's two major political parties, bolstered by the demographic subgroups that compose their most loyal and predictable constituencies. Over the past two decades, these groups have grown further and further apart. Klein (2020) observes that in the last half century of politics, while Americans have become more consistent in the party they vote for, it is not because they "like" their party more. On the contrary, most like their own parties *less* yet still vote in support of them "because we came to dislike the opposing party more" (10).

In the run-up to the 2020 presidential race, the nation's political tribes were afflicted by intraparty as well as interparty tribalism to such an extent that there were ruptures within factions as well as between them. Furthermore, despite internal discord within both, Republicans and Democrats remained "at war" with the "other" as well. The Pew Research Center documented fractures within both the Republican and Democratic Parties prior to the 2018 midterm elections ("Political Typology" 2017).

Republican Intraparty Sectors

The political typology found two distinctly different groups on the right—Core Conservatives and Country First Conservatives, who both overwhelmingly approved of Trump, but disagreed on much else—including immigration and whether it benefited the US to be active internationally. Core Conservatives, the most traditional group of Republicans, demonstrated an outsized influence on the GOP coalition; while they comprised 13 percent of the public—and about a third (31 percent) of all Republicans and Republican-leaning independents—they constituted a much larger share (43 percent) of politically engaged Republicans. This financially comfortable, male-dominated group overwhelmingly supported smaller government and lower corporate tax rates and believed in the fairness of the nation's economic system. A majority of this cohort (68 percent) supported American involvement in the global economy because it afforded the nation new markets and opportunities for growth.

Country First Conservatives, a considerably smaller segment of the GOP base, were older and less educated than other Republican-leaning factions. In addition, Country First Conservatives expressed unhappiness with the nation's course, were highly critical of immigrants, and wary of US global involvement. Approximately two-thirds of Country First Conservatives (64 percent)—the largest typology contingent of either party—reported that "if America is too open to people from all over the world, we risk losing our identity as a nation."

A third Republican group, Market Skeptic Republicans, diverged from the party's traditional support for business and lower taxes. Thirty-four percent of Market Skeptic Republicans indicated banks and other financial institutions had a generally positive effect on the country, the lowest percentage among Republican-leaning typology sector. Significantly, Market Skeptic Republicans embraced raising tax rates on corporations and large businesses. A large majority (94 percent) indicated the economy unfairly favored powerful interests, a view much closer to Solid Liberals (99 percent mostly unfair) than Core Conservatives (21 percent). Conversely, New Era Enterprisers were optimistic about the future and were more likely than any other factions to believe future generations of Americans would fare better than they had. Younger and somewhat less overwhelmingly white than the other GOP-leaning groups, New Era Enterprisers were also young, majority white and pro-business, and generally think that immigrants strengthen, rather than burden, the country.

Democratic Intraparty Sectors

The Pew Research Center also identified four distinct tribal factions within the Democratic Party. While all cohorts supported a social safety net, they diverged on government regulation of business, and government performance in general. And like the Republicans, Democratic contingents disagreed on US global involvement. In addition, the racial, ethnic, and income differences, historically intrinsic within the party, had accelerated. There were also two majority-minority Democratic-leaning typology groups, along with two more affluent, mostly white, groups.

"Solid Liberals" comprised the largest group within the Democratic coalition, with close to half (48 percent) of politically engaged Democrats and Democratic-leaning independents. In addition, the group was majority white, financially secure, mostly with college or post-graduate degrees, who expressed solid liberal attitudes on essentially all issues. In particular, their level of post-Trump donations set them apart from all other groups, Democratic or Republican. Close to half of Solid Liberals (49 percent) reported recent contributions to political candidates or campaigns while 39 percent had protested against Donald Trump's policy, again, the highest share of all groups within both parties.

"Opportunity Democrats" tended to agree with Solid Liberals on most significant issues. However, they were less affluent, less politically engaged, and less liberal—in attitudes regarding self-description of political activity. One area of difference between Opportunity Democrats and Solid Liberals was on corporate profits: 40 percent of Opportunity Democrats indicated most corporations made a "fair and reasonable amount of profit," compared with 16 percent of Solid Liberals. Opportunity Democrats also believed most people could advance with hard work.

"Disaffected Democrats" expressed highly positive feelings toward their party and its leaders while demonstrating cynicism about politics, government, and the current state of the nation. The financially stressed group supported activist government and a social safety net but believed the government in general to be "wasteful and inefficient." Also, a majority of Disaffected Democrats admitted their "side" had been losing in politics and less than half agreed that voting gave them a voice in government. Another majority-minority Democratic group, "Devout and Diverse" experienced more financial hardship than Disaffected Democrats. They were also the most politically mixed typology group with about a quarter leaning Republican and the largest segment of the "least politically engaged." Like Disaffected Democrats, Devout and Diverse voters were critical of government regulation of business and the most religiously observant Democratic-leaning cohort. Finally, they were the only Democratic group in which a majority (64 percent) believed it was necessary to believe in God to be moral and have good values.

In addition to the eight main groups in the political typology reported by the Pew Research Center in 2017, a ninth group—the "Bystanders"—appeared to be "missing in action politically." Essentially no one in this young, largely minority group was registered to vote, and most gave little or no attention to politics and government. Significantly, the study concluded by noting that, while both parties had intraparty schisms, a rhetorical binary of partisan-driven interparty hostility remained a defining characteristic of Republicans and Democrats toward the "other" party ("Political Typology" 2017).

A Temporary Truce Rather Than a Reconciliation

Joe Biden took the 2020 presidential nomination and, indeed the presidency, as a moderate Democrat with decades worth of experience and a political ethos constructed through a history of bipartisanship (see Hook 2019; and Emanuel 2021). Maurice Mitchell, the national director of the Working Families Party, conceded that the former vice president was "not a progressive." However, he also asserted that "even though progressives did not prevail in the presidency, our issues and our movement surely have." Colin Strother, a strategist for moderate Texas Democrat Henry Cuellar who narrowly defeated a Sanders-endorsed Democratic primary challenger, disagreed. Shortly after Joe Biden became the party's nominee, Strother argued that while the liberal segment of his party would still "get a seat at the table," they also "want a revolution" and "that's not how Washington works" (quoted in Weissert 2020b). Editor-at-large and co-founder of *Vox* Ezra Klein believes that in the last half century Americans have become more consistent in supporting their respective parties. However, confirming previous research, this support was not because constituents like their own party more, but because they dislike the opposing party more. Klein paraphrases this tendency: "Even as hope and change sputter, fear and loathing proceed" (2020, 11).

Ultimately, progressive and centrist Democrats did unite as a party behind their candidate in August 2020 and again the following November. However, it is doubtful that the consolidation was a sign of tribal reconciliation. Rather, the apparent liaison between the two Democratic coalitions was more likely a truce, albeit temporary, to unite in order to be sure that Donald Trump's Republican "tribe within the tribe" did not win.

Chapter 3

American Rhetorical Tribes

That tribalized political alliances have the potential to damage the United States, perhaps irreparably, has been a part of the nation's public conscience since its inception. Shortly after the American Revolution, John Adams observed that there was "nothing I dread so much" as a:

> Division of the Republic into two great Parties, each arranged under its Leader, and concerting Measures in opposition to each other. This, in my humble Apprehension is to be dreaded as the greatest political Evil, under our Constitution. ("From John Adams" 1780, 2021)

ORIGIN IN OTHERING

Yet, despite this fear, for over two centuries, American leaders have done little to discourage the rise of political parties. Chua and Rubenfeld (2018) suggest that while it would be "hard to imagine" representative democracy without interparty competition, Adams was "right to be apprehensive," particularly when the nation's political institutions and organizations are breaking down under the strain of partisan divisions.

The causes of America's resurgent tribalism are many. They include seismic demographic change, which has led to predictions that whites will lose their majority status within a few decades, declining social mobility and a growing class divide, and media that reward expressions of outrage. All of this has contributed to a climate in which groups in America—people of color and whites, conservatives and liberals, the working class and elites—feel under attack, pitted against others not just for jobs and spoils, but for the right to define the nation's identity. In these conditions, democracy devolves into a win-or-lose competition, one in which parties succeed by stoking voters' fears and defaulting to their ugliest us-versus-them binaries (Rosen 2018; Stalder 2018; Shermer 2012).

Americans on both the ideological left and the right tend to view their political opponents not as fellow Americans with differing views, but as enemies to be vanquished. And they have come to view the Constitution not as an aspirational statement of shared principles and a bulwark against tribalism, but as a cudgel with which to attack those enemies. As early as 2016, concerns were voiced over what would become of the Republican Party if Donald Trump won the nomination, let alone the presidency. Pete Wehner, a veteran of the George W. Bush White House, worried that a victory by Trump would be "catastrophic" to the party and a "terrible danger" to the United States. Bruce Haynes, a GOP operative in Washington, indicated that many in the party did not know "what to do" and were calling him "in tears," distraught because they could not support Trump because he was a "liar, a cheat and a racist" yet "everything" they had "ever cared for in politics" was "on the line and could be lost if I don't vote for him" (quoted in Stokols 2016; see also Marsh 2016).

THE FOUR PARTIES

By 2017, the emergence of what would eventually be called "Trumpism" was becoming apparent (Thompson 2020; Henninger 2021). An American "four-party system" had already been imagined, configured through warnings that Democrats were in danger of mirroring the tribalistic fracture already apparent in the Republican Party less than a year into Donald Trump's presidency (Costa et al. 2017).

"Resist Trump" Democrats, playing a "zero-sum game," maintained any win for the president was a loss for their party. To this end, under the banner of running against Donald Trump, Congressional Democratic candidates were breaking fundraising records, united through a campaign to unseat the president. In addition, a second coalition of Democrats speculated that Trump's election might be an opportunity to "lock in a compromise" with a president who seemed "happy to defy conventions." These included senators seeking re-election in conservative-leaning states such as Claire McCaskill in Missouri and Heidi Heitkamp in North Dakota, who realized that failing to support the president's tax cuts could be "political suicide."

Antholis (2017) maintained that pragmatic centrists could seek compromises with Trump Republicans, having "mastered the art of the deal." However, resisters could argue for the exact kind of Republican defeat progressives had predicted and for which they hoped. There has been speculation about how such a "four-party system" might fail:

How will this four-party system develop? The scenarios are endless. One could easily imagine Republicans failing to get any legislative accomplishments, leading to a massive GOP failing in next year's midterm elections. But a new four-party system could also make Trump formidable. With a solid 35 percent of support, he could lead the strongest remaining faction in American politics. (Antholis 2017; see also Rubin 2020b)

Identity and Value Clashes Between Parties

Research conducted by the Pew Research Center revealed that Americans had rarely been as polarized as they were prior to the 2020 presidential election. Hostility between Democrats and Republicans reflected the degree to which each party was at odds with the other on issues including the economy, racial justice, climate change, law enforcement, and international engagement. The research reported that champions of both Joe Biden and Donald Trump argued the differences between their candidates expanded beyond politics and policies. As an example, shortly before the election, close to 80 percent of registered voters in both parties said their differences with the other group were about core American values, and roughly 90 percent in both reported concerns that a victory by the other would lead to "lasting harm" to the United States (Dimonk and Wike 2020).

The United States was not alone in experiencing such breaches. The United Kingdom had polarized over Brexit; emerging populist parties disrupted European government systems while cultural conflict and economic anxieties "intensified old cleavages and created new ones in many advanced democracies." Even so, the 2020 pandemic revealed the pervasiveness of the divide in American politics with regard to other nations. In the summer of 2020, 76 percent of Republicans (including independents who leaned toward the party) reported the United States had done a good job dealing with the coronavirus outbreak, compared with just 29 percent of those who did not identify with the Republican Party. This gap was the largest breach found between those who supported the governing party and those who did not across fourteen nations surveyed. In addition, 77 percent of Americans indicated their country was now more divided than before the outbreak, as compared with a median of 47 percent in the other nations surveyed (Dimonk and Wike 2020; see also deFrance 2019; Schumacher 2019; and Stafford 2018).

American Exceptionalism

The Pew study also revealed that such American exceptionalism preceded the coronavirus pandemic. Americans were more ideologically divided than any of the nineteen other national publics surveyed when asked how much trust they had in scientists and whether scientists made decisions solely based on facts. Furthermore, such breaches had occurred in virtually every aspect of the public and policy response to the global epidemic. In particular, Democrats and Republicans disagreed over mask wearing, contact tracing, how well public health officials were dealing with the crisis, whether to get a vaccine once one became available, and whether life would remain changed in any significant way afterwards. Joe Biden's supporters considered the coronavirus to be a central issue in the election with 82 percent indicating it was very important to their vote. Conversely, supporters of Donald Trump ranked the pandemic as the least significant concern among six issues with only 24 percent indicating it was very important. Just 24 percent said it was very important.

While partisan media, social media, as well as cultural, historical, and regional divides were not confined to the United States, the nation's binary electoral system was still unique. The two-party system essentially merged legitimate social and political points of disagreement into a single argument, which exaggerated differences to such an extent that:

> When the balance of support for these political parties [was] close enough for either to gain near-term electoral advantage—as it has in the US for more than a quarter century—the competition becomes cutthroat and politics begins to feel zero-sum, where one side's gain is inherently the other's loss. (Dimonk and Wike 2020)

Such discord can reconfigure legitimate issues, many in need of democratic debate, into dialogic war zones to such an extent that genuinely nonpartisan concerns split again into opposing binaries and increasingly hostile camps. A particularly salient consequence of such interparty discord is that race, religion, and ideology merge into these deeply partisan tribes, often in unprecedented and discordant ways (see Saad 2021; Klein 2020; and Mitchem 2019).

IDEOLOGICAL FRACTURES WITHIN THE DEMOCRATIC PARTY

Edsall (2019c) suggests contemporary Democratic voters initially split into two distinct groups. The "progressive wing" was supportive of "contentious policies" on issues including immigration and health care and also "disproportionately white." A second group consisted of "somewhat liberal" voters. Issues of particular interest for these more moderate voters were "bread-and-butter concerns" including jobs, taxes, and health care reform.

Their majority was nonwhite, with almost half of its support coming from African American and Hispanic voters.

A third group was also configured. The first two contingents consisted of individuals who thought themselves to be "very liberal" and others who indicated they were "somewhat liberal." Both factions were two-thirds white and had substantial—but for the Democratic Party below average—minority representation. They were roughly a quarter African American and Hispanic. Alternately, those in the third group were Democratic primary voters who described themselves as moderate to conservative. This segment had the largest number of minorities; it was 26 percent Black, 19 percent Hispanic, 7 percent other nonwhites, and had the smallest percentage of whites, at 48 percent. Each of the three ideological groups also favored different sets of policies. On the left, the very liberal voters emphasized "the environment, protecting immigrants, abortion, and race/gender," while the moderate to conservative Democrats were "more concerned with job creation and lowering taxes" (Edsall 2019c).

The "Woke" Tribe

Goldberg (2018) describes a major change in American political behavior, driven primarily by "wokeness," a "digital era style of moral politics." The term euphemizes a narrow but "rapidly changing political ideology" of white liberals "remaking American politics"—or hoping to do so—in a more progressive or liberal trajectory. The baseline attitudes expressed by members of this group regarding racial and social justice issues "have radicalized to the extent that white liberals are currently the only demographic group in the United States to display a pro-outgroup bias." This group emerged as the only segment of the Democratic Party that expressed a preference for other racial and ethnic communities above their own. It is also significant that, as "woke ideology" has accelerated, this faction is generally comprised of white liberals who have pulled away from the opinions held by the rest of the coalition of Democratic voters—including minority groups, moderates, and other liberals within the party. In addition, the "revolution" in moral sentiment among this single segment of voters has led to multiple consequences ranging from changes in the norms and attitudes reflected in media and popular culture, to the adoption of novel political rhetoric and electoral strategies of the Democratic Party (see Martin and Ember 2019; and Beinart 2018).

"Woke" Democrats as Socialists

Nor has the development and emergence of "woke" Democrats occurred in a vacuum. The initiatives discursively set in motion by this tribal faction have, in turn, provoked pushback and countermeasures from conservatives and the Republican Party in general (Goldberg, 2018). In particular, this group has evoked retaliatory responses grounded in accusations of "socialism" from Republicans in search of a rhetorical weapon with which to attack their "enemy," the "other" mainstream political tribe. As an instance, it has been argued that the "woke" alliance within the party was generally responsible for the failure of the "blue wave" in November 2020. While Biden won the presidency with a sizable lead in both the electoral and popular votes, the party barely kept its majority in Congress, seeing multiple seats flip to the GOP, putting Democrats in danger of losing both the House and Senate in the next midterm election.

Griffin (2020) argues such a "politically correct" (PC) or "woke" culture created their "own monster" of "Trumpism" that survived outside of the presidency. For members of the "woke tribe," such charges might be considered progress and even provoke "stinging" responses back to anyone who might "stand in their way" of their "wokeness" (see Spaeth 2019). However, such rhetorical retaliation might be heard as offensive by other liberals, moderates, or any others within the Democratic Party "who are not blue enough" (Goldberg, 2018; see also Brooks 2019c; and Rennenkampff 2020). As a case in point, shortly after the 2020 election, Democratic Representative Abigail Spanberger warned that races were lost that "we shouldn't have lost." She also demanded Democrats never "say socialism ever again," warning they "need to get back to basics" and "if we run this [type of] race again we will get f***ng torn apart again in 2022." Missouri senator Claire McCaskill concurred, declaring that "as we circled the issues, we left voters behind and Republicans dug in" and that, perhaps arguing "'democratic' socialism is the good kind doesn't quite do it for the folks in Des Moines" (quoted in Harsany 2020; see also Bouie 2019).

Perhaps ironically, members of this party faction were often in problematic situations because their policy preferences appeared to exclude marginalized communities—with whom they were supposed to be allies. As an example, Black and Asian Democrats were significantly more supportive of restrictive immigration policies and less positive toward racial/ethnic diversity than their white liberal counterparts. In addition, Black and Hispanic Democrats were more sympathetic toward Israel than not and also more likely to be uncomfortable with contemporary social and gender-identity issues (Kuhn 2020; see also Goldberg 2018).

IDENTITY POLITICS AND POLITICAL LOYALTIES

The Democratic left also appears to be more influenced by identity politics than other cohorts within the Democratic Party. This has, in turn, influenced their view of the Constitution. A number of progressives, particularly those who are younger, appear to have turned against what were once "sacrosanct American principles." These include configuring free speech as an instrument of oppression—religious liberty as a conduit of discrimination and property rights as a shield for structural injustice. American Millennials are far more likely than older generations to say the government should be able to prevent people from saying offensive statements about minority groups, according to a Pew Research Center survey regarding global perceptions of free speech and media (Poushter 2015).

There are considerations based on this data for members of all political tribes. To illustrate, conservatives might consider that "making good" on the promises embedded in the Constitution requires "more than flag-waving":

> If millions of people believe that, because of their skin color or religion, they are not treated equally, how can they be expected to see the Constitution's resounding principles as anything but hollow?

In addition, liberals could revisit their "scorched-earth approach" to the nation's past. There is a "world of difference" between insisting the United States has failed to live up to its constitutional principles and saying that those principles are lies or smoke screens for oppression:

> Washington and Jefferson were slave owners. They were also political visionaries who helped give birth to what would become the most inclusive form of governance in world history. (Chua and Rubenfeld 2018)

Generational Tribalism

The "generational tribalism" evidenced through recent demographic research suggests that political polarization is often influenced by "age identity." Furthermore, such divisions are not necessarily driven by ideology. Younger Americans have grown up with crises including the invasion of Iraq, the response to Hurricane Katrina, and the 2008 financial crisis and so may believe they have legitimate reasons to feel animosity toward members of the "gerontocracy," many of whom belong to moderate and centrist cohorts within the Democratic Party.

A Pew Research Center study concluded the differences in partisan identification across generations was most apparent in the shares of liberal Democrats and conservative Republicans. Conservative and moderate Democrats and moderate and liberal Republicans tended to skew generationally closer across both parties (Manium and Smith 2017).

The generation gap in American politics has divided younger age groups, Millennials and Generation X ("Post-Millennials"), from the two older groups, Baby Boomers and the Silent Generation. In 2016, Millennials and Gen-Xers were the most Democratic generations. In addition, both had relatively large—and growing—shares of liberal Democrats: 27 percent of Millennials and 21 percent of Gen-Xers identified as liberal Democrats or Democratic-leaning independents. Millennials were the largest generation in the nation and the most diverse in the American history. They entered the job market during the worst recession since the 1930s. People under twenty-five faced unemployment rates more than double those of other age groups. By 2012, a record number of adults between eighteen and thirty-one were living with their parents. In the 2010s, as Trumpism was coalescing on the right, a rival political ideology was growing on the left, driven by young people. Millennials remained the most liberal and Democratic of the adult generations. They continued to be the most likely to identify with the Democratic Party or lean Democratic to such an extent that, by the 2018 midterms, substantially more Millennials than those in older generational cohorts favored the Democratic candidates in midterm congressional elections ("The Generation Gap" 2018).

Many in these factions were vested in Barack Obama as their hope for moving the nation center-left and more. Between 2013 and 2017, the median age of members of the Democratic Socialists of America dropped from sixty-eight to thirty-three. Others expressed a desire for a socialism that was closer to the New Deal. In 2019, Greta Thunberg, the Swedish teenager who inspired a global climate strike, told the United Nations "change is coming, whether you like it or not" (quoted in Behl 2019; see also "Greta" 2019). The median American age is thirty-eight. By 2020, the average age for a United States senator was sixty-five. Congress was among the oldest in history. Senate Majority Leader Mitch McConnell was seventy-eight and House Speaker Nancy Pelosi eighty. Such generational differences also produce distinct if not conflicting rhetorical worldviews as well as distinct and polarized factions within the two major parties. In the words of Patrick Fisher, a Seton Hall professor who specializes in the political dynamics of age, "Demographically, politically, economically, socially and technologically, the generations are more different from each other now than at any time in living memory" (quoted in Osnos 2020b, 15–16; see also Rosentiel 2009).

JOE BIDEN AS A COMPROMISE(R)

In 2016, Joe Biden and Barack Obama shared a basic belief that Americans sought unity in politics. Running for president, Obama referenced an "empathy deficit" and called attention to the inability of many Americans to "recognize ourselves in one another, to understand that we are our brother's keeper and our sister's keeper" (quoted in Osnos 2020a, 137). Four years later María Urbina, the national political director of the liberal grassroots group Indivisible, complimented presidential candidate Joe Biden on forging a "continuum of support that is deep and wide" through engagement with and consolidating the support of progressives including Jay Inslee, Bernie Sanders, and Elizabeth Warren (quoted in Smith 2020). The two dominant Democratic tribes within the Democratic party, centrists and progressives, appeared to willingly unite against the "existential threat of Trump," at least long enough to attempt a defeat of the incumbent president.

However, progressives anticipated the possibility a discourse-driven "paradigm" shift within their party should Biden be successful in his bid for the White House. Neil Sroka, a spokesperson for Democracy for America, a political action committee that endorsed Sanders in the Democratic primary, insisted the "realigning of the left and center" had "already happened" and that if Biden won, he would assume office with the "most progressive agenda a Democrat has ever been elected on in the history of the country" (quoted in Smith 2020; see also Beauchamp 2020). As an example, when Joe Biden released economic recommendations in August of 2020, they included ideas that worried some in in the banking industry. These included allowing banking at the post office and having the Federal Reserve guarantee all Americans a bank account.

Maintaining a Center-Left Profile

Still, in private calls with Wall Street leaders, the Biden campaign made it clear those proposals would not be central to his agenda. "They basically said, 'Listen, this is just an exercise to keep the Warren people happy, and don't read too much into it,'" one investment banker stated, referring to liberal supporters of Senator Elizabeth Warren (quoted in Linskey 2020b).

A reluctance to be pinned down on policy details was central to Joe Biden's campaign, grounded in a pledge to "restore the soul of the nation" rather than any particular "legislative holy grail" based in an "all-things-to-all-people approach." While sometimes making strong declarations in public, the former vice president also relied on aides to "soothe critics behind the scenes" (Sullivan 2020). That strategy, reflecting a decades-long career in which Biden presented himself more as mediator than ideologue, helped him unify his party's liberal and moderate wings behind the shared goal of defeating Donald Trump, albeit perhaps temporarily (Accetti 2020; Osnos 2020b; Haltiwanger 2020). However, this ethos could also become a point of contention in a Biden presidency, on topics from race to climate to trade (Hook 2019). As a case in point, some Black Lives Matter activists pressed for more concrete commitments from Joe Biden, worried they would "prove elusive" once he became president (see Voght 2020 and Lizza et al. 2020). It was also clear that Vermont Senator Bernie Sanders was speaking for his progressive tribe when he referenced Biden's endorsement of three months of paid family and medical leave and an expansion of child care should the Democrats take both Congress and the White House. Sanders warned the Democratic nominee that party liberals would "be damn sure" that Joe Biden would "follow through on the proposals that he is supporting right now" (quoted in Linskey 2020b).

A President for Republicans (Too) in a Politically Tribalized Nation

In the spring of 2020, Biden began describing himself as a "transition candidate," explaining:

> We have not given a bench to younger people in the party, the opportunity to have the focus and be in focus for the rest of the country. There's an incredible group of talented, newer, younger people. (quoted in Osnos 2020a)

Ben Rhodes, an adviser to Obama in the White House, said of the former vice president's unwillingness to take sides within his own party:

> It's actually a really powerful idea. It says, "I'm a seventy-seven-year-old white man, who was a senator for thirty years, and I understand both those limitations and the nature of this country." Because, no matter what he does, he cannot completely understand the frustration of people in the streets. That's not a criticism. It's just a reality. (quoted in Osnos 2020a)

Regardless, his general approach to campaigning continued to frustrate, if not baffle, many in the Democratic party, despite tribal affiliations. For instance, as he moved through the election cycle, Joe Biden continued to reference himself as a "transition candidate," who would be able to overcome generational and ideological rifts. Specifically, he chose to modify the narrative regarding the animosity between these political tribal factions, doing so through a bipartisan discourse. Perhaps not surprisingly, this was a disconcerting and itself a rhetorical position, too centrist for many Democrats and not enough so for others. Both contingencies were concerned that Biden was not "coming around" to their perspective of what the American presidency should do to further "their cohort's" agenda. Ironically, some of this tribe-centric partisan talk, critical of Joe Biden, was successfully co-opted by Republicans and turned into effective talking points with which to campaign against Democratic candidates (see Balz 2019; Graham 2020).

During an August 2020 interview with *New Yorker* columnist Evan Osnos, Biden spoke as a candidate whose job was to defeat Donald Trump rather than cater to completing blocs within his own party, which might weaken or thwart this goal. To that end, he configured weaponizing the term "socialism" as a rhetorical device with which Trump smoke-screened his own failures of leadership, particularly in the pandemic:

> Everybody knows, even people supporting him: this is all about his self-interest. It's all about him. . . . It has had profound impacts on people's ability to live their life. . . . They think that they will be materially better off if he's President. . . . He has gotten through, I think, to some degree—to about forty per cent [of Republicans]—saying, "The Democrats are socialists. They're here to take away everything you have." (quoted in Osnos 2020a)

This is not to dismiss that the Democratic nominee was averse to positioning himself, albeit by increments, in different directions within his own party's ideological spectrum and divided body. As an example, in 2012, while Barak Obama was weighing an endorsement of same-sex marriage, Joe Biden "beat him to it," saying at the time that he was "absolutely comfortable" with the concept. By his own account, Biden entered the Democratic primaries in 2019 with a narrow goal: to end the Trump presidency by uniting his party through a rhetoric of inclusion. Most Americans, he argued, did not want a revolution. At an early New York fundraiser, he promised not to "demonize" the rich and said that "nothing would fundamentally change." But, by March 2020, having effectively clinched the nomination, he appeared to frame his candidacy as one of change, akin to Franklin Roosevelt's New Deal. According to a senior aide to Bernie Sanders, Joe Biden told Sanders, in a phone call about a possible endorsement, "I want to be the most progressive President since F.D.R." (quoted in Osnos 2020a).

When queried about occasions when Joe Biden appeared, even within his own party, to swerve left," Barack Obama suggested that "from a forty-thousand-foot level" moderate and progressive Democrats were "not that different." Joe Biden and Bernie Sanders both wanted health care for all Americans, jobs that provided living wages, and universal education for children. Ultimately, in Obama's view, the perceived "movement left" was likely due to changed circumstances rather than a self-ascribed moderate or centrist ethos. A senior Obama administration official observed that Joe Biden's refusal to stake out tribal territory—beyond identity as "a Democrat" also contained a subtler message: "This country needs to just chill the f**k out and have a boring President" (cited in Osnos 2020a).

POLITICAL TRIBES

Republican

Beginning in 2018, multiple anti-Trump Republican groups began to coalesce including Reclaim Our Party, a super PAC targeting right-leaning independents and ambivalent Republicans with a message that it was alright to not support the president. By 2020, the two largest anti-Trump Republican groups were the Lincoln Project and Republican Voters Against Trump, both multimillion-dollar operations (see Parker and Costa 2020; Allan Smith 2020). They were joined by former Illinois Republican congressman Joe Walsh's Bravery Project and Stand Up Republic and its spin-off, Christians Against Trumpism and Political Extremism. Other push back organizations included the Republican Political Alliance for Integrity and Reform, known as Repair and helmed by former Trump administration officials and 43 Alumni for Joe Biden, organized by former staffers from President George W. Bush's administration (see Karni 2020). The sole raison d'etre of these party-less Republicans was to keep the current Republican president from securing a second term of office. They essentially co-existed in a loose and leaderless coalition without a tribal affiliation and so without a "figurehead" to whom they could show allegiance.

The result was the coagulation of the Republican Party during the 2020 presidential cycle into a rank-and-file endorsed super-tribe, "The Donald Base" (shortly to become "Tribe Trump"). The remains of what had been an already seriously incapacitated second party cohort was a neutralized, impotent, and shrinking "orphaned" faction of traditional Republican conservative voters with little organization, no leadership, and little if any power. As a case in point, suggestions about forming a third party or a new center-right faction were resisted even by some of Trump's "toughest Republican critics." This was because attempting to do so required "years if not decades" to access enough funds to have an impact, considering the Republican Party's "massive" Trump-centric "political infrastructure" (Reid et al. 2021; see also Matthews 2020).

It is likely that the aftershocks of Donald Trump's one-of-a-kind presidency will take years to place into full historical context. Some of the most pressing questions, particularly in the aftermath of the January 2021 attack on the Capitol and Trump's subsequent bipartisan impeachment, concern the future of the Republican Party (see Feuer 2021; Newman 2021). Some Republicans moved away from Trump, but many continued to fight on his behalf, including by voting to reject the electoral votes of two states won by Biden. In one sense, the "Tea Party" movement, which rhetorically coalesced during the 2009 "summer of rage" as a primarily Republican populist alliance, informed throughout by a "tear-down-the-house" mentality, is extinct.

The alliance, which at the height of its influence in 2011 was bringing in $20 million a year in contributions, buttressed by a 60-member strong caucus, went inactive in 2012. Its alleged demise could be attributed to the reality that a "mass uprising based" on think-tank inspired "small-government libertarianism" was simply "not so popular with most Americans" (Peters 2019). Even so, the Tea Party legacy—in practice, if not in theory—now threatens the stability of contemporary political parties in the United States.

Kabaservice (2020) maintains that "if the best guide to conservatism was once Arthur Schlesinger Jr.'s 'The Cycles of American History,'" in the current political culture, "it might be Leon Trotsky's 'The Permanent Revolution.'" The evidence for this conclusion is that "conservatism's familiar pattern of advance, consolidation, retrenchment and renewal has vanished" replaced by "something that looks like #MAGA Forever" (see also Williamson et al. 2011). It appears, then, that rather than imploding, the Tea Party has only been ghosting Republicans.

Democrat

Osnos (2020a) argues the tensions afflicting the Democratic Party reflect a clash between liberal meliorism, the "long view" of Biden and Obama politics, as well as "the impatient movement that Bernie Sanders labels a 'revolution.'"

The dominant Democratic discursively populated tribes, in this view, essentially claim competing virtues: one emphasizes realism, coalition-building, and practical politics, and the other the inescapable evidence that "reform" has failed to confront pervasive inequalities, the cruelties of American health care and incarceration, and ecological catastrophe. Barack Obama suggests tribalism within his party originates in "the traditional Democratic idea":

> You have a big-tent party. And that means that you tolerate, listen to, and embrace folks who are different than you, and try to get them in the fold. And so you work with not just liberal Democrats, but you work with conservative Democrats—and you are willing to compromise on issues. (quoted in Osnos 2020a; see also Dionne, Jr. 2020b)

The epicenter, then, of at least a substantial part of the tribal dissention within the party is that moderates can work with liberals because they share the same foundational beliefs, albeit with different timelines. Progressives, on the other hand, because their "it's now or never" timeline naturally excludes any plans that occur outside of their own discrete chronology, are less inclined to form intraparty coalitions. Obama countered the perception by some Democrats that compromise or tolerance, at least with or for those in their party with whom they did not agree, was a sign of weakness or, worse, an ideological failure (Osnos 2020a).

Shortly before the general election in 2020, there was speculation regarding the estimated 2 to 4 percent of the electorate who were still undecided two weeks before the general election and so might still be receptive to a unification narrative. One consultant in Portland, Oregon attributed the indecision to stubbornness, particularly among Bernie Sanders supporters, who, even at that late date, were refusing to endorse Joe Biden by "acting as though they're deliberative rather than idiots" (Judkis 2020). Ultimately, then, it appears that in order to be of consequence, any serious rhetorical management of the tribal ruptures within the Democratic Party tribe must address this troublesome contingency. Embedded in the worldview of at least one Democratic tribe is a default attitude to devalue, if not exclude, the norms of the other.

THE TRUMP EFFECT

Prior to the beginning of his presidency in 2016, Donald Trump split Republicans and Democrats more deeply than any president in thirty years. In 1994, when the Pew Research Center began asking Americans a series of ten "values questions" on subjects including the role of government, environmental protection, and national security, the average gap between Republicans and Democrats was 15 percentage points ("The People" 1994). Differences exacerbated considerably after Trump became president. By the first year of his presidency, the average partisan gap on those same questions had more than doubled to 36 points, the result of a steady, decades-long increase in polarization. Turnout in the 2018 midterm election, the first after Trump took office, also set a modern record. Even as he repeatedly cast doubt on the democratic process, Donald Trump as president proved to be an enormously galvanizing figure at the polls (Dimonk and Gramlich 2021).

Insurrection and Impeachment

Nearly 160 million Americans voted in 2020, the highest estimated turnout rate among eligible voters in 120 years, despite widespread changes in voting procedures brought on by the coronavirus pandemic. Joe Biden received more than 81 million votes and Trump received more than 74 million, the highest and second-highest totals in US history. By the end of his tenure in January 2021, fully 86 percent of Republicans still approved of Trump's enactment of the presidency while only six percent of Democrats gave their endorsement—the widest partisan gap in approval for any president in the modern era of polling (see also Porterfield 2021; Keeter 2021).

On January 6, 2021, during a "rally" outside the White House, Donald Trump continued falsely claiming the election had been "stolen" (Breuninger 2021). With Congress meeting the same day to certify Joe Biden's win of the presidency, Trump supporters attacked the Capitol in an assault that left five people dead and forced lawmakers to be evacuated until order could be restored and the certification could be completed. The House of Representatives impeached Trump a week later on a charge of inciting the violence, with ten Republicans joining 222 Democrats in support of the decision (Harper 2021; Leatherby et al. 2021). At the time, most Americans placed at least some blame on Trump for the riot at the Capitol, including 52 percent who said he bore a lot of responsibility for it. Once again, however, partisans' views differed widely: 81 percent of Democrats said Trump bore a lot of responsibility, compared with just 18 percent of Republicans (Dimonk and Gramlich 2021).

Acquittal and Acrimony

A 57–43 majority of the Senate voted to convict Trump, including seven Republicans who joined the fifty Democrats. Still, the final count fell short of the two-thirds majority necessary to convict the former president for "incitement of insurrection" (Weigel et al. 2021). At the time, Republican Senator Ben Sasse of Nebraska, who voted to convict, observed that while "tribalism is a hell of a drug" senators must nonetheless prioritize "our oath to the Constitution," which "means we're constrained to the facts." Lara Brown, director of the Graduate School of Political Management at George Washington University, maintained the vote to impeach Donald Trump would further "rend the Republican Party" and that Republicans talk about a "big tent" would likely "not be possible because no meaningful grey area" existed between Trump's contingent and other Republicans cohorts:

> It seems that the party is headed for many more months of in-fighting that will only be resolved by the 2022 elections, primary and general elections. And by resolved, I mean that one faction will likely prevail over the other, but which will win is hard to say. (quoted in Jackson 2021; see also Cillizza 2020)

The GOP's direction could depend to a considerable degree on what Donald Trump does "next." Nearly two-thirds of Americans (68 percent) said in January 2021 that they would not like to see Trump continue to be a major political figure in the years to come, but Republicans were divided by ideology. More than half of self-described moderate and liberal Republicans (56 percent) said they preferred for him to exit the political stage, while fully 68 percent of conservatives said they wanted him to remain a national political figure for many years to come (Dimonk and Gramlich, 2021). For all intents and purposes, by 2021 the Republican Party had effectively morphed into the Tribe of Trump.

An Exigence of Polarized Political Tribalism

DiSalvo (2012) argues that intraparty factions are sub-units capable of shaping ideological agendas within political parties, which then "try to move their party along the Left–Right spectrum" (7). Given the public's limited political knowledge, such party brands influence policy in a direction that is, regardless of affiliation, oppositional to positions held by centrist voters.

Clearly, one of the most pragmatic and consequential effects of entrenched American political tribalism is tumultuous, incessant, and increasingly angry public argument, enacted through contested elections, incivility, and acts of violence, some of which explode into domestic terrorism. This discord is driven by acrimonious disagreement over the nation's global persona and, significantly, over the meaning of being American (Shapiro and Fogel 2019). In light of the historical symbiosis between healthy democracies and healthy discourse, the resolution of such discord as well as rediscovering a national identity for the United States, including that of the nation's political tribes, may be a defining rhetorical exigence of the twenty-first century.

Chapter 4

Congressional Tribalism

Prior to the 1830s, congressional parties, rather than the electorate, chose American presidential candidates. During this period, the nation operated more like a parliamentary system in that congressional caucuses would single out candidates who were deemed electable. The first genuinely populist revolt in the United States was initiated by Andrew Jackson as an attack against the Democratic-Republican Party (as "Eastern elites") after it declined to select him in 1824. In 1832, a group of delegates supporting President Andrew Jackson met in Baltimore to conduct the first official convention of the Democratic Party, setting trends that lasted more than a century ("On This Day . . ." 2020; see also Miller 2021). Some have suggested, with little enthusiasm, that a return to privileging congressional parties' role in choosing candidates might counter the ascension of populists to the presidency (Cummings 2020; Clark 2020; Beinart 2016; Anderson 2013).

As recently as 2018 political parties appeared, at least on occasion, to be rhetorically holding the line against extremist factions, left or right. In a study of the 2018 primaries, Kamarck and Podkul (2018b) observed that congressional candidates described themselves in terms of the most common intraparty groups. Republicans generally self-reported belonging to one of four categories: Business/Establishment, Conservative, Tea Party, or Libertarian. Democrats overall sorted themselves into one of three categories: Progressive, Establishment, or Moderate. Additional results were revealing. Incumbents were excluded since, regardless of party affiliation, such candidates typically won their races. That said, on the Democratic side there were slightly more Establishment candidates than Progressive candidates, and Establishment candidates won more often. On the Republican side, the Establishment candidates did even better, winning their primaries 40 percent of the time compared to 24.8 percent of the time for Conservative candidates.

THE MIDTERMS

However, there were precedents for factional division within the two American "big tent" political parties, notably from a conservative right and a liberal left. Significantly, during the midterm elections of 2010, the Tea Party challenge to Republican Party incumbents produced a contingent of House Republican Conference insurgents with essentially uncompromising positions that stalled government, drove a Speaker of the House from office, and accelerated Congressional dysfunction. A similar rupture developed after Bernie Sanders's strong showing for progressives in the 2016 Democratic primaries (Brownstein 2020b; Kelley 2018). Both factions within the separate major parties exemplify rhetorical perspectives that continue to modify, shape, and influence the contemporary political landscape in the United States.

2018 Midterms

In the run-up to the 2018 midterm elections, what had initially been the "paralyzing" partisanship characterized by accelerating tension between Democrats and Republicans finally ruptured. Party divides were rhetorically cleaved into "schisms within the parties" and, in some instances, "schisms within schisms" (Seib 2017). As an example, Democrats splintered over whether to reconfigure Senate rules to prevent the ascension of Neil Gorsuch to the Supreme Court (Godfrey 2017; Tau 2017) as Republicans battled over the fundamental fairness of the US economic system ("Political Typology . . ." 2017). While such polarization accelerated during the first two years of the Trump presidency, Republican Representative Tom Cole of Oklahoma suggested, "He didn't create them. He walked into it." Dissension within the parties evidenced ideological battles within each. In addition, at the time, Republicans discursively battled over the trajectory of their support for a health care bill. A Pew Research study revealed that that even in a political landscape substantially scarred by partisanship, the divisions within the Republican and Democratic coalitions were as important a factor in American politics as the divisions between them ("Political Typology . . ." 2017).

In some cases, these fissures were not new—evident in a half dozen previous Pew Research Center typology studies conducted over three decades. Yet, especially within the GOP, many of the divisions centered on the issues that had been front-and-center for Donald Trump since he first launched his presidential campaign ("Political Typology . . ." 2017). Several distinct factions had taken shape at this point (Seib 2017). These included the "President's Tribe," frequently populated by a base with minimal government experience and little allegiance to the Republican Party. Instead, voters who were primarily outside of the Beltway as well as anyone who best served his personal interests were afforded most of Trump's attention. Essentially an independent force, since his office had been secured with limited support from Republican Party leaders, he continued to surround himself largely by constituents with limited interest in government, which in turn provoked more loyalty to Donald Trump than to a Republican Congress.

A second tribe, the Governing Republicans, included party members who celebrated the potential to control American government and believed it was imperative to demonstrate success at governing, even if that meant accepting compromises with Democrats. The Freedom Caucus formed a third group, composed by the House of Representatives' most conservative Republicans. For example, this sector of the party blocked a bill to repeal and replace Obamacare because it failed to meet their principles.

On the other side of the aisle, tribal cohorts within the Democratic Party included the Never-Trump Democrats, often given voice by Senator Bernie Sanders. This bloc generally refused to cooperate with any of the tribes within the Republican Party. Party Chair Tom Perez also spoke for this tribe when he rallied Democratic protestors by insisting that Donald Trump had not legitimately won the 2016 election. The Maybe-Sometimes-Trump Democrats were moderate to conservative Democrats, many from states the president won, who occasionally expressed a willingness to work with the Trump administration on selected issues. Senators Heidi Heitkamp of North Dakota, Joe Manchin of West Virginia, and Joe Donnelly of Indiana were members of this tribe as evidenced by their willingness to break with the majority of their party to support Trump's choice of Judge Gorsuch for the Supreme Court ("Senate Democrats . . ." 2018). While largely united in opposition against the president, Trump's election provoked a wave of political activism within the left-leaning liberal Democratic faction, with an enthusiasm not replicated among other segments in the Democratic base. In addition, Democrats were also internally divided over US global involvement, as well as some religious and social issues ("Political Typology . . ." 2017).

Of the five tribal segments in play at the time, Seib (2017) maintained that a congressional combination of centrist governing Republicans and Democrats willing to cross alliance boundaries to work together was the "likeliest path to legislative achievement amid factionalized Washington." To that end, Democratic Senators Heitkamp, Manchin, Mark Warner, and Claire McCaskill, and Republicans Bob Corker, John McCain, Rob Portman, and Lamar Alexander suggested a possibility existed for developing a bipartisan rhetoric through which congenital interparty and intraparty discord might be addressed.

TRIBALISM AS A "BLAMING GAME"

Both Republican and Democratic Parties have had relatively little public vetting of intraparty conflicts until recently. Republicans in particular have not attempted to manage tensions between those with significantly different ideas or geographic bases than those of their leadership, despite the "noise" made by the "Tea Party" and, a decade later, the Freedom Caucus, albeit regarding tactics rather than ideology (Teles and Saldin 2021). They have not done so in great part because the dominant "Team Trump" cohort—and its leadership in particular—generally manages intratribal conflict through intimidation and oppression rather than deliberative discussion.

Conversely, Democrats are engaged in an increasingly contentious intraparty battle between a polarized liberal-to-progressive faction and a moderate-to-center "mainstream 'Biden Wing'" faction. Both have well-organized memberships, clearly structured and occasionally charismatic leadership, delineated participation corridors, user-friendly social media networks, and impressive sources of funding. And, as of the 2020 election cycle, moderates have become an "embattled majority," having been "put on notice that they are in the crosshairs of the party's left wing," as evidenced by congressional losses, some of which took establishment leadership by surprise (Teles and Saldin 2021).

Beginning with the 2018 primaries, Democratic Party leaders cautioned that embracing progressive-backed programs such as Medicare for all and the Green New Deal would produce losses. This resulted in narrowing their focus to centrist issues such as saving the Affordable Care Act and defeating Donald Trump. While Joe Biden won the presidency, crucial down-ticket losses in the House and Senate resulted in a "knives are out for the left" reaction from party leaders and moderates. As a case in point, Majority Whip James E. Clyburn of South Carolina spoke against running on defunding the police, while Florida Representative Donna Shalala argued she lost her bid for re-election because of the rise of "The Squad." This, in turn, drew media attention, which "reinforced" arguments that the Democratic Party was dominated by socialism (Jacobs 2020). Virginia Representative Abigail Spanberger argued that Democrats, should never again use the word "socialism" because doing so caused the loss of "good [party] members" (Dowd 2019).

Primarying

During the primaries, New York Representative Alexandria Ocasio-Cortez, when queried about Joe Biden as the possible nominee for her party, insisted "I don't want to go back. I want to go forward." The Green New Deal advocate referenced Biden's approach to global warming by asserting she would "be damned if the same politicians who refused to act then are going to try to come back today and say we need to find a middle-of-the-road approach to save our lives." Waleed Shahid, speaking for the left-leaning Justice Democrats, concurred and worried that "so-called 'centrist' Joe Biden would turn Democrats into the party of 'No, we can't,'" and predicted 'there is going to be a war within the party' which 'we [progressives] are going to lean into'" (quoted in Murdock 2019).

Democratic freshman Representative Ilhan Omar, a member of the progressive Democratic "Squad" (Izadi and Epstein 2019; "AOC, Omar, Pressley, Tlaib" 2019), who had been challenged by Antone Melton-Meaux as too divisive and "overly focused" on building a national profile, ultimately retained her seat in the August 2020 Minnesota primary. Ocasio-Cortez and Rashida Tlaib of Michigan, also members of the "Squad," faced similar opposition and also won their primary races earlier in the year. The victory for Omar afforded the freshmen group a more secure foothold in the caucus and more power as they pushed back against the party's centrists (Fandos 2020a).

Additional primary wins by other Democratic liberals included Jamaal Bowman in New York, Cori Bush in Missouri, and Marie Newman in Illinois, all of whom unseated moderate incumbents. Newman defeated Representative Dan Lipinski, a conservative Democrat who opposed abortion rights and the Affordable Care Act. Bush's campaign explicitly benefited from the momentum claimed by progressives in 2020 and since 2018 (Foran 2020). A documentary about her 2018 campaign and that of challengers like Ocasio-Cortez, "Knock Down the House," also contributed to their national profile (Dargis 2019). All won their national races in November ("U.S. Election" 2021). Like Ocasio-Cortez, each challenger had the backing of Justice Democrats, whose executive director Alexandra Rojas insisted "the Squad is here to stay, and it's growing" (Fandos 2020a).

Progressive Democrats were not hesitant to take on their centrist colleagues who threatened left-leaning (or those re-purposed as liberals in a "primary-ing" battle) incumbents during the 2020 state primaries. Notably, incumbent Senator Ed Markey easily won Massachusetts's Democratic Senate primary, defeating a member of one of the most preeminent families in Democratic politics through a show of force for the party's left wing, not a uniformly popular outcome within the party. Graham (2020) argues that while the "AOC progressives" were in sync with fellow Americans regarding "hating Trump" and so considered him a divisive president, "The Squad" and their advocates within the party were "completely out of step on policy." From this perspective, most Americans did not want to replace their private insurance with Medicare for all, had little interest in paying higher energy costs to "bring about the Green New Deal windmill utopia," and were not in favor of "defunding cops or funding reparations." Regardless, the "social justice warriors" of the Sunrise Movement, Justice Democrats, and Democracy for America made these issues mandatory to such an extent that any Democrat hoping to win their endorsements in a primary who rejected them did so "at your peril."

Case in Point: Joe Kennedy III

Representative Joe Kennedy III became the first in his family, an American political dynasty, to lose a congressional campaign in their home state (Hook 2020). Overall, Kennedy claimed that he would be a better senator, who could both deliver for his state and build the party across the country. He also criticized Senator Ed Markey, who had been endorsed by "The Squad," for spending less time at home in Massachusetts than any other member of the state's congressional delegation, even when Senator Elizabeth Warren was running for president (Anthony Brooks 2020). A *Boston Globe* and Suffolk University poll a year earlier had Kennedy leading Markey by 14 points in a hypothetical matchup. In addition, Kennedy led among voters in every sub-group, including younger and older voters (Pindell and Graham 2019). Polls showed him with a double-digit lead while public perceptions of Markey included that he was "more likely to be seen at a Starbucks in suburban Washington than a Dunkin' Donuts near his home in Malden." Former Congressional Representative Michael Capuano described Joe Kennedy's candidacy as "designed around the idea that a vote for Kennedy was an investment in his seemingly limitless political future, while Markey was already on his way out the door." Yet by the last month of the campaign, as mail-in voting began, polls showed Markey had taken the lead (Pindell and Graham 2019).

There were signs that Kennedy was frustrated by this downturn when he told CNN in August 2020 that the coronavirus pandemic "without question hinders a challenger" since it limited his ability to connect in person with people, which he viewed as one of his advantages in the race. Nonetheless a masked Kennedy extensively canvassed Massachusetts and picked up the endorsement of House Speaker Nancy Pelosi, a "surprise move" during what had become a contentious race by September 2020. One rhetorical device employed by Pelosi was the spotlighting of Kennedy's effort to help win back the House in 2018 by campaigning and fundraising for Democrats in tight races across the country, which helped deliver Democrats the House majority.

In advocating for Kennedy, Pelosi asserted that "the times" demand "we elect courageous leaders." She also tacitly appealed to liberals in the party by insisting that Kennedy "knows that to achieve progressive change, you must be on the front lines leading movements of people" (quoted in Caygle and Ferris 2020). Even so, Markey won voters and shattered the Kennedy political mystique in the deeply Democratic state of Massachusetts by successfully persuading the liberal faction of the party. This included building an "implausible connection" with young insurgents through Ocasio-Cortez, as well as endorsements from Elizabeth Warren and other progressive and center-left congressional candidates such as Missouri's Cori Bush who had ousted incumbents elsewhere (Hook 2020).

Ocasio-Cortez, who advocated the Green New Deal with Ed Markey at one point, accused Joe Kennedy of being "a progressive in name only" (LeBlanc 2020). Pelosi's endorsement "infuriated many progressives," who had faced mounting resistance from the Democratic establishment as they launched their own primary challenges against sitting members. For instance, Ocasio-Cortez, who had actively and vocally endorsed left-leaning challenges to moderate Democrats since her own 2018 "insurgent campaign," called out Pelosi with "no one gets to complain about primary challenges again." Furthermore, the House Speaker's support of Kennedy over Markey countered the party's default policy against backing challengers, which Ocasio-Cortez condemned as "like less a policy and more a cherry-picking activity" (Caygle and Ferris 2020).

Kennedy also struggled to articulate his message while Markey essentially rebranded himself as a progressive warrior on climate change while advocating for other "revolutionary priorities" of the Democratic Party's more liberal cohort. In so doing, the incumbent harnessed support from liberal leaders to overcome a challenge from his younger rival, a grandson of Robert F. Kennedy by a margin of nearly 11 points (LeBlanc 2020). Ultimately, Senator Markey did a "masterful" (and more effective job) of campaigning, rebranding himself so that voters believed the incumbent was "someone he is not" (Murray 2020b).

Ed Markey had successfully embellished and even occasionally exaggerated ideological differences between himself and Kennedy who, in truth, held essentially the same view as Markey on most major issues. As an example, both supported the Green New Deal and Medicare for all. Markey's "come-from-behind" victory has been attributed to an aggressive campaign of support from liberals, led by progressive politicians and organizations. This coalition went "all in" to defend him in part to demonstrate to other Democrats who might "venture into progressive waters" that they would have political cover. The high-profile paradigm campaign also functioned to warn other moderates who might challenge other "Squad-backed" candidates that they would be similarly targeted (Robillard 2020).

Markey stepped into the political vacuum created by the departures of progressive icons Elizabeth Warren and Bernie Sanders from the presidential primary. In short, Democrats within the "left-leaning" tribe of their party were "devastated" by the collapse of those two campaigns, resulting in a disappointed and agitated faction of newly unemployed former progressive staffers and volunteers—many of them Millennials and Gen-Xers—young high school and college activists with time and energy in excess. Ed Markey received their undivided attention as evidenced by a tweet from one of Warren's former staffers (which later became a viral source of campaign funding for Markey):

> Here is my #1 hot take as a newly-free Warren staffer: THE F**KING CO-AUTHOR OF THE GODDAMN GREEN NEW DEAL MIGHT LOSE HIS SEAT IN THE SENATE TO A MODERATE AND YOU'RE ALL JUST SLEEPING ON IT. (Murray, 2020)

The Markey campaign also spent almost half a million dollars airing an ad that only featured Ocasio-Cortez (and not Markey) leading up to the race against Kennedy. Evan Weber, co-founder of the Sunrise Movement, observed that the incumbent was "very eager" to "fight that fight with us" and "did a lot of work to rile up young people and the youths and progressives." Specifically, Markey ran a "policy-centered campaign" that foregrounded the Green New Deal and climate issues and remained laser focused in order to "rile up young people and the youths and progressives" (Murray 2020b).

The support of Chuck Schumer and moderate Joe Manchin for Markey, along with the incumbent's friendship with Ocasio-Cortez, demonstrated that any Senate race would pivot on generational rather than subjective policy differences with a "youthful Kennedy" and his unprecedented "family brand" facing off against Markey's four decades of service and lengthy record (Rogers 2020; Everett and Caygle 2019). Also, many Democrats considered Markey and Kennedy so "aligned ideologically" as center-left moderates, that it was unclear why Kennedy was challenging the incumbent in the first place. Markey supporter and conservative West Virginia Democratic Senator Joe Manchin even queried "what's the fight?" Others, however, were more than willing to discursively stretch depictions of the two as representatives of ideologically opposed tribal blocs: one (very) liberal and the other moderate at best.

Specifically, Senator Markey deflected Joe Kennedy's "shine" by "projecting the power of some of the party's brightest stars," the foremost being Alexandria Ocasio-Cortez, whose presence alone was instrumental in creating the narrative of Kennedy as "not liberal enough" (Rogers 2020). In a video posted on the Markey campaign's YouTube account, she imagined a future party with Ed Markey as "a proud and strong progressive champion" for working families not just in Massachusetts, but across the country:

Ed Markey ... is one of the strongest progressives that we have in the United States Senate. And in a time right now, when we have to have conversations not just about holding this administration accountable but changing the Democratic Party for the future, Ed Markey has a very critical role in making sure that climate change, as well as a bevy of other issues—health care and beyond—are critical core issues in how we fight for working people and working families in the United States." (Graham 2020)

Markey responded in kind, stating he was "proud to partner" with Ocasio-Cortez and "honored" that she chose to endorse his candidacy over Kennedy. More than that, Markey was "fortunate" to call the New York congresswoman his "friend and colleague" and, again, reminded his constituents how "I am proud to have her support" (Graham 2020).

The coveted endorsement from the New York congresswoman undercut one of the biggest premises of a Kennedy challenge to Markey: the call for a generational change from the incumbent, then 73, to Kennedy, then 38. At 29, in 2018 Ocasio-Cortez became the youngest woman ever to be elected to Congress (Hess 2018). Often photographed in "retro-hip Nikes," Markey discursively aligned himself with New York's Ocasio-Cortez, "the party phenom," as well as the Sunrise Movement, a primarily youthful group focused on combating climate change, "to show he was of the times." This point was spelled out in an Ocasio-Cortez ad in which she exclaimed "when it comes to progressive leadership" that it was "not your age that counts" but rather "the age of your ideas" followed with the assertion that "Ed Markey is the leader we need" (Murray 2020a).

When initially considering whether or not to challenge Senator Markey, Joe Kennedy was warned that, in addition to the incumbent, he would also have to take on and defeat Chuck Schumer, Elizabeth Warren, the Senate Democrats' campaign arm, and "maybe Alexandria Ocasio-Cortez." The congressman and grandson of Robert F. Kennedy was told he would likely "confront a buzz saw of Washington Democrats" if he challenged the Massachusetts senator, a move that would be "a massive distraction" for the party in a safe Democratic state when party focus needed to be on the battle against Republicans for both the White House and the Senate majority.

At the same time, moderate New Hampshire Senator Jeanne Shaheen insisted that the kind of "intraparty" fighting that could result from such a challenge was "not good in the long term." Such a campaign would most likely be detrimental to Joe Kennedy, in that as a "survivor of the [Ted] Kennedy-[Jimmy]Carter fight" during the 1976 presidential campaign, Senator Shaheen recognized "how long those [negative] sentiments last" (Everett and Caygle 2019; Davies 2019). Kennedy certainly encountered the "buzz saw" effect up-front and personally as he campaigned to unseat Ed

Markey. Time will show to what extent his political career was damaged by the "brush up" with the self-identified Liberal tribe of his party in general and the "The Squad" in particular.

A uniquely salient—and surprising to the Kennedy campaign—discursive device employed by Markey and his team was the weaponization of Joe Kennedy's name. Drew O'Brien, a former adviser to John Kerry and Boston Mayor Thomas Menino, indicated that liberals not only succeeded, during the Massachusetts campaign, in redefining the Kennedy name for the electorate but rhetorically created an "astounding" transformation of Ed Markey into the "darling of the young Sunrise Movement and the progressive Movement" (Murray 2020). Initially reluctant to capitalize on the Kennedy legacy, it became an issue after the incumbent strategically cast voters' choice as between supporting a "son of the working class" or an "entitled scion" (Graham 2020).

Markey also inverted former President John F. Kennedy's famous call to action declaring "it's time to start asking what your country can do for you." Joe Kennedy's campaign countered by explicitly identifying their candidate as the heir to the legacy of his grandfather Robert F. Kennedy and great-uncles John F. Kennedy and Ted Kennedy. Building on this legacy, the narrator of one television ad argued that Joe Kennedy's fight for health care for all, jobs and opportunity, and racial justice were "in his blood" (Rogers 2020). Although the Democratic challenger finally "embraced" his family name, it "came too late." The progressive factions of his party had metaphorically positioned Ed Markey as one of themselves. The transformation was a success and the Senator won as the "most all-out AOC candidate in the race" (Graham 2020).

In sum, the 2020 Massachusetts primary resolved in Markey's favor, in great part because of his successful discursive appeal to and rhetorical enactment of a tribalistic "liberal versus moderate" intraparty binary. Furthermore, this point was not missed by Donald Trump who, after Markey's clearly progressively backed victory, presidentially tweeted "see, even a Kennedy isn't safe in the new Radical Left Democrat Party" followed by "Pelosi strongly backed the loser!" (LeBlanc 2020). Ultimately, Joseph Kennedy III lost in every precinct in East Boston, home territory. He had been successfully primaried.

Moderates Push Back

Centrist Democratic tribal leaders accelerated efforts in the 2020 election cycle to protect incumbents from what they considered legitimately perceived threats from the progressive tribal faction. Notably, they hoped to reassure anxious moderates who witnessed firsthand Ocasio-Cortez topple moderate incumbent Joe Crowley in 2018 and then lead successful assaults against many other "not liberal enough" congressional candidates. New York's Crowley, once seen as a possible successor to Nancy Pelosi as Democratic leader of the House, experienced a "shocking" primary defeat to the "political newcomer," an organizer for Bernie Sanders's 2016 presidential campaign, who ran on a platform of generation, racial, and ideological change. Crowley's defeat by Ocasio-Cortez, albeit in a low turnout district, was considered the "most significant loss for a Democratic incumbent in more than a decade" and one that would "reverberate across the party and the country" (Goldmacher 2018; Martin 2020b).

Graham (2020) believed the impacts of the "trophies being collected by Team AOC" with candidates including Ayanna Pressley in Boston, Jamaal Bowman in New York City, and Cori Bush in St. Louis during congressional elections would be felt immediately among Democrats already in office. The "Democrats these progressives took down were not Blue Dog moderates like Joe Manchin in West Virginia" but "solid liberals" such as Massachusetts's Mike Capuano (see "Mike . . ." 2021). While the progressive tribe celebrated turning "purple seats blue," some in the party, albeit tongue-in-check, observed:

> Nobody is happier to see hardcore liberals being defeated by far-left crazies more than the GOP. You see Trump's tweet Wednesday morning? He couldn't contain his glee. [It read] "See, even a Kennedy isn't safe in the new Radical Left Democrat Party,' Taxes up big, no 2A. Biden has completely lost control. Pelosi strongly backed the loser!" (Graham 2020)

Delaware Senator Christopher A. Coons fended off a similar challenge in September 2020, defeating activist Jessica Scarane to win the Democratic nomination for a second full term. Elected in 2010 to the seat once held by former vice president Joe Biden, Coons had established a moderate profile while Scarane, a member of Democratic Socialists of America, ran on a platform that included Medicare for all and a Green New Deal. Despite anticipating that a Democrat leaning and "suburb-heavy state" would welcome a more liberal representative in Washington, Scarane's progressive message "hit a wall" with Delaware's Democrats. Coons secured the endorsement of his party as well as an endorsement from Biden. He also indicated he would not side with Republicans who would block a potential Biden agenda if Democrats won control of the Senate in November. In addition, he promised that "if Minority Leader McConnell . . . uses the filibuster to block progress. . . . I'm not going to stand by and watch" (Weigel 2020b). Coon's victory signaled the end of primary campaigning run by progressives that unseated three House Democrats and won a string of victories down the ballot (Weigel 2020b).

CAUGHT IN THE MIDDLE

In the run-up to the partisan fight over President Trump's push to install Judge Amy Coney Barrett on the court, California Senator Dianne Feinstein, the ranking Democrat and the oldest member of the Senate, kept a low profile, rarely engaging directly with the press. Fandos (2020b) reports that progressive Democratic activists, many of whom argued that she mishandled the confirmation process for Justice Brett M. Kavanaugh as well as the 2017 hearing on Barrett's confirmation to an appeals court, considered pushing for Feinstein's removal.

Brian Fallon, a leader of a liberal advocacy group that lobbies Democrats to prioritize federal courts, referred to the concerns about Feinstein's competency as "further evidence" of how Democrats "ought" to frame committee leadership. The Senator's default negotiating strategy of seeking compromise with Republicans could hurt Democrats if they won back the Senate and Joe Biden was elected president:

> Dianne Feinstein is not somebody who inspires any confidence whatsoever that there will be sufficient attention on an issue that should be a priority of a President Biden . . . she will probably be an enabler and an accomplice to the obstruction efforts that created all of these vacancies for Trump to fill in the first place. (Fandos 2020b)

Meagan Hatcher-Mays, the director of policy for a progressive Democratic grass-roots group, also criticized Senator Feinstein's apparent lack of control over the Kavanaugh hearing, suggesting that her "genteel" demeanor was from another time and anachronistic in a twenty-first century Senate. Feinstein's signature politeness was configured as an artifact from a long-gone era: "She handled him with kid gloves . . . thanking him for being there. You don't have to do that!" (Fandos 2020b). Conversely, Feinstein's moderate defenders insisted their Democratic colleagues confused Feinstein's "patrician gentility for senility." For instance, Rhode Island's Senator Sheldon Whitehouse observed that while it was not in Senator Feinstein's "nature" to be "tangling with an obstreperous Lindsey Graham," the Republican Chair of the Judiciary Committee, "she brings a perspective, a dignity, a long history of bipartisanship, good will and an exemplary record on issues involving women, which are particularly germane" (Fandos 2020b).

This resulting controversy over Dianne Feinstein's role further evidenced tension between the centrist and liberal Democrats within their party. Furthermore, Republicans looked to, if not encouraged, the continuing intraparty conflicts regarding Feinstein's role in the Senate Judiciary Committee as a vulnerability within the opposition party which they were "eager" to exploit (Fandos 2020b).

TRIBAL STRATEGIZING FOR THE FUTURE

During an interview shortly before the November 3 presidential election, Alexandria Ocasio-Cortez, "the" voice for young "disciplined" and "pragmatic" progressive Democrats, prioritized winning the White House for Joe Biden before advocating her liberal left-centric agenda. When asked if Bernie Sanders should be offered a cabinet position in a Biden White House, Ocasio-Cortez argued that progressive Democrats must "make sure that we win this White House" so that afterwards they could effectively lobby to push the more conservative (but still Democratic) Biden administration to "appoint progressive leaders" (Coleman 2020; Cole 2020).

Down ballot, the polarized left contingent took a number of primary wins over establishment Democrats. As a case in point, Missouri Black Lives Matter activist Cori Bush unseated 10-term Representative William Lacy Clay, and Jamaal Bowman, a New York former middle school principal, "took down" 16-term Representative Eliot L. Engel, the chairman of the House Foreign Affairs Committee. Both won their races in November, albeit in strongly Democratic districts (Nilsen 2020). Justice Democrats, the group that launched Ocasio-Cortez's 2018 candidacy, won five of the nine primaries it participated in during the 2020 cycle. Notably, during the Trump presidency, "far-left" candidates "managed to unseat five establishment Democrats, portending future intraparty conflict (Bade 2020).

Safe Seats

Polarization in American congressional politics has been exacerbated by weak parties, subject to control by unrepresentative voters on their fringes and those who fund them (Anderton 2020). This power derives from changes in the basic role of primaries at the presidential level as well as their interaction with "safe seats" in Congress. Such elections are generally characterized by low turnout and disproportionately high participation by polarized or "orphaned" voters. The same is true of caucuses. In particular, Donald Trump was selected as the Republican presidential candidate in 2016 by less than 5 percent of the US electorate. A similar dynamic manifested in both parties' congressional elections. The Tea Party's insurrection within the Republican Party after 2009 was driven by candidates who generally won races with only a 12 percent to 15 percent participation rate. And in 2016, Alexandria Ocasio-Cortez, the "leading voice" of her party's left-leaning sector, won a primary against the incumbent Joe Crowley, a centrist Democrat, with only an 11 percent turnout in New York's 14th congressional district, meaning more than 80 percent of voters stayed home (Cummings 2020).

A mitigating factor in such low turnout districts is the steady increase in "safe seats" for both parties in the House and Senate (Mutnick 2020; DeSilver 2013; Rosentiel 2006). As a result, if a seat is safe for the party, the only election of consequence is the primary. Polarization follows as primary voters pull candidates toward the fringes, with losing the election as the ultimate penalty for a candidate who ignores such voters. This, in turn, creates incentives to "demonize opponents and embrace extreme policies" to such an extent that both Democratic and Republican politicians, instead of responding to their actual constituencies, tailor their issues and positions for voters, albeit from the outer margins of their parties. A potentially toxic alchemy results whereby primaries and caucuses pull the candidates to the extremes, but those same candidates need their entire party to win in the general election:

> They know that if they move to the center, they're going to get attacked in the next primary. So instead, they try to move more moderate voters toward the extremes, so that there will be less pressure on them from party leaders to moderate their views once elected. [So] the polarization of Congress [does not] follow the polarization of the population, it preceded it . . . candidates get pulled to the extremes by primary voters and then attempt to mainstream those extremist views to make it easier for their party to win the general election. (Cummings 2020)

Congressional Dissonance

The dissonance evidenced by the ascension of the Tea Party in 2010 as well as the presidential campaign of Bernie Sanders in 2016 foreshadowed and informed intratribal discord between and within the political parties. For Republicans, tribes have coalesced into an essentially permanent state of tension between an increasingly silent and virtually invisible rank-and-file faction and the increasingly polarized right contingent of outspoken Republicans who constituted first the Tea Party Caucus and then the Freedom Caucus. On the Democratic side, the polarized left activism inspired by the Sanders campaign has the potential to turn any future Democratic majorities into mirror images of the problems that have plagued the Republican majority. As a case in point, a large number of progressive/liberal/left members of Congress could fairly easily prevent leadership from entering into cross-party compromises on big issues like budget and entitlements (Kamarck and Podkul 2018b).

On the last morning of the February 2021 impeachment trial of Donald Trump, Senate Republicans successfully countered Democrats' demands to call witnesses. This after Washington Republican Representative Jaime Herrera Beutler—who had supported impeachment—revealed GOP leader Kevin McCarthy acknowledged Trump dismissed pleas for help during the violent insurrection by his supporters at the Capitol on January 6 (Cathey 2021).

The tense exchanges that began immediately after the acquittal underscored an intra-party tribalism endemic among Republicans, between cohorts who were devoted to the former president and those who argued the party needed to move beyond a disgraced ex-president in order to be politically relevant in the future. To illustrate, although the call for witnesses to bolster the House argument failed, a major rupture within the party immediately revealed itself through rhetorical attacks on Jaime Herrera Beutler by the former president's acolytes. Specifically, Trump advocate Representative Marjorie Taylor Greene of Georgia threatened-by-tweet of "the gift that keeps on giving" and warned Herrera Beutler that "the Trump loyal 75 million are watching " (Jackson 2021; Egan 2021).

As evidenced by the ascension of Tea Party Republicans in 2010 and progressive Democrats in 2016, intraparty tribalism is endemic to American political culture. This sectionalism has provoked Republicans into an organic tension between moderates or centrists within their party and those conservatives who first populated the Tea Party and then the Freedom Caucus (DeSilver 2013). The progressive discourse initially inspired by Sanders's 2016 challenges to moderate Democrats has generated similar discord with centrists. This has occurred to such an extent that, without intraparty rhetorical arbitration, future Democratic majorities may replicate the disturbing images and mimic the anti-democratic actions that have so recently convulsed the modern Republican Party (Karmarck and Podkul 2018a; Kabaservice 2020).

Chapter 5

Mediated Tribalism

EIGHTEENTH-CENTURY MASS MEDIATED POLITICS

In 1787, James Madison observed that easy access to communication available to small republics was precisely what had allowed mob majorities to engage in the "violence of faction" and so quickly overcome minority voices. He argued that a greater variety of American parties and interests could deter this tendency of emergent mobs to subvert representative democracy as it struggles to take hold early in its evolution cycle. In addition, he believed the geographical expanse of the new country would prevent such mobilization (Madison 1787; Hamilton et al. 1787, 2014). That said, at the time of the nation's founding, "new media technologies," including what James Madison described at the time as "a circulation of newspapers through the entire body of the people," united citizens throughout the former colonies. Furthermore, much of the mass media of the time was partisan. As a case in point, the *National Gazette*, published by James Madison, also carried his personal attacks against adversaries, the Federalists (Rutland and Mason 1983; Pasley 2000).

However, unlike the social mediated political coverage that dominated two centuries later, the medium of choice for political information, newspapers of the time, generally functioned as platforms for reasoned arguments by elite political actors. Madison maintained that newspaper journalists would channel their information into information corridors through which to facilitate a "commerce of ideas." While no doubt a naïve take on the suasory impact of mass mediated information delivery systems situated within the twenty-first century, Madison, perhaps with good reason, believed that his contemporaries would take the time to read complicated arguments (including the essays that became *The Federalist Papers*), allowing "levelheaded reason" to spread slowly across the republic of the United States (Rosen 2018a; Berkowitz 2019; Lorenz 2018).

Contemporary Mass Media Politics

The twenty-first century dominant mass media conduits of political information including Twitter, Facebook, and other social media delivery systems would likely have been severely criticized by James Madison and the other inventors of American democracy as toxic to their conceptualization of a representative constitutional system (Rosen 2018b). To illustrate, the twenty-first century warp speed delivery of public discourse, which, in turn, makes time, space, and even place increasingly irrelevant, enables virtual versions of mob democracy to emerge and dominate as quickly as the messages can be tweeted, Instagrammed, or constituted within a multitude of digital mass media delivery systems. In particular, intentionally incendiary, inflammatory, deceptive, or simply false messages tend to "travel farther and faster than arguments based on reason" and so undermine critical thinking, which foundations the process, itself an essential component in a healthy democratic system (Rosen 2018a).

Mass media influences the rhetorical enactment of foundational principles of democracy, specifically trust, informed dialogue, a shared sense of reality, mutual consent, and participation. Technologically driven time and space compression, combined with the monetizing of public attention, has accelerated this influence, particularly with respect to digital delivery platforms. In short, "social media" is massive both in reach and influence, as well as integral to American political life (Deb et al. 2017). Media theorist Marshall McLuhan suggested that while "print technology created the public," electronic technology "created the mass." From this perspective, "the public" consists of "separate individuals" with "separate, fixed points of view." In contrast, "the new technology demands we abandon the luxury" of "this fragmentary outlook" (McLuhan and Fiore 1996).

Klein (2020) suggests contemporary media offers an "explosion of choices" that allow an individual access to the political media you really want." In this way, competing polarized media narratives of political identity, conflict, and celebrity pose, and on occasion answer, voters' questions about "why your side should win and the other side should lose" (147).

MEDIATED COMMUNITIES

Two decades ago, Brooke (1999) suggested that expecting digital platforms to be "inherently democratic" was unrealistic. Instead, consideration should be focused on the types of "communities"—or tribes—that might be facilitated online:

> Too often, hopes and anxieties replace analysis in our descriptions of cyberspace and we end up assuming that we can . . . wish all the nastiness of the world away by entering cyberspace. It is . . . easier to take the path of least resistance, to invest cyberspace with . . . dreams of democratic utopias or fears of cyberstalking. . . . Reality is somewhere in the middle. (24)

Extreme mass mediated partisanship predicts belief in political "fake news" more strongly than even a conspiracy mentality as well as the perceived credibility of a source (independent journalism versus fraudulent messaging). As such, polarized tribal messaging may more accurately predict propaganda or unsubstantiated political news/opinions than a conspiracy mentality (Farago et al. 2019).

"FAKE NEWS" VERSUS "THE FACTS"

Incompatible Trust Levels

One of the few concepts that Republicans and Democrats could agree on during Donald Trump's tenure as president was that they did not share the same set of facts. A 2019 Pew Research Center survey revealed that close to three-quarters of Americans (73 percent) said most Republican and Democratic voters disagreed not just over political plans and policies but over "basic facts." Much of this disconnect evolved from and was facilitated by a news media that, if critical of Donald Trump, the then president routinely disparaged as "fake" and the "enemy of the people." Republicans specifically expressed widespread and growing distrust of the press with distrust expressed "in" 20 of 30 specific news outlets. Conversely, Democrats trusted a majority of the same sites. The two dominant political parties also placed their trust in "two nearly inverse media environments." Republicans overwhelmingly preferred a single outlet—*Fox News*—even as Democrats used and expressed trust in a multiple and wider range of sources.

Some of the media organizations Trump criticized most vocally saw the biggest increases in GOP distrust over time. The share of Republicans who said they distrusted CNN rose from 33 percent in a 2014 survey to 58 percent by 2019. The proportion of Republicans who said they distrusted *The Washington Post* and *The New York Times* rose 17 and 12 percentage points, respectively, during that span. In addition to their criticisms of specific news outlets, Republicans also questioned the broader motives of the media. In surveys fielded over the course of 2018 and 2019, Republicans were far less likely than Democrats to say that journalists act in the best interests of the public, have high ethical standards, prevent political leaders from doing things they should not, and deal fairly with all sides. Notably, Trump's staunchest GOP supporters often had the most negative view. Republicans who strongly approved of Trump, for example, were much more likely than those who only somewhat approved or disapproved of him to say journalists have very low ethical standards (Dimonk and Gramlich 2021).

Political Misinformation and Media Dependence

Apart from the growing partisan polarization over the news media, the former president's time in office also saw the dominance of misinformation as a concerning new reality for many Americans, regardless of party tribal affiliation. Half of adults said that made-up news and information was a major problem in the country, exceeding those who said the same thing about racism, illegal immigration, terrorism, and sexism. Fully two-thirds believed made-up news and information had a big impact on public confidence in the government (68 percent), while half or more said it had a major effect on Americans' confidence in each other (54 percent) and political leaders' ability to get work done (51 percent). A November 2020 survey revealed six in ten adults believed made-up news and information had played a major role in the "just-concluded election" (Dimonk and Gramlich 2021).

Conspiracy theories often became media content during Donald Trump's tenure, in many cases amplified by the president himself. Nearly half of Americans (47 percent) said in September 2020 that they had heard or read a lot or a little about the collection of conspiracy theories known as QAnon, up from 23 percent earlier in the year. In addition, most of those aware of QAnon said Trump seemed to support the theory's promoters. In particular, he frequently made disproven or questionable claims as president. News and fact-checking organizations documented thousands of his false statements over four years, on subjects ranging from the coronavirus to the economy. Perhaps none were more consequential and persuasive than his repeated assertion of widespread fraud in the 2020 election he lost to Democrat Joe Biden. Even after courts around the country had rejected the claim and all 50 states had certified their results, Trump continued to say he had won a "landslide" victory. The false claim gained widespread currency among his voters:

in a January 2021 survey, three-quarters of the former president's supporters incorrectly said he was definitely or probably the rightful winner of the election. (Dimonk and Gramlich 2021; Megerian 2021).

MASS MEDIATED INFLUENCE

Senator Ed Markey won the 2020 Massachusetts Democratic Senate primary, defeating a member of one of the most powerful families in Democratic politics in a show of force for the party's progressive wing. An endorsement from the *Boston Globe* proved critical to reassuring moderates that they had little reason to replace the incumbent with Joe Kennedy. Specifically, the paper created ideological gaps between the two despite minimal differences (Robillard 2020). On the "other side of the aisle," *Fox News*' Sean Hannity and Donald Trump, Jr. complained American media had abandoned their obligation to educate the public "on both sides" to instead serve as activists for the "left wing mob." This false equivalency argument was further perpetuated when the younger Trump insisted that "as a result," the "[liberal] media" will do "whatever is necessary" to "protect Joe Biden," including giving him billions of dollars worth of "free cover-up" (Trump, Jr. 2020).

Media Bias as Persuasion

This theme was expanded and revised by Kathleen Parker, a self-described conservative political columnist for the *Washington Post*, who observed that when President George W. Bush won a second term in 2004, the "[mainstream] media were aghast" and befuddled when attempting to figure how or why anyone had "voted for him." A similar reaction allegedly occurred when these same reporters attempted to deconstruct Donald Trump's "near-reelection" in November 2020 as well as how they had misjudged what became major Republican successes in House races:

> It's a valuable exercise, if it means anything. We know that Joe Biden's election made perfect sense to most in the Beltway media, as would have Hillary Clinton's, as did Barack Obama's, as did Bill Clinton's. That's because most of them supported the Democrats through undisguised, selective coverage. (2020)

In this view, a liberal pro-Democrat slant permeates "mainstream" journalism (meaning a majority of traditional corporate analog and digital media platforms, content generators, and corporations—except, certainly, *Fox News*). Although Americans, including presidents, have had "trust issues" with producers of mass mediated content "long before Trump turned it into an 'enemy of the people,'" the former president developed a cottage industry during his time in office, through which to generate and mass-deliver "fake news" content. Ostensibly this was done "to protect" himself from "incoming" information that he wished to ignore. Parker concludes that while such mischief may have "worked to his advantage," Trump's appropriation of, for example, Twitter (until he was excommunicated from his preferred social media platform post-insurrection) had divided the nation "more than ever" to the extent that:

> [Americans are] more contemptuous and distrustful of the 'other' and doomed if we don't do something about it. Earnest efforts post-2016 to better understand the American voter, with editors essentially embedding reporters outside their comfort zone, were well-intentioned if not nearly enough. Biden has promised that unifying the country will be a priority of his administration. I trust his intentions, but he can only do so much without the media's cooperation. I'm not suggesting that reporters should relax their watchdog role, but . . . none of us [is] more important than the people we're supposed to serve—the readers, television viewers and online followers who expect us to trust them to judge unfiltered facts that we present in good faith. (2020)

It should be noted that "media" bias is likely considerably more complex (or simply different) than Kathleen Parker's implied "liberal"/anti-Republican "Beltway" filter suggests. Moreover, her commitment to a "good faith" journalism of "unfiltered" facts (without vetting or critical assessment or checks) is troublesome. Nevertheless, her basic point is valid.

Preferred Mass Media Platforms

In a late 2019 survey conducted as part of Pew Research Center's Election News Pathways project, *Fox News* and *CNN* were named by the largest segments of Americans as their preferred political news sources—16 percent and 12 percent, respectively. A half a dozen other news outlets—*NPR*, *NBC News*, *ABC News*, *MSNBC*, *CBS News*, and *The New York Times*—were named by at least 2 percent of adults.

About half (49 percent) of respondents identified one of these eight outlets as their main source for political and election news. The long list of all other individual outlets, named by fewer than 2 percent of respondents, included larger sources like *The Washington Post,* the *BBC,* and Rush Limbaugh, as well as more niche sources such as *One America News, The Young Turks,* and individual local newspapers. Some of the remaining respondents named social media sites (4 percent in total) or a medium without any specific outlet specified ("radio," "the Internet").

Interestingly, individuals who considered *Fox News* or *MSNBC*—signature networks for the polarized right and left, respectively—as their main political news content providers were equally partisan or biased in favor of that source over others. Half of the eight sources named by at least 2 percent were much more likely to be named by Democrats and independents who leaned Democratic than by Republicans and GOP leaners: *MSNBC, The New York Times, NPR,* and *CNN*. Again, and notably, *Fox News* was the only platform in the top eight that was far more likely to be named by Republicans than by Democrats. Those who named *Fox News* and *MSNBC* also displayed roughly the same high levels of partisanship. About nine in ten of those whose main source was *Fox News* (93 percent) identified as Republican, very close to the 95 percent of those who named *MSNBC* and identified as Democrats. Similarly, about nine in ten of those who named *The New York Times* (91 percent) and *NPR* (87 percent) as their main political news source identified as Democrats, with *CNN* at about eight in ten (79 percent).

Finally, the three major broadcast news networks—ABC, CBS, and NBC—had more of a mix of Democrats and Republicans among those who named these outlets as their main sources for political news. For example, the makeup of those who named NBC News as their main source was 57 percent Democratic versus 38 percent Republican (Grieco 2020). This suggests that constituents who preferred the signature partisan network delivery systems for news and information content over traditional broadcast content were likely to be less bipartisan, more tribal, and possibly even more likely to judge the "truth" value of that content from a biased rather than critical standpoint.

The New York Times was a main source for a comparatively large share of young adults.

People whose main political news source was *The New York Times* or NPR were most likely to be under age 50. Looking across the eight most commonly named main sources for political and election news, NPR and *The New York Times* had greater appeal to younger Americans. About six in ten of those who identified NPR (64 percent) or *The New York Times* (63 percent) as their primary political news source were under age 50. *The New York Times* had the highest proportion of adults ages 18 to 29 who named it as their main source, at 29 percent. Those aged 30 to 49 were most likely to name NPR (49 percent). Among those who named *MSNBC, CBS News,* or *Fox News* as their main source for political news, about seven in ten were ages 50 and older.

Other demographic differences stood out among those who named each of these eight outlets as their main source for political and election news. Women were much more likely than men to favor network TV, as they made up about six in ten or more of those who cited CBS (70 percent), ABC (60 percent), or NBC (58 percent) as their main source for political news. Those who named NPR and *The New York Times* as their primary source tended to be more educated, with about seven in ten in each group having at least a bachelor's degree (68 percent and 72 percent, respectively). And while those who named *Fox News* as their main news source were predominantly white (87 percent), nearly half of those who relied on *CNN* were some other race or ethnicity (47 percent).

Media Consumer Bias

Cognitive predispositions, particularly in the form of confirmation biases, may influence decisions made by individuals when they interact within mass media platforms and attribute meaning to the content generated therein. As a case in point, individuals tend to discount information that undermines past choices and judgments, a thinking bias that impacts domains of information, understanding, and persuasion ranging from science and education to politics. The mechanism underlying this "fundamental characteristic of belief formation" pivots on failing to consider the strength of others' disconfirming opinions to alter confidence in judgments, "yet adequate for referencing when opinions are confirmatory" (Kappes et al. 2012; Nickerson 1998).

It follows that cognitive processes beyond those set in motion through interaction with "liberal" or "conservative" media (or specious rhetorical devices such as content saturation) inform political persuasion. Specifically, if Tweeted or Facebooked or streamed information tracks with beliefs already held by its consumers, then it may indeed impact the intended receiver's/ audience's partisan behavior. This effect may account for why an argument, even if it is well evidenced and critically sound, will still be dismissed by a portion of the voting public as "fake news." In such cases, the argument is simply because the intended audience/receiver already disagrees with its conclusions—before the reasoning is ever deconstructed (heard or read). Conversely, other mass mediated messages, regardless of their brevity (as is often the case with social media content), may successfully target intended audiences despite minimal if any effort on the part of a source to account for either soundness or ethicality of the content. Taibbi (2019) argues that in this way mainstream media gaslights and intentionally divides Americans by passing off a "twisted wing of the entertainment business" as "the news." As a result, digital media manipulates election coverage, frequently configured as a tirade or a confessional, to create anger and in some cases even paranoia and distrust.

The interdependence between rhetoric, democracy, and the channels through which persuasive messages are mediated between speaker and audience is well documented (Abbot et al. 2016; Hauser 2004; Golden et al. 2004; McChesney 1999). As society—local, national, and global—has advanced, so have discoveries and use of digital technology. Accordingly, as such advancements are assimilated, cultures have discovered novel ways to integrate day-to-day activities and public life. This synthesis has produced technology-driven "public spaces" within which digital content is produced and launched. Political actors have exploited the rhetorical possibilities of such digital spaces and discourse to successfully target particular constituencies without constraints of time or space or, increasingly, critical assessment. In particular, political figures rely on these digital media platforms to launch persuasive messages most often when political upheaval or campaigns grounded in extreme tribalized partisanship are in effect (Gregory 2020).

Trump's Discourse of Unity and Division

Donald Trump's most efficient and effective campaign rhetorical strategy during the 2020 election cycle was to discursively frame Joe Biden, and so all Democrats, as a left-leaning socialist whose tendencies would prove fatal to Americans. The incentive for developing and defaulting to this rhetorical device was simple. Without essentially changing "a word" (and being sure "that word" was used "over and over and over"), the then president solidified his own base while distracting and dividing the "enemy," in this case the Democratic Party. Specifically, he appealed to extreme partisan tribalism within his base (coalesced around "Trumpism" rather than "republicanism") while distracting and dividing Democrats—from each other—which in turn bolstered his own tribal leader ethos.

During the summer of 2020 the Trump campaign unleashed a rhetorical "fusillade" across various media platforms—including his "medium of choice," Twitter. During this "tweet assault," which instantaneously shot to 88 million followers, the former president demanded unwavering allegiance and executed relentless assaults against Biden specifically and any Democrat by implication. At one point, Trump tweeted that "Bernie Sanders admits he forced Joe Biden to move 'a whole lot' to the left on healthcare." Also, a campaign email noted how Biden had praised Alexandria Ocasio-Cortez, arguing that because the democratic nominee was "too weak to stand up to the radical left," he had "completely surrendered to them." A *Fox News* cable television ad queried about the "radical left wing mob's agenda" and warned it might well "take over our cities, defund the police, pressure more towns to follow" and that, damningly, "Joe Biden stands with them" (Smith 2020; Denham 2021).

Donald Trump and his acolytes frequently relied on Twitter-mediated rhetorical devices of victimization, resentment, and revenge, discursively reframed into civic virtues. Kelly (2020) deconstructs this discursive technique as "ressentiment" (re-sentiment), a "condition in which a subject is addled by rage and envy yet remains impotent, subjugated and unable to act on or adequately express frustration." A reliance on this mass mediated strategy empowered the Trump campaign to deflect the "affective charge of animus without forfeiting the moral high ground of victimhood" to his (and his audience's) "oppressors."

The efficacy of the Twitter media platform derives from its simplicity as well as privileging of "simple, impulsive and uncivil" discourse with which targets may easily be assaulted, often without concern on the part of the user for accountability. These three attributes were well evidenced in the former president's Twitter-chatter while in office. Ott (2016) suggests that Donald Trump's dominant rhetorical presidential persona was created from within this Twitter-world, which, in turn, generated a "post-news" and "post-truth" public arena. It is also within this rhetorical space that Donald Trump successfully "othered" fundamentally anyone with whom he disagreed. Among others, the former president rhetorically divided from the press, immigrants, foreign adversaries, welfare recipients, those within his own party he did not like, and, certainly, "the" other major political tribe, the Democratic Party (Ott and Dickinson 2019).

MEDIATED DISINFORMATION

Joan Donovan, research director of the Shorenstein Center on Media, Politics and Public Policy at the Harvard Kennedy School, maintains that while there are multiple reasons for why people participate in deliberate disinformation campaigns, certain individuals are more attracted than others, most often those driven by extremist ideologies. In such cases, narratively targeted individuals are motivated by the "clout and influence" they receive from "very small universe of like-minded individuals." Others are "incentivized by money" to such a degree that mediated deceptive information (intentional lying), including the generation and dissemination of "fake news," becomes a lucrative business, "especially if you're good at it" (Heim 2021; Li and DiFeliciantoni 2021; Buncombe 2018; Goldsmith 2017; "Revealed . . ." 2019 . . .).

Intentional disinformation substantially constituted the rhetorical vision within which Donald Trump's base participated during the January 6, 2021 insurrection against the United States Capitol. For many in his faction, Trump's incessant, massively mediated, and digitally platformed false narrative that liberal Democrats had committed voter fraud and stolen "his" presidency was an unquestioned truth. Indiscriminate obedience to this fabrication so enthralled his followers that they chose to move from symbolic action into an organized violent act, historically unprecedented in content, scope, and origin (Cronin 2021). This concerned Facebook CEO Mark Zuckerberg to such an extent that he and others removed Trump's content from their social media platforms. It has been argued doing so was the right course of action in that the former president co-opted social media platforms as rapid delivery systems for an intentional disinformation narrative meant to inflame, incite, and, ultimately, provoke violence (Heim 2021; Needleman and Wells 2021; Conger et al. 2021).

The President Is Not "Anyone"

When queried about concerns that massive, mediated platforms such as Twitter or Facebook could deny access to the President of the United States and so "anyone," Joan Donovan, research director of the Shorenstein Center, replied that the former president was certainly "not anyone" in that he utilized Twitter to politically oppress. Nor was he "a private citizen"; rather at the time of the insurrection he was still a "sitting president":

> If this was happening in any other country, we might see other world leaders call out for removal of this person's account, knowing that they are mounting a private takeover of government. (Heim 2021)

Donovan continued that she would prefer Zuckerberg's Facebook and Jack Dorsey's Twitter, as well as other social media behemoths, did not dominate the direction, flow, and content of socially mediated mass communication (Heim 2021). However, since that was the case, it was imperative that the "enormous responsibility" that comes with such "large-scale" broadcast technologies be regulated at the "level of the federal government" (Heim 2021; Shieber 2021; Zitser 2021). While FCC "content and carriage" regulation of major digital platforms is speculative at best, Twitter and Facebook have both banned Donald Trump, the former permanently and the latter "at least" until 2023 (Yoo 2018; Colarossi 2021; Conger and Isaac 2021).

Digital Mass Media and Democracy

In *Rich Media, Poor Democracy*, communication theorist Robert McChesney argued that America's "hypercommercial" corporate media-system contradicts the communication requirements of a healthy democracy. In addition, he suggested that any literal reform of the media must be part of a broader movement to democratize the core institutions of society including media corporations because the more powerful they become the poorer the prospects for participatory democracy" (1999, 2). Two decades later, Shorenstein Center on Media, Politics and Public Policy research director Joan Donovan maintains that "disinformation" has really "worn out its purpose" and created a space driven by public and political will such that regulation of content and interventions to do so by social media companies is possible:

> [Because of] this interaction effect between millions of people seeking information and bad actors who will use that vulnerability to their advantage. . . .You don't get 100,000 domains related to [COVID]-19 without a big chunk of people thinking they can monetize this pandemic . . . so it's not just talking about [regulating] speech. This is the economy now. (Heim 2021; Guttman 2020; "Revealed . . ." 2019 . . .)

A REPUBLICAN ALLEGORY FOR DEMOCRATS

The fate of a fractured Republican Party unable to consolidate its moderate and radical factions into a confederation rather than antagonistic tribes and, so finally, at war with itself could be an allegory for the Democratic Party (Warren 2021; Goldmacher 2021; Balz 2017). The insurrection at the US Capitol early in 2021 represented the extreme pathology that underscores not only the extent to which American political parties are estranged from each other but also an end state of unresolved acute tribalism within an American political party. The media was a not-so-silent and willing accomplice throughout the entire process (McEvoy 2021; Coyle 2021; Frenkel 2021). As an instance, online radicalization, from *Fox News* to Facebook, consolidated into a massive, profit-friendly, user-biased disinformation culture that "fanned the flames of fury" into mediated alternative realities of perpetual dissent and, ultimately, violence. Accordingly, such forums have distorted into "antisocial websites" that "peddle hate and fear mongering" to such an extent that certain segments of the electorate become "radicalized enough to believe they have to storm the Capitol and attack police officers" (Seltzer 2021; McDonald et al. 2017; Neumann 2013).

CNN Global Affairs analyst Susan Glaser suggests the media is often challenged because the "unthinkable becoming reality" is difficult to report to such an extent that it becomes complicit in a "mass delusion event." One fundamental rhetorical technique for countering this tendency is a commitment to "plain language" so that reporters focus primarily on deconstructing, clarifying, and describing rather than judging or embellishing. Jeffrey Goldberg, editor-in-chief of *The Atlantic*, suggests American journalists become "foreign correspondents," noting that while it is "easy" to "describe the Arab spring" or unrest in the Middle East, "we have to import some of that language into describing what's going on domestically because that is what's happening domestically" (Stelter 2021; Aistrope 2016; "Applying Private Sector . . ." 2016).

Thin and Strong Democracy

Barber (1984) configures contemporary American democracy as "thin," a system of representative governance with democratic values that are "provisional, optional, and conditional." Such a system generally fails to develop an ethos from which citizenship, or democratic participation, can emerge. Alternately, a "strong democracy" facilitates political equality and citizen engagement, both signature attributes of a healthy system, through political discourse. From this perspective, digital media simultaneously thrives within and perpetuates "thin" rather than "strong" democracy. This process is accomplished through seven axes: speed, simplicity, solitude, pictoriality, lateralness, informationality, and segmentation, all of which have "ambiguous implications for democracy" (Barber 2002).

Specifically, the speed of digital mass media discourages deliberation while providing rapid access to that information, which would empower citizens to be more "quickly appraised of world events" if they made the effort to do so. As a result, immediacy is prioritized over patience or introspection and personal gratification over social transformation. This in turn facilitates simplistic thinking whereby citizens, with easier access to information, construct a world based on "reductive and reactionary responses" than critical assessment. In this view, digital technology tends to initially isolate because it is constructed for a single user (e.g., one person at one terminal). The result is that ideologically homogenous virtual echo chambers rather than deliberative discursive communities become the norm (Cinelli et al. 2021).

Digital technology also impacts democracy through pictoriality or mediated images, often constructed and delivered for visceral impact rather than as a complement to substantive argument. While lateralness enables digital technology to link users without mediators or gatekeepers, it also empowers and encourages citizens to make decisions about substantive issues without mediation of experts or input from others outside of the "echo chamber" culture. There is also concern that mediated information is often "raw data" presented and consumed without consideration of context, already compacted and so often distorted because of its speed and immediacy. Lastly, digital media platforms routinely target their messages to particular segments of individuals as "consumers" rather than citizens.

This characteristic of digital media may particularly counter the development of a strong democracy as it utilizes "specific rhetorics" within which Americans are intentionally targeted to perceive themselves as singularly unique entities and so possessing few shared interests with their "neighbors, coworkers and others." Consequently, rather than message content, social media is primarily focused on what digital delivery platforms decide to do with that content. To that end, instead of remaining neutral, "media capitalists" generally enact decisions based on which content to "amplify, elevate, and suggest" and so ultimately promote to users/consumers. This default business model, which "promotes scale above all," favors messages of "extreme, divisive content," again generally contraindicated for a healthy democracy (Eisenstat 2021; Wheeler et al. 2020). That many contemporary media companies tend to act on behalf of corporate rather than democratic interests and so configure Americans as consumers rather than citizens, accelerates tribal divisions between and within American political cultures, including those of the Democratic Party.

WEAPONIZED MEDIA PLATFORMS

Barber (2002) argues that media technology, manifest in digital delivery systems and platforms, may be used for any outcome determined by who controls it, including corporations and private owners of platforms. Given this model, which promotes profit and divisive content regardless of its truth value, regulators could begin to alleviate some concerns. As a case in point, it would be useful to specify who should benefit from Section 230 of the Communications Decency Act which states that "no provider or user of an interactive computer service shall be treated as the publisher or speaker of any information provided by another information content provider" ("Section 230" 2021). It follows that identifying social media corporations—many of which algorithmically select what speech to amplify in order to persuade users to consume content that foregrounds hate groups and conspiracy theorists—as "Internet intermediaries" who should receive immunity from consequences is "absurd":

> [That] the few tech companies who steer how more than 2 billion people communicate, find information, and consume media enjoy the same blanket immunity as a truly neutral Internet company makes it clear that it is time for an upgrade to the rules. They are not just a neutral intermediary. (Eisenstat 2021)

Because it has been argued that Section 230 has been over-interpreted to provide blanket immunity to all Internet companies ("Internet intermediaries") for any third-party content they host, it would be beneficial to define more accurately "Internet intermediary." It would also be useful to clarify the responsibilities of "digital curators" who decide what content to foreground and amplify and how to manage voters' (consumers') content. Because digital media platforms generally self-regulate, policies will likely not change to favor moderation until the "entire machine is designed and monetized." Until then it is possible that media platforms will continue to be weaponized into "aiding and abetting those intent on harming our democracy," regardless of the political tribe or party cohort to which they belong (Eisenstat 2021; Wheeler, et al. 2020).

Constraints and Possibilities

Communication theorist Robert McChesney observed in 1999 that expectations regarding an emerging Internet as the conduit of a "golden age of competitive capitalism" had not been met (182). A *New York Times* op ed argued at the time that the lesson of the Internet was that "the big get bigger and the small fade away" (Hansell 1998). Although McChesney noted that in a less "dubious" political culture, the "Internet" could be of "far greater democratic use than it is or likely will be" in the future, he was not optimistic:

> Those who think the technology can produce a viable democratic public sphere by itself where policy has failed to do so are deluding themselves . . . dominant forces in cyberspace are producing the exact type of depoliticized culture that some Internet utopians claimed the technology would slay. (1999, 182)

Klein (2020) contends that a fundamental dilemma of mass mediated journalism is to decide "what to cover to become the shaper of the news rather than a mirror held up to the news," concluding that ultimately American news media "isn't just an actor in politics," it is also "arguably the most powerful actor in politics" (164). To this point, there are certain outcomes, uniquely adapted to pervasive digital and social media platforms, which facilitate public polarization and its manifestation as political partisan tribalism, including that which exists within and between American political parties. These include the creation of echo chambers and filter bubbles which either mirror one's ideas back within seconds and, more egregiously, deflect ideas before one has a chance to reflect on or deconstruct them.

The ease-of-access design of social media platforms, along with a general partisan media slant in analog channels, has exacerbated these inter- and intraparty political divisions and polarization. Additionally, social media algorithms reinforce the divisions and create the echo chambers that perpetuate increasingly extreme or biased views over time. Social media often functions as an accelerant, strategically used to create and deliver viral posts with intentionally false or poorly vetted information. Such content—roughly understood by the public as "fake news"—may be re-created and disseminated by state and private actors, often intentionally. Both threaten American public life through a relentless onslaught of frequently distorted messaging, most of which is inaccurate at best.

Regardless, such rhetoric shrinks and distorts the public sphere, a crucial space within which to enact democracy. This does not bode well for a nation that depends on public critical and ethical discussions of multiple and competing perspectives in order to determine what knowledge constitutes truth. There is also frequently an intentional "confusing" of popularity or celebrity with legitimacy. This is an easy mash-up in the viral world of Facebook, Twitter, and Instagram, where, for the most part, anyone for fundamentally any reason may essentially say anything about anyone to anyone instantly, contextualized by photos, graphics, and memes. Within such media cultures, groundless assertions may be propagated, often embellished by trolls, hackers, and bots. On occasion, populists—perhaps not surprisingly often in "speech protected" liberal democracies—prefer "direct messaging" their electorates, rather than vetting through deconstructing or expert gatekeepers. In doing so, protocols are frequently ignored, dissent and marginalized voices silenced. Ultimately, these digital behaviors may become soft power strategies, enacted to distort support for a particular leader or ideology or to shade what is likely a veiled manipulation of a public (Deb et al. 2017).

First Strike Capability

Those who occupy polarized ideological or affective spaces within their respective political parties may be uniquely vulnerable to mediated "political capture," and so manipulated by expertly packaged propaganda grounded in disinformation and covert influence. Developing content for such specious digital platforms becomes light lifting for well-financed, technically sophisticated public actors and organizations. That unvetted and possibly invented speech acts, as well as symbolic behavior of any kind, may be virtually produced and delivered 24/7 is troublesome for a political culture that embraces, is constituted by, and is dependent on free and open exchanges of information. Such messages may be instantaneously and widely consumed by essentially any audience as first strike weapons delivering hate speech, humiliation, and abuse to and between marginalized, vulnerable cohorts. Virtually any "othered" populations, including many within the political culture of the United States, are potential casualties of such digitalized discursive attacks. Nowhere was this more obvious than during the run-up to the 2020 American presidential election.

Chapter 6

Caucuses, Primaries, and Convention

A PARTY DIVIDED

The intraparty divisions within the blocs or tribal sectors that constitute the Democratic Party impacted the 2020 election cycle through distinct and frequently conflicting priorities, ideologies, and rhetorical behaviors. Perry Bacon, a senior writer for the political data and journalism blog *Five Thirty Eight,* configures the "Democrats divided" Party during the 2019–2020 election cycle as six discrete factions on a liberal-to-conservative continuum. From this standpoint, the term "progressive" has lost its utility, "essentially meaningless" when used alone because it describes so many different types of Democrats. Accordingly, multiple descriptors reflect contemporary Democratic politics through foregrounding "disagreements playing out among party elites in the real world, which aren't well captured by 'liberal vs. moderate'" or other "broad terms" (2019).

The Super Progressives

This cohort leans "very liberal" on economic and identity/cultural issues and vocally anti-establishment. They attack both Republicans and Democrats, the former by default and the latter when they see "defects." Members of this faction argue the party is too centrist and too cautious. The group advocates exceedingly liberal policies on economics (for example, health care for all Americans) as well as very liberal stands on issues around identity and race such as abolishing the Immigration and Customs Enforcement Agency. Moreover, its members aggressively push their vision even when other Democrats balk. Super Progressives include Representatives Ayanna Pressley, Mark Pocan, Rashida Tlaib, Alexandria Ocasio-Cortez, and Ilhan Omar.

The Very Progressives

This contingent is "very liberal" on economic issues, "fairly" liberal on identity issues, and skeptical of the Democratic establishment. Members share beliefs with the first group, regarding economics in particular. However, they are a "little less aggressive and less focused" on issues of identity and "more willing to play nice" with the party establishment. Members also support economic liberalism along with Super Progressives and are "worried" that the party is "too cozy" with corporate America. Very Progressives include Bill de Blasio, Jeff Merkley, Bernie Sanders, and Elizabeth Warren.

The Progressive New Guard

This coalition is also liberal on both economic and identity issues but "electability" of candidates and the appeal of ideas to the political center are important as well; they generally rose to prominence after Barack Obama was elected president. Bacon (2019) suggests the majority of Democratic members of Congress and Democratic governors are in this group or the next. Both contingents are often in the position of "responding" to ideas posed by the two previous cohorts instead of "driving the party's vision themselves." This segment is distinguished by a "kind of performative wokeness," regarding racial and other issues. Its members are skilled at speaking to a broad coalition of Democrats regarding gender and racial issues. In addition, they are not as "dismissive" of the "young activists" advocating projects such as the Green New Deal, as the next faction. The group intentionally casts a "wide net" to not only "working-class swing voters" but also those in "purple" states, realizing the significance of appealing to nonwhite voters and white millennials "who might not vote at all" without inspirational candidates. Members of this group include Stacey Abrams, Cory Booker, Pete Buttigieg, Julian Castro, Kamala Harris, Jay Inslee, and Beto O'Rourke.

The Progressive Old Guard

This faction is "solidly center-left" on both economic and identity issues and also concerned about the "electability" of candidates. Like the previous group, it pays attention to the ideas of the political center and share similar views on policy in general. The bloc generally rose to prominence before

Obama was elected president. However, unlike the previous group, the old guard is less willing to "placate the party's most progressive wings." The defining phrase of this group might be "how do you pay for that?" Its members are also "deeply concerned" about the party "going too far left" in part because they believe Democrats' success pivots on swing voters. Members of this segment include Joe Biden, Dianne Feinstein, Nancy Pelosi, and Chuck Schumer.

The Moderates

This alliance is generally more conservative and "business-friendly" than previous groups regarding economic policies and "somewhat liberal on cultural issues as well as frequently anti-establishment." Supported issues include expanding background checks for gun purchases and components of ICE. Many in this group represent competitive (purple) districts and states. Others may be, "in their hearts and minds, just more conservative" than other Democrats. On some occasions, they might contrast themselves from the previous groups just to "play up their differences" and inform their constituents essentially, "I'm a Democrat, but not that kind of Democrat." Members include Josh Gottheimer, Conor Lamb, and Abigail Spanberger.

Conservatives

In general, this segment is skeptical of liberal views on both economic and cultural issues and usually supportive of abortion limits. The segment is usually from conservative-leaning areas. It is the smallest of the groups but also increasingly important in winning gubernatorial races as well as seats in state legislatures in the West and the South. Bacon (2019) suggests that this segment will:

> punch above its weight in the national debate about where the Democrats are headed—because these Democrats will likely be those pushing loudest for it to avoid the policy stands of the Very Progressives and the Super Progressives. And they will have a compelling argument—by being elected.

Members include (Governor) John Bel Edwards and Joe Manchin.

Chapter 6

THE PRIMARIES

The 2020 Democratic Presidential Candidates

The chasm between moderate and left-leaning Democrats expanded throughout the 2016 campaign due in part to the candidacy of self-described Democratic socialist Bernie Sanders (Kelley 2018). The fissure widened exponentially over the next four years into a "practical versus ideological" tribal binary. By 2020, the intraparty breach had become a defining feature of the presidential race.

The separate campaigns involved the most progressive, largest, and diverse groups of candidates in four decades (Hurt 2019; Detrow 2020; Watson et al. 2020). What constituents actually believe can differ from the candidates' opinions of their own ideology and legislative record. When *Business Insider* asked Americans to rank the 2020 presidential candidates based on ideology, a majority described Bernie Sanders as the most liberal candidate in the Democratic field—by a wide margin. Senator Kamala Harris, Senator Cory Booker, former Secretary of Housing and Urban Development Julián Castro, and Senator Elizabeth Warren were considered the next most liberal candidates. Joe Biden was positioned as the most centrist of the entire group followed by Senator Amy Klobuchar and former mayor Pete Buttigieg. Representatives Seth Moulton, Eric Swalwell, John Delaney, and Tim Ryan, and Senator Michael Bennet were considered the least liberal candidates in the field (Relman and Hickey 2019).

The BBC described a "tension" which was dominating American Democratic presidential primaries, between the "so-called progressive wing of the party, led by Bernie Sanders and Elizabeth Warren" and the "moderates like Joe Biden, Amy Klobuchar and Pete Buttigieg" (Zurcher 2020). Maurice Mitchell, the national director of the Working Families Party and a leader in the Black Lives Matter movement, suggests Joe Biden was seen by progressive Democrats during the primaries as "running a retrograde candidacy." The result was that the Democratic nominee was simultaneously accused of being a "socialist puppet and a neoliberal shill." Younger, highly educated, more ideological social media savvy voters configured Joe Biden as a "creature of the ancient régime and a cheerleader of the national-security state, with such timid appetites for change that, when he won on Super Tuesday, the price of health-care stocks went up."

Liberals were further dismayed that the most diverse presidential field in American history winnowed down to a "white man in his eighth decade." Still, Joe Biden's centrist ethos, while not representative of the party's progressive agenda in full, may have provided him with a "Rooseveltian moment." While not the "progressive star" progressives had hoped for, he nonetheless could "be a product of either your most cynical thinking" or "your most optimal thinking" (Maurice Mitchell: Osnos 2020a).

The Field Narrows and Divides

By the February 3, 2020 Iowa primary, a dozen Democratic candidates remained. These included Joe Biden, Elizabeth Warren, Bernie Sanders, Pete Buttigieg, Michael Bloomberg, Amy Klobuchar, and Andrew Yang. Other candidates included Tulsi Gabbard, Tom Steyer, John Delaney, Michael Bennet, and Deval Patrick (Oliphant 2019). By the New Hampshire primary a week later, it appeared that none of these candidates had created a broad cross-party coalition. Instead, each occupied a corridor of factionalized support too narrow to establish advantage in the race, which foreshadowed further disunity. The resulting "war of attrition" for the nomination had the potential to produce a "brokered convention," as the candidates divided the Democratic base "along lines of race, class, generation, and ideology" (Brownstein 2020b). Specifically, Iowa elevated two Democrats with fundamentally different visions for their party regarding the role of government, and the trajectories of their possible presidencies. Bernie Sanders essentially called for restructuring the American government and economy "in a more progressive way":

> Our message to Wall Street and the insurance companies and the drug companies and the fossil fuel industry and the military industrial complex and the prison industrial complex [is] change is coming. (Detrow 2020)

While Pete Buttigieg also planned to improve the nation's economy and political system, he would do so within an already established framework of "big" but "incremental" changes. This provoked criticism from Sanders that Buttigieg represented the "status quo," to which he pushed back as a moderate:

> I respect Senator Sanders, but at a moment like this when the message goes out that you're either for a revolution or you must be for the status quo, most of us don't know where we fit and would rather be part of a movement that makes room for all of us. (Detrow 2020)

Buttigieg also presented himself as a necessary liaison between the liberal Sanders and the centrist Biden:

> We do not have to be tribal in our politics of the future. And in fact, in order to solve our big problems, we're going to have to recognize that there are options somewhere in between a revolution and the status quo. In order to govern, as

well as to lead, we've got to enlist the energies of people from my party, independents and some number of people who are accustomed to being in the other party. (Garrison 2020)

As a candidate who positioned herself as more centrist than Pete Buttigieg, Amy Klobuchar argued she was a wiser choice to represent the moderate cohort. Because of her congressional experience in building coalitions and advocacy, as president, Klobuchar could actually get legislation passed:

> Bernie and I work together all the time. But I think we are not going to be able to out-divide the divider in chief. And I think we need someone to head up this ticket that actually brings people with her instead of shutting them out. (Detrow 2020)

In contrast, Joe Biden, who had not finished strong in Iowa, warned that neither Buttigieg nor Sanders were equipped to defeat Trump. While Biden indicated he had "great respect" for Pete Buttigieg, he was nonetheless concerned that the former South Bend, Indiana mayor's governing inexperience posed "a risk." Furthermore, if Sanders became the nominee for the party:

> Every Democrat in America up and down the ballot . . . will have to carry the label Senator Sanders has chosen for himself. He calls himself a democratic socialist. Well, we're already seeing what Donald Trump is going to do with that. (Garrison 2020)

One incident spotlights how Democratic leaders at this point moved toward an "open war" with one another," an intraparty "strife" that impacted additional primary campaigns. Infighting focused largely on what had been experienced by some as the "failed" caucus process in Iowa. Groups were at odds over who deserved blame, and increasingly bitter over the rules governing who would be allowed into future nationally televised candidate debates—a process that could enable billionaire Mike Bloomberg to participate in future debates. As an example, supporters of Bernie Sanders openly criticized the Democratic National Committee, revisiting grievances from the divisive 2016 primary race in which he had played a prominent role (Wierson 2020). In that campaign, Sanders's backers, based on hacked internal DNC emails, argued the entire system was "stacked against" their candidate. At the same time, Hillary Clinton's base blamed Sanders and his bloc for failing to sufficiently rally his base on her behalf in the general election ("Hillary . . ." 2016; "Elizabeth . . ." 2017).

Progressive Opposition

It has been argued that the 2020 primaries were seen, in great part, as a contest of ideas, with Sanders and Elizabeth Warren on one side and Democrat Joe Biden on the other. In this view, Biden won the nomination because Democratic voters decided that, as a moderate, he'd be more successful against Donald Trump in the general election than Sanders or Warren or other candidates (Waldman 2020). By and large, the majority of Joe Biden's competitors, notably Sanders and Warren, were self-identified liberal progressives embracing the Green New Deal, Medicare for all, free public college, and decriminalized borders. These appeals were particularly cogent for millennials and Generation Z, who by 2030 would be on track to be the majority of American eligible voters (Osnos 2020a; Brownstein 2020a).

In 2018, twenty millennials were elected to Congress, including Alexandria Ocasio-Cortez, a Sanders supporter and also a self-described democratic socialist who upset a moderate Democrat in the Bronx, albeit in a very low voter turnout election. But Biden believed that his peers had missed a crucial lesson of the midterm elections: forty-three House districts had moved from Republicans to Democrats, as some older, moderate voters recoiled from Trump's party:

> We won by not going after the opponent but after the issues underlying what the opponent supported. They were running against Obamacare, and all of a sudden you heard them say, "I didn't say I was for doing away with that." (Osnos 2020b)

Moderate-left (or "Progressive Old Guard") Biden had a chance with some "fed-up" Trump voters, according to pollster Samuel Popkin with farm bankruptcy nearing a thirty-year high (Osnos 2020a).

Joe Biden's primary campaign discourse stopped short of calling for revolution. For example, instead of Medicare for all, he would augment Obamacare, by lowering the Medicare eligibility age from sixty-five to sixty, and adding a "public option," an idea, perhaps ironically, that was considered radical during the Obama presidency by moderates or even conservatives less than a decade later. Biden's polling revealed that a majority of potential Democratic primary voters identified as moderate or conservative rather than progressive and that more than half were over the age of fifty. This was salient data for any Democrat who wished to win not only a party nomination but a national election. Anita Dunn, a senior Biden adviser, acknowledged that while young people were important to winning the 2020 presidential election, so were "white people above the age of sixty-five" because it was "their demographic which actually gave the election to Donald Trump last time" (Osnos 2020a; Martin and Glueck 2020a).

DEBATES

Refusing to "Go Negative"

Although some configured Joe Biden's victory in the primaries as a fluke or the result of luck, his refusal to "savage" debate opponents and engage in tribalistic attack rhetoric was instead strategic. In the words of one Biden adviser, "if the only way to get the nomination was to destroy all these other people, he [Biden] was going to inherit a party that wasn't going to win anyway" (Osnos 2020a; Glueck 2020; Karni 2020). Within days, Biden had gone from the edge of campaign oblivion to victory. He had received help from Elizabeth Warren, who swiftly dispatched Bloomberg as a viable candidate, denouncing his derogatory comments about women.

Biden clearly benefited from electorate fears of Bernie Sanders as well as Donald Trump and, perhaps more significantly, because of his refusal to engage in rhetorical tribalism against other Democratic progressives. Once it became clear that he was in a two-person race, the prospect of nominating Sanders became increasingly unappealing to many moderate Democrats—including some fellow candidates, older Black voters in states such as South Carolina, and big-money donors. Even as his rivals said that he was "too old, too conciliatory, and too tainted by his record," Joe Biden resisted responding with aggressive negativity and spending "all day trying to win the latest Twitter war" (Osnos 2020b).

Tribal Demographics

Intraparty tribalism was foregrounded before and during the primary debates. Candidates assessed the "overall mood" of the voters regarding whether they preferred a "politically cautious nominee" who vowed to "restore normalcy" to the White House, or a more confrontational standard-bearer with an ambitious and disruptive reform agenda. On the eve of the first Democratic presidential primary debate in June 2019, demographics of the ten candidates mirrored those of their constituents as well as competing opinions regarding their party's future. A Pew Research Center report at the time indicated that nearly half of all Democrats and Democratic-leaning independents (46 percent) described their political views as liberal while 39 percent said they were moderate, and 14 percent identified as conservative ("6 Facts . . ." 2019).

Miami, Florida

Early in the Democratic debate cycle, during a "race to see who could get furthest to the left," intraparty tribalism was foregrounded when Vermont's Bernie Sanders attacked essentially all of the other candidates for being "too conservative," including fellow progressive Massachusetts Senator Elizabeth Warren during the June 2019 first round of debates in Miami, Florida. Conversely, moderates Minnesota Senator Amy Klobuchar and South Bend, Indiana former mayor Pete Buttigieg insisted "ultra-progressives" such as Sanders and Warren would take the party over the "progressive cliff " and so continue the Trump presidency into a second term (Lockhart 2020).

Westerville, Ohio (Otterbein University)

Shortly before the October 2019 primary debate in Ohio, the Democrats' populist wing appeared increasingly in control of the race, bolstered by polls, increased cash flow and "with only a 'wounded' leading candidate, Joseph R. Biden, Jr., standing in its way." Senator Elizabeth Warren had risen in the polls while both she and Senator Bernie Sanders were dominating in fundraising as Joe Biden's numbers had slipped in a way that troubled his supporters.

Left-leaning tendencies were also part of former Texas Representative Beto O'Rourke's reinvented ethos as he assumed a novel political identity for himself of a gun-control activist as well as a critic of the Democratic Party's generally cautious platform on the issue. Other Democratic challengers felt pressure to use the Ohio debate to prevent the remaining primaries from being defined by the binaries of a Warren/"progressive" or a Biden/"moderate." Strategies for doing so were generally limited to either directly damaging Warren's campaign or by other candidates proving themselves to be better alternatives to Joe Biden's centrism. As a case in point, McManus (2020) suggests left-leaning priorities that dominated the Democratic primaries between June 2019 and April 2020 included Medicare for all, the Green New Deal, abolishing immigration and customs enforcement, and raising the taxes of the wealthy (McManus 2020). In addition, Pete Buttigieg had moved in previous weeks to position himself as a center-left alternative to both Joe Biden and Elizabeth Warren, using television ads in Iowa. Others were also looking to Iowa for a breakthrough, including Senators Kamala Harris, Cory Booker, and Amy Klobuchar as well as Tom Steyer, a former hedge fund investor who re-branded himself as a reform-minded outsider.

At this point in the primary campaign, Joe Biden was a clear favorite only in South Carolina, and advisers counselled him to look for success with voters in larger, more diverse states. To that end, he counted on the older and more centrist African American and Latino voters who had helped Hillary

Clinton hold the line against Bernie Sanders during the 2016 Democratic primaries (Burns 2019b). Biden signaled he would enter the debate on the offensive and that he had to become "more aggressive" as polling indicating an "anti-establishment" preference was trending, with voters rewarding candidates for defying conventional limits of political discourse and "pushing boundaries in really productive ways" (Burns 2019b; Bycoffe et al. 2019).

Sean McElwee, a prominent activist who co-founded the nonprofit think tank Data for Progress, initially and harshly criticized Biden at the outset of the primaries. However, after he demonstrated a willingness to meet with outspoken party progressives and refused to engage in intraparty tribalistic discourse, McElwee's opinion of Joe Biden changed:

> I think a lot of people who just s**t on the Democratic Party haven't spent a lot of time talking to mainstream actors within the Democratic Party ecosystem [which is] very liberal. I think people should just take a step back and look at what Biden has done. A.O.C. is someone I like a lot. She said that she wouldn't vote for him in the primary, and that in a different country she would be in a different party from him. And he could have responded to that by being, like, "F**k you." But instead he responded to that by being, like, "How about you come in and write my climate policy?" (Osnos 2020a)

Las Vegas, Nevada

During the February 2020 Las Vegas debates, one political analyst observed that the candidates had attempted to "destroy each other" without providing any "useful information" during the process. Intraparty ruptures had become so obvious during the vitriolic exchanges that voters could "forget that old bromide about there being more that unites them than divides them."

Reporter Brian Williams suggested that all of the candidates agreed on climate change as a global "existential crisis," rather than uniting to address that concern, they sniped at each other "on petty differences." In particular, each candidate constructed their campaign messaging to their specific liberal or centrist tribal segments within the Democratic Party. Early in the primary cycle, candidates initially staked out narrow ideological niches within the two dominant progressive and moderate factions in order to distinguish themselves from other contenders. As an example, Sanders discursively joined his "Bernie Bros" from 2016 while Elizabeth Warren caucused with her bloc to call out Sanders's sexism. At the same time, Mike Bloomberg appealed to his moderate faction of business leaders and criticized Sanders as a communist. Amy Klobuchar embraced rural voters, Pete Buttigieg championed young people outside the Beltway, and Joe Biden embraced minorities (Kahn 2020).

Even early on, pandering to such intratribal bickering was likely "destructive and defeatist" in that doing so hindered a realistic chance of Donald Trump's defeat by a Democrat. As a case in point, common action from the party to address paramount global issues such as the climate crisis would likely be improbable if not impossible:

> The candidates [all] need to do much more. Unity has to occur now, not in July at the national convention, if there is to be any hope of stopping the nightmare of four more years of Trump. (Brian Williams: Kahn 2020)

THE CONVENTION

Intraparty Tensions: Reservations and Warnings

The ideological differences between the pre-convention energized liberal wing and the post-convention more dominant centrist wing of the Democratic Party were harmonized ahead of the convention through what William Galston of the Brookings Institution calls "pretty skillful internal party management by the Biden forces." But, he added, "I think that's a truce, not a peace treaty" (Balz 2020a). Prior to the beginning of the convention in August 2020, McManus (2020) expected "mostly moderate messages" to be delivered by Biden and his running mate, Kamala Harris. Rather than "fiery" discourse, it was likely convention rhetoric that would focus on pragmatic rather than ideological goals such as winning the presidency and managing the coronavirus. When he introduced Harris, the junior senator from California, as his running mate, Biden said Americans deserved a president and a vice president "willing to lead and take responsibility" unlike "as [Trump] says, 'It's not my fault.'"

Both Senators Sanders and Warren spoke while Ocasio-Cortez appeared on a 60-second video. Sanders appealed to his contingent to vote for Biden, suggesting that without a unified Democratic Party, not only might the United States succumb to another four years of Trump, but progressive efforts would have been wasted:

> This election is about preserving our democracy. During this president's term, the unthinkable has become normal. [Trump] has tried to prevent people from voting, undermined the U.S. Postal Service, deployed the military and federal agents against peaceful protesters, threatened to delay the election and suggested that he will not leave office if he loses. Together we have moved this country in a bold new direction. Our movement continues and is getting stronger

every day. But, let us be clear, if Donald Trump is re-elected, all the progress we have made will be in jeopardy. (Weissert 2020b)

There were still serious reservations about the former vice president among liberals at the convention, several of whom had indicated that, should he be elected, they would push back on issues including health care, climate change, education, and criminal justice. Others refused to back the Democratic Party platform because it did not support Medicare for all, a symbolic move that nevertheless suggested possible intraparty breaches to come (Herndon and Ember 2020). In a sign of the "tensions simmering behind the scenes at the convention," some "left-wing activists" organized a #LetAOCSpeak campaign, with a petition circulated by the Young Delegates Coalition asking the DNC to allot the New York Representative Alexandria Ocasio-Cortez more speaking time. The petition read:

> We call on you to have Representative Alexandria Ocasio-Cortez give the keynote address at the Democratic National Convention or, at minimum, have as much time to speak as is given to Republican John Kasich. AOC is one of the Democratic Party leaders who is most respected by young Democrats and progressives. (Bade 2020)

Ultimately, Ocasio-Cortez's 97-second DNC speech to second the nomination of Senator Bernie Sanders for president spotlighted her prominence in the party as a "far left force." It also functioned as a "shout-out" regarding issues to which attention "must be paid" should Joe Biden and his centrist bloc win the November election:

> In a time when millions of people in the United States are looking for deep systemic solutions to our crises of mass evictions, unemployment and lack of health care [and] out of a love for all people, I hereby second the nomination of Senator Bernard Sanders of Vermont for president of the United States of America. (Bade 2020)

Ocasio-Cortez galvanized the progressive alliance of her party hoping to keep Democratic centrists like Biden from co-opting her coalition's priorities. An equally crucial effort was directed at increasing progressives' congressional numbers in 2021 and so expanding their power to pressure the legislature as well as the next president into embracing policies such as the Green New Deal and Medicare for all. Corbin Trent, a former Ocasio-Cortez aide, warned at the time that the party was united behind Joe Biden "right now" to defeat Donald Trump but that after the election there could be a very different goal:

They won the nomination, so they get to pick the game plan [but] that doesn't mean that they get to pick the game plan in the midterms, when we start primarying their a**es. And it don't [sic] mean that they get to pick the game plan when we start recruiting for 2024 and we primary their a**es off. (Bade 2020)

Uniting Against Trump

Nonetheless, the official party platform incorporated elements from both liberal and centrist tribal segments, the result of joint task forces seeking intraparty agreement on issues including health care and climate change. Biden had endorsed climate goals that came close to the Green New Deal that Ocasio-Cortez had supported. He also agreed to consider additional benefits and less expensive premiums for the public health insurance program he wanted to add to Obamacare. Unlike in 2016, Donald Trump become the single factor that united the principle intraparty units within the Democratic Party so that Joe Biden and Kamala Harris—"both practical politicians"—moved with their party "not as far left as Warren or Sanders, but far enough to keep progressive leaders on board" (McManus 2020; Kelley 2018).

A major theme that emerged out of the convention was that segments within the polarized tribe began to unite not to support the presumptive nominee but to defeat the incumbent president. As an instance, a pair of liberal groups, the Working Families Party and the Center for Popular Democracy Action, chose to endorse Joe Biden's candidacy as a "vehicle to topple Trump." Both backed different candidates during the primaries, with the Working Families Party endorsing Elizabeth Warren and then backing Bernie Sanders after the senator from Massachusetts pulled out of the race, while the Center for Popular Democracy Action had lined up behind Sanders.

Leaders of both alliances indicated their endorsements were the "lesser-of-two evils," that they would prefer to work with Biden than Trump, but "still expect a Biden presidency would require considerable outside pressure for him to make liberal policy." National director of the Working Families Party Maurice Mitchell maintained that although his organization had major differences with the former vice president, Joe Biden nonetheless offered "better solutions than Donald Trump" (Linskey 2020c).

While the Democratic primary race began as a tribal skirmish within the party, by the time the convention began, a treaty was brokered. For the moment, ideologically polarized cohorts united behind Joseph Biden for the singular purpose of stopping Donald Trump from achieving a second term in office as President of the United States. Accordingly, the diverse alliances within the party coalesced through a shared purpose, with an often-warring moderate establishment and galvanized liberal factions agreeing to deliver the White House to Biden (Balz 2020a). Uniting against Trump had operated throughout as the singular issue that kept the Democratic Party from fracturing. This became more obvious with the diverse lineup for the first night of the convention, when in the name of unity, former candidates—by and large all of the original Democratic nominees for the 2020 presidency—lauded Joe Biden (Herndon and Ember 2020).

Taking "One for the Team"

On the first day of the virtual 2020 Democratic National Convention, Bernie Sanders assumed the role of uniter rather than spoiler (Chotiner 2020; Krugman 2020). Four years earlier, he had emerged from his own, albeit unsuccessful, residential campaign a liberal superstar. At the time, his base was so loyal—and so openly antagonistic toward Hillary Clinton—leaders considered whether they needed to panic about the future of the Democratic Party over the next several years (Milbank 2016; Frizell 2016).

Four weeks after Clinton won the 2016 nomination, Bernie Sanders still hadn't endorsed the presumptive nominee, vowing to "take our campaign for transforming the Democratic Party into the convention" (Alcindor 2016; Phillips 2016). Four years later, he withdrew from the presidential race and endorsed his former rival as soon as Joe Biden became the presumptive nominee, a striking departure from Sanders's first presidential bid (Rubin 2020; Collins 2020). This time, rather than creating intraparty discord by perpetuating his own campaign, Bernie Sanders "took one for the team," telling Biden "we need you in the White House" and that he would "do all that I can do make that happen." Because the election was "the most important in the modern history of this country" and "in response to the unprecedented crises" Americans faced, an "unprecedented response" was imperative. That response, according to Sanders, was that "we need Joe Biden as our next president" as the leader of a "movement like never before of people who are prepared to stand up and fight for democracy and decency and against greed, oligarchy, and bigotry" ("Bernie Sanders . . ." 2020).

A recurring discursive strategy utilized by Sanders was to rally the liberal bloc who had supported him during the primaries to give their allegiance to Joseph Biden, at least until Trump was defeated. Addressing his base, Sanders expressed gratitude for his followers, insisting that "our movement continues and is getting stronger every day." In addition, he observed that, while disagreeing with his former rival over health care, Joe Biden was worthy of support. Sanders also reminded his coalition not only of their goals but of their success in mainstreaming those goals:

Many of the ideas we fought for that just a few years ago were considered radical are now mainstream, but let us be clear. If Donald Trump is re-elected, all the progress we have made will be in jeopardy. At its most basic this election is about preserving our democracy. ("Bernie Sanders . . ." 2020)

He also warned constituents who supported candidates other than the former vice president of consequences if the party remained at war with itself. Not only would Trump remain in office but the progress Bernie Sanders and his cohorts had made during the past four years would be in jeopardy. Because of this, he promised to reach across ideological lines within his own party as well as with Republicans:

I will work with progressives, with moderates, and yes, with conservatives to preserve this nation from a threat that so many of our heroes fought and died to defeat. My friends, I say to you, to everyone who supported other candidates in the primary and to those who may have voted for Donald Trump in the last election, the future of our democracy is at stake. The future of our economy is at stake. The future of our planet is at stake. We must come together, defeat Donald Trump, and elect Joe Biden and Kamala Harris as our next president and vice president. My friends, the price of failure is just too great to imagine. ("Bernie Sanders . . .", 2020; Ember, 2020a)

PRESIDENT-ELECT BIDEN

Incorporating Others' Perspectives

Once it became apparent that he was going to be the Democratic nominee, Joe Biden's discourse embraced some of his fellow progressive primary candidates' arguments. In the "usual course" of a Presidential campaign, a Democrat leans left during the primary and then "marches right" in the general election. Biden went the opposite direction. A year after assuring voters that "nothing would fundamentally change," Biden "leaned left" or at least slanted in that direction, as he argued that America was due for "some revolutionary institutional changes." As an example, within weeks after winning the nomination, he had adopted Elizabeth Warren's plan to ease student debt and overhaul the bankruptcy system. In addition, Biden embraced a modified version of Bernic Sanders's plan for tuition-free college and eased his opposition to federal funding for abortions (Osnos 2020a; Glueck 2020c; Epstein and Goldmacher 2020; Kaplan 2020).

Progressives Push Back

While former vice president Joe Biden's primary win united tribal factions of Democrats behind a goal of defeating President Trump and combating the coronavirus, there were concerns that the detente might not last past the November 3 election, no matter who won the presidency. Biden won the nomination despite rejecting calls from more liberal candidates to endorse a Medicare for all health care system, extend free public university tuition to everyone, and overhaul the economy to eventually eliminate fossil fuels. Their calls were not without merit, as progressives defeated establishment Democrats in congressional primaries in Illinois, New York, and Missouri. As a result, demands were immediately made on Biden to implement policies originally situated firmly within the polarized left block, if he won the presidency (Thomas and Collins 2020).

After working diligently to put Joe Biden so close to achieving the presidency, some in this liberal contingent immediately discussed "planning to give him hell the minute he sets foot in the White House." Unlike with Barack Obama, there would be no "honeymoon" when it became clear that his ability to "cut deals with Republicans"—central to Biden's campaign—"would be hemmed in from day one." Former staffers to progressive Charles Booker, who campaigned from a platform of criminal justice reform but had narrowly lost his race to centrist Amy McGrath in Kentucky's Senate race, immediately caucused for a liberal-centric congressional chamber. In addition, the liberal version of Republican's Freedom Caucus was under consideration while Medicare for all advocates argued for formation of a PAC to put single-payer advocates in office and "fight the policy's enemies" (Otterbein 2021).

Joseph Geevarghese, executive director of the Bernie Sanders-founded group Our Revolution, argued "our movement is ascendant." To that end, he warned that Joe Biden and Kamala Harris faced almost certain challenges legislatively from the left in 2024 if they governed as "Third Way-ers" or engaged in "Clinton-esque triangulation." Democratic California Representative Ro Khanna insisted he was "confident that progressives will have a big, big role in a Biden administration." To that end, liberals had to continue to "push for their values, and advocate for people to join the administration [that] are progressive" (Otterbein 2021).

Sanders Speaks

After dropping out of the primaries in April 2020, Bernie Sanders simultaneously championed his progressive coalition while directing his base to unify behind Joe Biden. Embedded in a call of support for Biden was a mandate that the former vice president and now Democratic nominee more openly embrace their movement. A long-standing question among Sanders's base had been whether a majority of their alliance, some of whom had been leery of Biden's record, would endorse him. As a case in point, according to Evan Weber, a co-founder of the youth-led climate-focused organization Sunrise Movement, the Biden campaign really did the "least outreach of any of the major front-runners" to their organization in the entire election cycle (Khalid 2020).

With Sanders no longer in the presidential race, a substantial portion of his left-of-center alliance hoped that the president-elect would choose one of their ideological allies to be his running mate such as Massachusetts Senator Elizabeth Warren or California Representative Karen Bass (Ember and Herndon 2020). Doing so would address their concerns that Biden would govern as the former vice president had spent most of his career, anchored in Democratic establishment politics.

Once Biden secured the nomination, Sanders began "moving far more quickly than he had in 2016," to back Biden almost immediately because he had "a better relationship with Joe Biden than I had with Hillary Clinton." Faiz Shakir, Sanders's former campaign manager, observed that, post primaries, Bernie Sanders was "confident" that Joe Biden was in a strong position to win the election, but that there were positions on issues such as raising wages, creating jobs, and expanding health care coverage that his campaign needed to address. When asked how confident he was that the center-left Democratic nominee could defeat Donald Trump, Sanders indicated that while there was "a strong chance" for victory, he pointed out that "Biden's views" were not his; that "my program was much more progressive" and that "he's got to do a better job in getting it out, to be honest with you" (Ember 2020b).

HOLDING THE CENTER

Prioritizing Unity: Kamala Harris as Vice President

Joe Biden consolidated the support of fellow candidates, winning the backing of Amy Klobuchar, Pete Buttigieg, and Beto O'Rourke ahead of Super Tuesday in March 2020. Other former candidates, including Kamala Harris, endorsed him as well ("Bernie Sanders . . ." 2020). Even so, the pressure to accommodate the demands of progressives within his own party became a crucial constraint for Joe Biden, as he campaigned to become president of the entire nation. An agile if not paradoxical rhetorical high-wire act was required if the centrist former vice president was to maintain enthusiasm for his candidacy from the left bloc within his own party while gaining a majority of votes from the "rest of the country." Significantly, millions of those votes belonged to Americans who shared Donald Trump's discursive vision of the Democratic party as so dominated by "socialists and extremists" that Biden was inevitably and irreparably out of touch with Republicans, particularly in pivotal states such as Michigan, Wisconsin, and Pennsylvania (Ember 2020b).

The choice of Kamala Harris, a center-left California Senator, fit the bill. A majority of progressives opted to applaud rather than criticize the Democratic nominee's choice for vice president, momentarily opting for the unity of consensus rather than tribalistic division, hyper-focused with an electoral priority of removing the incumbent from office. Evan Weber, political director for the climate advocacy group the Sunrise Movement, which had endorsed Senator Sanders's candidacy, acknowledged that the decision for vice presidential running mate was "always up to the vice president [Biden]" rather than the Democratic Party and so a "personal [choice] of his" (Ember and Herndon 2020).

This public support for Harris spotlighted the gravity of the situation, wherein liberal Democrats, at least for the moment, prioritized party unification behind Joe Biden over their faction's demands for change in order the defeat Donald Trump (Ember and Herndon, 2020; "Does Biden-Harris?" 2020).

All Things to All Democrats

Bernie Sanders had cautioned the Biden campaign, both in public and private, that their nominee, a centrist, must do more to excite the liberal sector. He emphasized, in particular, that the Democratic nominee should work harder to appeal to young voters and Latinos, both blocs that had overwhelmingly supported the Vermont Senator in the primary but had not evidenced such a connection with Joe Biden. Shortly after Biden's nomination, Sanders suggested the former vice president would be "the most progressive president since FDR" if he followed through on his agenda (Waldman 2020). Nonetheless, after the primaries, Biden was still confronted by the partisan left in his party for his "conservative" stances while Republicans attacked him as intractably "liberal" in the worst sense.

As a case in point, Biden's health care plan was "far more ambitious" than the Affordable Care Act. However, since the plan was not argued as Medicare for all, it was discursively framed (and derided by some) as "the moderate alternative." This in turn was "evidence" of the Democratic nominee's ethos as a "cautious moderate." In Viser's (2020b) view, Joe Biden's centrist positioning carried risk, not the least in the Democratic primaries. He was not the candidate riding the left's energy and vowing to start a revolution like his chief rival Sanders or the one who would make history such as Barack Obama had done or the several female candidates Biden had defeated, including his eventual running mate Kamala Harris.

In addition, his centrist, and on occasion (particularly from a Republican standpoint) center-left profile was bolstered by refusing to "abolish ICE" when it was broached during the primaries and at the time became a Republican shibboleth with which to condemn the Democrat of possibly "running to the left." Nor did Joe Biden endorse policies that might "defund the police." Rejecting such epithets demonstrated that he was clearly more moderate than some in his party, "an insulation that has given him the ability to keep steadily moving on policy." Such positions provided additional evidence that a Biden presidency might reverse the shift traditionally expected once a campaign has been won. Rather than appealing to particular niche segments within the party through promises of "ideological fealty" (then returning back to center) once the nomination was secure, Biden did the opposite "in substance if not in rhetoric" (Waldman 2020).

Intraparty Compromises

Throughout the primary season, Joe Biden generally occupied moderate/centrist territory for Democrats, thwarting left-leaning calls for universal health care and free college and refusing to join many in the party with the Green New Deal—even so, creating a path to securing the nomination (Shear and Crowley 2020; Liasson 2019). Liberals anticipated that, after a Biden win, they could still force the moderate president to endorse some of their priority proposals. Mondaire Jones, who won his New York state congressional primary (and went on to win running as the progressive candidate in a "left-leaning" district), argued that his contingent had to leverage their membership in a way that would guarantee concessions from a Biden White House on issues like criminal justice reform and health care (Otterbein 2021).

Some leaders of grassroots activist organizations credit Biden for recognizing the need to accommodate the left sector of their party. "The Biden team was clear you needed to engage those folks," according to George Goehl, executive director of the grassroots organizing group People's Action. "That was very practical political thinking" (Balz 2020a). A key strategy of Biden's was the to embrace the full breadth of the party. To that end, his team constructed one of the most liberal platforms in the party's history. This included concerns advanced by Senator Sanders and Senator Warren in their primaries, such as lowering the age for Medicare and strengthening the former vice president's position on student debt forgiveness. In addition, a symbolically significant task force hybrid team was announced that included former secretary of state and party moderate John F. Kerry and liberal Representative Alexandria Ocasio-Cortez.

A day after Bernie Sanders dropped out of the presidential race, Biden, by then the presumptive Democratic nominee, made an overture to the liberal coalition in his party by announcing two policy proposals including lowering the age of Medicare eligibility and forgiving student debt for low-income and middle-class families who attended public colleges and universities and some private institution. Biden lauded Sanders as a "powerful voice" whose movement "changed the dialogue in America." The former vice president also indicated he was "proud to adopt" such policies and that Senator Sanders and his left-of-center contingent could "take pride in their work in laying the groundwork for these ideas" (Khalid 2020).

To demonstrate their platform unity, Sanders agreed to joint task forces with Joe Biden on criminal justice, economics, education, health care, immigration, and climate change, crucial tests of whether the "left and center factions of the Party could get along." Biden stated that he wasn't going to engage in an "ideological jihad" with Sanders:

> I said, "Bernie, if you want these set up in order for me to insist that I be for Medicare for all . . . this is not where it's going to go." But I said, "I'm open, I hear you, I'm ready to listen." (Biden: Osnos 2020b)

Biden also recruited Alexandria Ocasio-Cortez to chair the climate task force, alongside former Secretary of State John Kerry. Others included Varshini Prakash, of the Sunrise Movement, which during the primary had graded Biden's climate plan an F. Also, while Sanders and his team wanted all-clean electricity by 2030, as a sign of cohesion and willingness to compromise, they "were happy to settle for 2035." The biggest unresolved point of contention was fracking. "It's not like I walked out of there with Bernie's Green New Deal in hand, and I did not expect to," Prakash said. "But it was a lot more collaborative, actually, than I was anticipating" (Osnos 2020b). Finally, Joe Biden accepted the nomination at the virtual Democratic convention on August 29, 2020, spotlighting the symbolic unification of his party around himself and his running mate, Senator Kamala Harris, "even as sharp differences" remained "below the surface" (Glueck 2020c).

A "Big Tent" Approach

Conversely, some progressives including liberal Ritchie Torres, who won both his New York primary as well as the congressional seat in November, argued all Democrats would likely support such propositions "on their own" because the party is far more progressive now than it was . . . even 10 years ago. The progressive renaissance in America . . . has expanded the realm of what can be achieved politically [and] I think the left has given a future Democratic president greater freedom to govern.

Consequently, while he "might think he's returning Americans to "normalcy" through a "back to the past of American foreign policy," Joe Biden "is doing the opposite" (Ashford 2020). When Biden was nominated as the Democratic candidate, he committed not only to rebuilding America, but also to "build it back better." Although Biden's foreign policy would be "better" than Donald Trump's "destabilizing force," Trump's "unusual presidency" would facilitate both an opportunity as well as a rhetorical space for Americans to question "flawed and outdated assumptions about the world."

As an example, while the "agenda of the far-left" might be configured as Democratic leaders' "worst nightmare," Speaker of the House Nancy Pelosi, a former progressive activist herself, has argued the party needs a "big-tent approach" that enables moderates to represent their districts and reach out to conservatives. In this view, that the party has not followed this advice is one of the reasons Medicare for all has "gotten hearings but no votes in the House" (Seib 2018).

FiveThirtyEight's Perry Bacon explained his rationale for partitioning the 2020 Democratic Party into six contingents (two on the left, two in the center, and two to the right). While the two most liberal groups have a "ton of new policy ideas and energy" and remain "determined to push the party left," the Democrats have a majority in the House in part because of moderate Democrats winning in closely contested districts. Therefore:

> The party probably needs more moderate, and even some conservative, Democrats to gain ground in gubernatorial and Senate seats. Trapped in the middle are the party's congressional leaders and most of its presidential contenders, facing pressure from the party's left and the right. (2019)

These categories and this conclusion, specifically that moderates in Congress and the presidency are under siege from two distinct ideological camps within their own party, inform a principal leitmotif of *Democratic Disunity*. While the Democratic "left" and the Democratic "right" see each other as having very little in common ("shared substance" in Kenneth Burke's nomenclature), they are in truth united through their division, in that both are joined in attacking the center (Burke 1969; Durham 1980). Further deconstructed, this means the Democratic Party is still fundamentally two discrete tribalized cohorts: moderates and everyone else. Regardless of this intraparty bisection, Democrats, first and foremost, coexist and cooperate with Republicans who at this point remain, up and down the ticket, Tribe Trump (Bacon 2021; Blake 2021; McCarthy 2021; Martin 2021). As such, the sooner the "big tent party" realizes the center holds only if well supported, the better.

Chapter 7

The Election

Beginning with his 2016 ascension to the presidency, Donald Trump and the Republican Party began rhetorically constructing a palpable fear of Democrats' "turning to socialism." This implied accusation assaulted Biden, Kamala Harris, and fundamentally all candidates up and down the Democratic ticket throughout the 2020 election cycle. As the 2018 midterm elections approached, the White House warned of disaster if Democrats' failed socialist policies continued. Trump issued a "blistering op-ed" at the time, accusing Democrats of bringing danger to "every single citizen." In his view, the "centrist Democratic Party" was dead, replaced by "radical socialists" determined to reinvent the American economy "after Venezuela." In addition, a democratically controlled Congress would legislate such a "radical shift in American culture and life" that "every single citizen" would suffer "misery and decay" (Trump 2018).

Trump insisted that government-run health care mandates were not only "menacing to our seniors and our economy" but worse because of Democrats' "absolute commitment to end enforcement of our immigration laws by abolishing Immigration and Customs Enforcement." It would follow that "millions more" would "cross our borders illegally" and take advantage of health care meant only for taxpaying Americans:

> Today's Democratic Party is for open-borders socialism. This radical agenda would destroy American prosperity. Under its vision, costs will spiral out of control. Taxes will skyrocket. . . . I am committed to resolutely defending Medicare and Social Security from the radical socialist plans of the Democrats. For the sake of our country . . . this is a fight we must win. (Trump 2018)

2018 ANTECEDENTS

Although Democrats at the time had witnessed a rise in "self-identified socialists" running for—and winning—seats and realized some in the party might have even suggested an overthrow of capitalism, none had attained national office on that platform (Kurtzleben and Malone 2018). Democrats at large still remained committed to a free market economy. Accordingly, in the United States "socialism" frequently conflated notions of public care programs run from tax revenues and generated by free market enterprise, as opposed to a rigid and possibly even an "un-American" system with solely state-owned businesses (Lockie 2018).

Unprecedented in American politics, a wave of Democratic candidates began referencing themselves as "socialists." Some won, many lost, but others created "even in defeat" rhetorical spaces "for those who run in the next cycle, and the one after that." As a result, any "political revolution" would "happen incrementally" because the Democratic "establishment"—even in its more "progressive quarters"—was still frightened that they would receive "blowback" from moderates (Krieg 2020). Candidates such as Ben Jealous, Democratic nominee for governor in Maryland and 2016 Sanders supporter, rejected the association—twice noting his "venture capitalist" work and eventually becoming more direct in his denials. During a news conference before the midterms, he responded to a direct question about whether he identified as a socialist with "Are you f***ing kidding me?" Also, Elizabeth Warren, like Bernie Sanders at the time, rumored to be considering a 2020 presidential primary run and a vocal advocate of Medicare for all, asserted she was "capitalist to my bones" (Krieg 2020; Harwood 2018).

Evolving Attitude

However, attitudinal change—as well as conflicting interpretations about who and what messages belonged in certain rhetorical spaces and how they should be framed—was on the horizon. For the first time in Gallup's measurements, in 2018 Democrats viewed socialism more positively than capitalism. While attitudes toward socialism among Democrats had not changed materially in a decade, with 57 percent holding a positive view, their attitudes toward capitalism slipped to 47 percent positive, lower than in any of three previous studies. Significantly, 57 percent of Republicans perceived capitalism more positively with only 16 percent expressing positive perceptions of socialism, with little sustained change in their views of either since 2010 (Newport 2018).

For decades, the former "ran scared" of the ambiguously defined term while the latter weaponized it, often to challenge Democrats' patriotism. Krieg (2020) suggests that although it is tempting to attribute the socialist resurgence in 2018—as well as its notoriety two years later—to acolytes like Sanders and Alexandria Ocasio-Cortez, the reality is complex. To illustrate, time and timing configured a different political horizon, including the lack of money due to a stagnant economy for wage-earning workers, younger ones in particular, whose initial political memories coalesced during the 2008 financial crisis also informed the political realities. Combined, these intimidated and threatened newly political millennials with inescapable student debt, a cruel private health insurance system, and global environmental destruction (Krieg 2020).

It is also instructive that "democratic socialist" is not the same identity as "social democrat." As a case in point, Sanders and company are more accurately described by the latter in that they rarely call for a hard stop to capitalism, preferring instead modifications and limits. In contrast, "democratic socialists" maintain that capitalism is organically incompatible with democratic ideals, ultimately transitioning to socialism, albeit often without time constraints (Barrett 1978; "What Is Democratic Socialism?" 2021; Hiatt 2020).

INTERNAL RUPTURES, EXTERNAL ASSAULTS

It is not surprising then, that during the 2020 presidential election, national political culture cleaved into polarized rhetorical visions of "socialism," which by November were in full view. The term was a default rhetorical device with which Republicans bludgeoned Democrats in general; it also facilitated intraparty tribalism within the Democratic Party. The different configurations of the word emboldened Republicans to situate policies favored by "liberal groups" (fundamentally all Democrats) under the "socialism" banner. Trump labeled Democratic candidate (and future vice president) Kamala Harris's views as "communist" after claiming her immigration policy pivoted on nothing less than her desire to "open up the borders" of the United States (Tankersley 2020).

Using Democrats' Words Against Their Own

One powerful rhetorical device used in the intraparty moderate-versus-liberal conflict between Democrats was again appropriated into a discursive weapon for Republicans during the national and down-ticket 2020 races. Specifically, Joe Biden was rhetorically re-created as a dupe of socialists and alt-left leaning Democrats, mirroring concerns within its own ranks. The "socialism" accusation was echoed in the rationale undergirding Texas Representative Kevin Brady, the top Republican on the Ways and Means Committee, when he asserted:

> In my district, I hear a lot of fear about the dramatic turn the Democratic Party has taken toward socialism. My constituents are fearful when they see proposals to defund the police, abolish our immigration and customs enforcement, when there is burning and looting in cities, and concerns over the Green New Deal. (Tankersley 2020)

Four years earlier, Donald Trump co-opted Bernie Sanders's attacks against Hillary Clinton for failing to be "liberal enough"—particularly after she had won her party's nomination—into laser-focused rhetorical weapons. Trump made Sanders's criticism of Clinton his own by creating a shared identity of being unified against Hillary Clinton with the Vermont Senator's base. The Republican nominee effectively appealed to a substantial portion of Bernie Sanders's supporters with appeals that they join him in their mutual dislike for the Democratic nominee by refusing to vote at all, or, better yet, opt for "revenge voting" for Trump as a sort of rhetorical punishment because Hillary Clinton was "not liberal enough" (Kelley 2018).

Republicans capitalized on this intraparty "progressive versus moderate" schism, which by 2020 had produced two distinct rhetorical tribes. Identical discursive devices—including the words "liberal" and "socialist," which in 2016 united many in Clinton's own party against her for not being liberal (or socialist) "enough"—were written, spoken, and tweeted. In this instance, Republicans configured the concepts as absolute "devil-terms" through which they rhetorically created all Democrats as "liberals" and so "socialists" (Weaver 1953, 1985). As a result, in the Republican "newspeak" of 2020, descriptors for self-identified tribes within the party such as "moderate or centrist" disappeared while "liberal or progressive" became synonymous for unelectable. The platforms of Joe Biden and Kamala Harris, which situated both as Democratic centrists, were discursively re-created in this manner (Lybrand and Subramaniam 2020; Herndon 2020c; Murdock 2019).

The Republican Leitmotif

In the August 31, 2020 edition of his *Fox News* program, Sean Hannity referenced Kamala Harris as Joe Biden's "radical running mate" and alluded to fissures within the Democratic Party, attributing the violence that accompanied many of the "Black Lives Matter" protests to a particular segment of that party:

The far left radical base of the Democratic Party, well, they're rioting in nearly every city run by liberal Democrats for decades. Not only did high-profile Democrats and so-called journalists encourage this kind of violence daily, but they also enabled destructive riots to spiral out of control, in city after city. They ignored or mitigated the violent protests and minimized the damage. (Trump, Jr. 2020)

Hannity insisted all Democrats, including Joe Biden, are "one mind" and had become nothing less than a "propaganda media wing" for the "Democratic radical socialist party."

On the same program, Donald Trump, Jr. asserted that Americans were unable to defend themselves from looting and would be subjected to arrest, jail, and loss of their businesses because Democrats "have lost control to the radical left." Trump Jr. insisted Joe Biden was "a sock puppet for the left so they can get Kamala, and Bernie and AOC and those crazy policies." He concluded that ultimately theirs is "a radical leftist agenda" with Joe Biden acting as "a fake moderate to sell it" (Trump, Jr. 2020; Nichols 2020). Speaking at an October 2020 rally, Donald Trump asserted that, if elected president, Joe Biden and his far-left allies would turn America into a socialist state. The Democratic candidate had forged "a corrupt bargain in exchange for his party's nomination" and had already "handed control to the socialists and Marxists and left-wing extremists" like his vice-presidential candidate. Another line of argument was the then president's claim that Joe Biden's running mate, Senator Kamala Harris, was a communist and that the Democratic ticket offered nothing less "a choice between a socialist nightmare and the American dream" (Tankersley 2020).

During an October 13 rally Trump assured supporters that Joe Biden would turn the nation into a socialist state should he win the presidency. He also condemned the Democratic candidate's "corrupt bargain" that Biden had traded for the party nomination. Alluding to Kamala Harris, Trump insisted that Joe Biden had been duped by "socialists and Marxists and left-wing extremists like his vice-presidential candidate" and so would force America into a socialist state if given the chance. As he had four years earlier during his first presidential campaign, Donald Trump strategically played to the "progressive-hard left"/"moderate-center" tribal division within the Democratic party (Kelley 2018) as a discursive strategy. In this case, the then president directed a crucial portion of the Florida electorate to share in his rhetorical vision that Joe Biden, a career-long Democratic moderate, would enact a radical socialist agenda if elected. NBC News election day exit polls reported that close to 55 percent of Florida's Cuban American vote went to Trump ("NBC News Exit Poll" 2020). At least a portion of this victory came from his deceptive but successful framing of the Democratic nominee as "Castro-Chavista," rhetorically linking the Democratic presidential candidate to Fidel Castro of Cuba and Hugo Chavez of Venezuela. Ultimately, at least in part because a majority of the Cuban American Latinos shared in the president's vision that America would become a socialist country if Biden were elected, Donald Trump won the battleground state of Florida's 20 electoral votes (Sesin 2020).

When he formally launched his 2020 presidential campaign in June of 2019, Trump "circled back to a word he has used publicly at least 118 times since becoming president":

> No matter what label they use, a vote for any Democrat in 2020 is a vote for the rise of radical socialism and the destruction of the American Dream," Trump said at his 60th rally since being sworn in. (Trump: Rieger 2019)

Republicans wielding "socialism" or "communism" as assault weapons is neither a novel nor particularly original campaign strategy. Notably, "red baiting" successfully discredited Democratic (and other) policies and people for close to one hundred years. Of note, a 2019 Gallup poll indicated 43 percent of Americans considered it a "good thing" to have "some form of socialism" in the United States, an 18-point increase from a 1942 survey on socialism (Younis 2019). Notably, while 34 percent of Americans reported "no opinion" about socialism in 1942, only 6 percent had no opinion (Younis 2019). Those numbers suggest that a large portion of the electorate, particularly those in Tribe Trump were receptive to, if not enthusiastically available for, rejecting or accepting one political party over another—as well as its presidential candidate—based on the rhetorical power of one word.

DEFINING MOMENTS

Writing in September 2020, columnist E. J. Dionne, Jr. tacitly acknowledged the existence of confrontational tribes within the party when he advised to "never underestimate the Democrats' capacity to tear each other apart." However, he argued that such tendencies would likely be minimized or even disappear, albeit temporarily, during the election because "confronting a pandemic and an economic catastrophe" would unify factions to such an extent that "every Democrat, from center to left, would understand that blowing it this time would cause irreparable damage to themselves and to the country." Democrats would probably unite to defeat Donald Trump. Furthermore, while the "differences across the party's wings are real," opportunities existed for compromise between, for example, single-payer health care and "simply expanding Obamacare." In addition, the escalating economic crises produced an exigence that mandated a united rhetorical front from which Democrats could create a single policy that "could look simultaneously like realism to centrists and a 'New Green Deal' to progressives" (2020a).

Still, Republicans were incessant in their accusations that Joe Biden was a "Trojan horse," a diversion to mask Democratic socialist policies being pushed "from the left wing of the Democratic Party." Furthermore, since joining the ticket, the party had amended their claim to include Kamala Harris as "instrumental in doing the pushing" (Rossi 2020). That theme was foregrounded in the vice-presidential debate.

Vice-Presidential Debate

During the October 2020 debate, Republican vice president nominee Mike Pence insisted Americans must scrutinize Harris's record to see evidence of the Democratic vice-presidential nominee's extremely liberal tendencies. This included that, as a California senator, Harris had spoken against fracking and co-sponsored the Green New Deal. This was clearly evidence of her bias and a predictor of how she and equally ultra-liberal Joe Biden would rule the nation. Furthermore, the Green New Deal was "essentially the same plan" as Harris had co-sponsored with "AOC (Alexandria Ocasio-Cortez) when she submitted it in the Senate." Pence accused Harris of putting "your radical environmental agenda ahead of American auto workers and ahead of American jobs":

> But Senator you said it didn't go far enough on climate change, you put your radical environmental agenda ahead of American auto workers and a head of American jobs. I think the American people deserve to know that it's probably why Newsweek magazine said that Kamala Harris was the most liberal member of the United States Senate in 2019, more liberal than Bernie Sanders, more liberal than any of the others in the United States Senate. ("Kamala . . ." 2020)

This, despite the fact that the policy was primarily in line with the rapid phase-out of oil, gas, and coal that the federal government's National Climate Assessment scientists argued was necessary to avoid ecological collapse and countless human deaths. Nonetheless, the vice president relied on configuring Kamala Harris as recklessly demonstrating disrespect for the American people because she, and so by default, "all" Democrats "want to abolish fossil fuels and ban fracking" (Kaufman 2020; Phillips 2020; "Tracking . . ." 2021). Furthermore, Harris was criticized for some of her "too liberal" or "not liberal enough" positions as she campaigned in the primaries. Some voters, even within her base, were confused regarding Harris's stand on different issues during her presidential campaign, even seeming to have a "new, have-it-every-which-way approach." Fundamentally, the concern was most likely moot, because once Kamala Harris joined Joe Biden on the same presidential ticket, they were also likely joined over policy with a Biden slant. Mike Pence's accusations of socialism aside, if Harris moved in any "new" ideological direction as vice president, it would likely have been "even further to the center of her party" (Phillips 2020; "Tracking . . ." 2021).

During a post-debate interview on *60 Minutes*, Harris "could not conceal her amusement" when asked if she would pressure Joe Biden to adapt a "socialist or progressive perspective" if they won the presidential election. Citing a 2019 ranking from the non-partisan organization GovTrack, CBS News anchor Norah O'Donnell told the vice-presidential hopeful that she was "considered the most liberal United States senator" in 2019, pointing out that she supported policies like the Green New Deal, Medicare for all, and legalizing marijuana. "Joe Biden doesn't support those things," O'Donnell said. "So, are you going to bring the policies, those progressive policies you supported as senator, into a Biden administration?" Harris responded:

> What I will do, and I promise you this, and this is what Joe wants me to do, this was part of our deal: I will always share with him my lived experience as it relates to any issue that we confront, and I promised Joe that I will give him that perspective and always be honest with him.

When O'Donnell followed up with "And is that a socialist or progressive perspective?" Kamala Harris paused, seemed surprised ,and then "cracked up, 'No!'" and concluded:

> No, it is the perspective of a woman who grew up a Black child in America, who was also a prosecutor, who also has a mother who arrived here at the age of 19 from India, who also, you know, likes hip-hop.

Despite O'Donnell pressing the issue, Harris indicated she did support Biden's positions (Rossi 2020).

RUTH BADER GINSBURG

Joe Biden's Disengagement

Early in his campaign for the presidency Joe Biden, who had staked his candidacy largely on returning the nation to normalcy, by protecting institutions and forging bipartisanship, situated himself as a centrist, with appeals to Republicans as well as Democrats. Campaigning in the fall of 2019, he stated, "I'm not prepared to go on and try to pack the court, because we'll live to rue that day," arguing that doing so would cause the Court to lose its credibility.

He spoke in Wisconsin, shortly after Justice Ruth Bader Ginsburg's death in September 2020, a state that Donald Trump won by about 27,000 votes four years earlier, the first Republican to do so since 1984. At this time, he directly targeted Obama voters who had abandoned Hillary Clinton in favor of Trump four years earlier, never mentioning the Court vacancy or the "political earthquake" that followed the Justice's death. This was in part due to Biden's belief that most voters were not galvanized by the intensifying animosity between Democrats and Republicans regarding the Court (Nagle 2020). While acknowledging the gravity of the issues, there were also other concerns that mitigated Joe Biden's decision to disengage from a rhetorical war with Trump over adding more Justices to the Supreme Court so close to November 3:

> It's a legitimate question but let me tell you why I'm not going to answer that question: Because it will shift the focus. That's what [Trump] wants. He never wants to talk about the issue at hand and he always tries to change the subject. Let's say I answer that question, then the whole debate's going to be about what Biden said or didn't say, Biden said he would or wouldn't. (Linsky and Viser 2020)

During the September 2020 Wisconsin campaign, Biden's consensus-centric rhetoric configured the presidency as branded by Donald Trump, a poser, who claimed to be a "man of the people" but was in truth simultaneously part of and in thrall to wealth and Wall Street. Biden reminded Wisconsin voters that, with their help, he would be the first president in years who had not attended an Ivy League school, having received a bachelor's degree from the University of Delaware and a law degree from Syracuse University: "I think it's about time that a state school president sat in the Oval Office [because].... If I'm sitting there, you're going to be sitting there, too" (Linsky and Viser 2020; Graham 2020).

He also appealed directly to Trump's base, but through a broad inclusive message:

> I know many of you are frustrated. You're angry [and] you believe you weren't being seen, represented or heard. I get it. It has to change. And I promise you this: It will change with me. (Linsky and Viser 2020; Easley 2020a)

Party Angst

This approach contrasted sharply with the "bubbling anger" among many Democrats over Republican tactics regarding the Supreme Court, "a fury that began with the polarized left but appeared to seep into the party's mainstream" (Linsky and Viser 2020; Kass 2020). Biden's strategy raised the question of how he would react if Senate Republicans rejected his pleas to step back from the brink and instead push ahead with confirmation hearings. Linsky and Viser (2020) warned that if that happened Biden would face substantial pressure from the "liberal flank" of the Democratic Party "to adopt the more belligerent stance he has been studiously avoiding." Such pressure was suggested when Senate Minority Leader Chuck Schumer did a joint appearance with Alexandria Ocasio-Cortez, after Justice Ginsberg's death was announced. When asked about expanding the Supreme Court, Schumer responded, promising that "once we win the majority, God willing, everything is on the table" (Linsky and Viser 2020; Goldiner 2020).

At the time Elizabeth Warren also announced the formation of a coalition of civil rights groups focused on goals such as expanding the Supreme Court, ending the filibuster, and terminating the electoral college and granting statehood to D.C. (Gontcharova 2020). Other progressive Democrats argued that even if most voters cared little about the court itself, Ginsburg was unique: a justice who was crafted into an action figure, became the subject of movies, and evolved into a pop culture sensation known as the Notorious RBG. Her death, they argued, could galvanize voters in a unique way, especially women younger than 40:

> Everything the last four years has led to this moment. No Democratic response should be off the table, including expanding the Supreme Court. We are in a life-and-death struggle for the soul of our country, and we should use any means necessary. (Rachel Carmona, chief operating officer of "Women's March" quoted in Linsky and Viser 2020)

Some progressive Democrats, anticipating few legislative options to block a confirmation, considered "threatening moves" that were historically considered off limits. For example, in order to secure the White House and Senate, some argued for expanding the Supreme Court by adding new justices and filling those slots with liberals. That reflected a broader anger at what many in the party felt was a breakdown in the rules of American democracy—from gerrymandering to the electoral college, from the filibuster to attacks on voting. That had also prompted more support for moves including ending the filibuster and creating statehood for Puerto Rico and the District of Columbia, which are heavily Democratic ("Is It Possible . . ." 2020; Gordon 2021).

DEBATES

Through most of his half-century Senate career, Joe Biden positioned himself as a mediating, moderate voice both in the Democratic as well as national political cultures (Tankersley 2020). Still, even as he pursued the presidency during the 2020 campaign with a pledge to "soothe the nation's wounds and lower its collective temperature," Biden was challenged to deflect a charge foregrounded by Donald Trump's accusation during their first debate that he was a pawn of "far left" Democrats, violent agitators who had the party's nominee "wrapped around their finger" (Flegenheimer and Glueck 2020). Joe Biden's public identification as a Democratic centrist mirrored a discursive presidential campaign strategy of "coffee table conversation on policy" rather than a "bloody knife fight threatening to wound the party" (Kapur 2020). This rhetorical mode clearly dominated both of the presidential debates through which he engaged Donald Trump.

Cautions from Democrats

On the eve of the first presidential debate, intraparty sparring began between the moderate and liberal Democratic factions regarding Joe Biden's appeals to Republicans. There were concerns about their nominee's appeals to the "conscience" and "hearts" of Senate Republicans in response to their push for a rapid confirmation of Amy Barrett to the Supreme Court as a replacement for Ruth Bader Ginsberg. The Democratic presidential candidate rhetorically sidestepped liberal colleagues' concerns and appeased Republicans by defaulting to a message of bipartisan comity and national unity when he spoke of the "great respect" he had for "a number of my former Republican colleagues" and that he hoped "they will do the right thing" and so "de-escalate" the rapid escalation over his party's concern that Donald Trump was determined to pack the Supreme Court. While clearly concerned about the speed at which the confirmation appeared to be heading, Biden focused instead on the impact of the Supreme Court on health care, as the most effective strategy for appealing to swing voters tired of political divisiveness and relentless focus on the coronavirus pandemic (Lerer 2020a).

However, progressives, younger voters, and women, considered the core of the Democratic Party, worried an expanded conservative majority on the court would be an "existential threat" to abortion rights, climate change legislation, and gun control. Oregon's Democratic Senator Jeff Merkley, a primary advocate for ending the filibuster, a proposal initially considered by the party's center-left faction shortly after Ruth Bader Ginsburg's death, insisted "this whole situation with the court intensifies the understanding of how much the November election matters." Still, Biden refused to comment on Judge Barrett or proposals championed by progressives to expand the court, dismissing those questions as distractions that played into Donald Trump's agenda "because it would shift all the focus" and so give the president "what he wants [which is] never [to] talk about the issue at hand" (Lerer 2020a).

Biden's moderate allies maintained that the Senate fight did not resonate with independents, who were wary of partisan conflicts and considerably more concerned about the economy and the coronavirus rather than the Supreme Court. Representative Mark Pocan, a Wisconsin Democrat, cautioned that if Joe Biden relied on a more aggressive rhetorical stance against Republicans in "places like Wisconsin"—because voters were tired of partisan warfare in Washington—independents could be repelled. Other Democrats argued that Biden should avoid the "unpredictable dynamics" of a confirmation battle. Elevating the expectations of Democratic voters, because of the "all-but-inevitable failure of their efforts to stop the nomination" would likely demoralize the party's base in the midst of voting. Barbara Boxer, a former Democratic senator from California, believed that since the Senate was "tied in knots" she did not consider it "smart for Joe Biden to get in the middle of that mess." Also, because Democrats were already energized prior to Justice Ginsburg's death, there was little to be gained by actively joining in rhetorical combat over Amy Barrett's confirmation (Lerer 2020a; Sprunt 2020).

Cleveland: September 19, 2020

Throughout his first presidential campaign, Donald Trump simultaneously relied on and contributed to a discursive "progressive versus moderate Democrat" motif, which had been a key component in the "perfect storm" of elements that coalesced to overwhelm Hillary Clinton four years earlier (Kelley 2018). This rhetorical technique was foregrounded again during the first presidential debate on September 29, 2020, when Donald Trump alluded to serious division within the Democratic Party by warning that Joe Biden's party "wants to go socialist medicine and socialist healthcare" and that "they're going to dominate you, Joe." Biden countered metaphorically that such division was non-existent saying "the party is me" and that "right now, I am the Democratic Party." Trump still insisted that a critical split existed between Democrats by replying "not according to Harris," an exaggerated reference to Trump's deceptive configuration of the Democratic vice-presidential nominee's ties to socialism.

When Biden responded with "it is not" to moderator Chris Wallace's question about Republican's concern that modifications to Obamacare would end private insurance, Trump interjected "that's not what your party says, by the way" and that Biden "agreed with Bernie Sanders, who's far left, on the manifesto, we call it" and "that gives you socialized medicine." The president pursued his line of discourse by demanding that the Democrat respond to Trump's claim. Biden responded with "there is no manifesto, number one" after which Trump interrupted with "he [Biden] just lost the left" and continued to over-talk Biden by insisting the Democratic nominee collaborated with Bernie Sanders "on a plan that you absolutely agreed to and . . . they call it socialized medicine."

During the session in which Chris Wallace asked the candidates to comment on why Americans "trust you over your opponent to deal with race issues," Donald Trump claimed that he did not think Biden had "any law enforcement" behind him and argued that the Democratic candidate could not "even say" the phrase law enforcement because if Biden said those words he would "lose all of your radical left supporters." The president continued to bait Biden through innuendo demanding an explanation for refusing to "say the words" and then offering his own answer to the question:

> Because you know what? If [Portland had] called us . . . we would put out that fire in a half an hour. But they won't do it, because they're run by radical left Democrats. If you look at Chicago . . . Seattle . . . Minneapolis, we got it back, Joe, because we believe in law and order, but . . . the top 40 cities are run by Democrats, and in many cases the radical left. And they've got you wrapped around their finger, Joe, to a point where you don't want to say anything about law and order . . . the people of this country want and demand law and order and you're afraid to even say it.

When Wallace asked both candidates whether the nation-wide increase in homicides was "really a party issue," Trump returned to rhetorically configuring Joe Biden as in thrall to a radical left and increasingly powerful segment of the Democratic Party. The president said that even though such violence was "like nobody's ever seen" and "crazy," Biden nonetheless "doesn't want to say law and order" because he is afraid of losing "his radical left supporters" and "once he does that, it's over with." Trump also warned that "our suburbs would be done" and problems would beset Americans "like you've never seen before" if Biden ever became president and it ran the "way he would want to run" ("Donald Trump and Joe Biden 1st Presidential Debate" 2020a; Kapur 2020).

While Joe Biden distanced himself from some of the priorities of his party's left wing—and Vermont Senator Bernie Sanders—during the first debate, there was no sign that he had alienated his party's liberal and grassroots activists. Shortly after the first debate, Sanders spotlighted the crucial goal of a unified Democratic Party when he emphasized it was "terribly important" that Joe Biden be elected. As evidence of party unity, campaign digital director Rob Flaherty said Biden had raised $3.8 million at the debate's end in his "best hour of online fundraising" (Peoples et al. 2020).

Senator Christopher Coons warned Joe Biden early on in the 2020 presidential campaign that the Democratic nominee needed to prepare for constant and incendiary attacks designed to simultaneously harm Biden and increase the potentially lethal division between Americans and within the Democratic Party into mutually hostile and political tribes. While Biden did sustain such attacks from Republicans and, on occasion, within his own party, he generally responded with calls for cooperation rather than animosity. For example, directly addressing the country's deep polarization and causing some discomfort in the process, Joe Biden spoke to this division at a cross-party fundraising event when he said, "to those of you who are Republicans, I promise I'm not going to embarrass you" (Viser 2020b). Nor did Biden demonstrate animosity toward the progressive members of his own party as he firmly but respectfully defended his personal ethos as a moderate. To illustrate, when baited by Trump to call out the "moderate versus socialist" rift in the Democratic Party, Biden replied only that he had "defeated the more liberal elements of the Democratic coalition" in elections (Viser 2020b). In a Miami October 2020 interview, he identified himself as a "moderate" and "the guy that ran against socialists" (Blow 2020).

Nashville, Tennessee: October 22, 2020

During the second and final presidential debate, Donald Trump again attempted to conflate Joe Biden's platform with Bernie Sanders's attempts to forge a single-payer health network in Vermont. The president argued that when Joe Biden, actually a "very liberal governor," spoke about a "public option" he was really talking about "destroying" Americans' Medicare and Social Security to such an extent that "this whole country will come down." Again, refusing to respond to Trump's discursive baiting, Biden replied that during the primaries he "beat all those other people" simply "because I disagreed with them" ("Donald Trump and Joe Biden Final Presidential Debate" 2020). Trump again played the "democratic socialist" card against Biden when he insisted that although "180 million people out there" had "great private healthcare" a President Joe Biden would continue "Obamacare" and so "terminate all of those policies":

> These are people that love their healthcare. People that have been successful, middle-income people. . . . They have 180 million plans, 180 million people, families. Under what he wants to do, which will basically be socialized medicine, he won't even have a choice, they want to terminate 180 million plans. We

have done an incredible job at healthcare, and we're going to do even better. Just you watch. ("Donald Trump and Joe Biden Final Presidential Debate" 2020b)

This rhetorical stream was picked up when moderator Kristen Welker asked Joe Biden a "follow-up" related to Donald Trump's accusation that the former vice president wanted to force socialized medicine on Americans. "It's ridiculous," Biden responded to Welker's query about how he would respond to citizens who had concerns about his healthcare plan as imagined by the incumbent president. Biden compared Trump's depiction to believing a "public option that people can choose" was a "socialist plan":

> I think healthcare is not a privilege, it's a right. Everyone should have the right to have affordable healthcare, and I am very proud of my plan. It's gotten endorsed by all the major labor unions, as well as a whole range of other people who, in fact, are concerned in the medical field. This is something that's going to save people's lives. And this is going to give some people an opportunity to have healthcare for their children. How many of you at home are worried and rolling around in bed tonight, wondering what in God's name you're going to do if you get sick, because you've lost your health insurance and your company's gone under? We have to provide health insurance for people at an affordable rate, and that's what I'll do. ("Donald Trump and Joe Biden Final Presidential Debate" 2020b)

Again, Trump was insistent on spotlighting the Democratic nominee as a closeted socialist, noting that for "47 years" and then "as vice president for eight years" Biden "didn't do anything." Trump continued, with references to Kamala Harris as even more enthralled to socialism than Joe Biden:

> He [Biden] wants socialized medicine. And it's not that he wants it. His vice president, she is more liberal than Bernie Sanders and wants it even more. Bernie Sanders wants it. The Democrats want it. You're going to have socialized medicine, just like you want it with fracking . . . he goes to Pennsylvania after he gets a nomination, where he got very lucky to get it. And he goes to Pennsylvania, and he says, "Oh, we're going to have fracking." ("Donald Trump and Joe Biden Final Presidential Debate" 2020b).

The Legacy of Extreme Partisanship

Much as he did in 2016, albeit not as successfully, Trump and his Republican apparatus attempted to again secure the American presidency by mortally rupturing the Democratic Party. The "progressive versus moderate" schism had by 2020 crevassed into two distinct and increasingly combative rhetorical tribes. The same discursive devices—"liberal" and "socialist"—which in 2016 successfully united many in Clinton's own party against the Democratic nominee for president—again rhetorically functioned as absolute "devil-terms," although with a different outcome (Weaver 1953, 1985). Within the Republican "newspeak" lexicon of 2020, descriptors for self-identified tribes—notably "moderate or centrist"—were switched out for "liberal or progressive," which, particularly during the down-ticket elections, configured as metaphors for "unelectable." Joe Biden and Kamala Harris, once they occupied the two top tiers of the 2020 Democratic ticket, were essentially caught in the same rhetorical trap (Lybrand and Subramaniam 2020; Herndon 2020c; Murdock 2019). Although they survived to win the presidency, intraparty tribalism had taken hold, already mutated into a monolithic structure in one party and embedding as divisively viral in the other.

Chapter 8

The Legacy of Intraparty Tribalism

As the 2020 election cycle began, historian Michael Kazin predicted a continuation of tribal antagonism within the Democratic Party would impact the campaign regardless of who won the party's nomination. From this perspective, whoever was nominated to run against Trump was likely to be even more unpopular for left-leaning party members than Hillary Clinton was in 2016. This would be the case even "if it's a progressive" for the liberals:

> We've had 40-plus years of mostly neoliberal governance, and American power is declining. Trump has just accelerated that decline. That produces a lot of anxiety, a lot of disenchantment with the powers that be, and that may continue to help the left. So there are going to be crosscurrents. It's hard to know who will benefit. (Levitz 2019)

Rampell (2020) argued that during his presidency, Donald Trump had been repeatedly successful at persuading millions of Americans that his positions are "not a bad deal." To illustrate, it appears Trump considered his anti-immigrant, anti-trade, anti-government base as representative of "America writ large" rather than that they were likely "not even representative of all Republicans." At the same time, Bernie Sanders had also fully assumed a de facto leadership of his cohort of liberal Democrats, even as Trump continued to wield the full power of the American presidency through his increasingly influential and exponentially growing faction of conservative Republicans. Both Sanders and Trump had coalesced their blocs, hardening and positioning their respective segments of the American electorate into political tribes that were not only at odds nationally but at odds with factions in their respective parties. Whatever degree of success Trump attained by November 2020 was directly connected to his ability to increase antagonism between the national political tribes as well as to further congeal his own "tribe" while further rupturing an already damaged Democratic tribe. The incumbent managed to do so in part by lasering his own rhetoric, persuading both liberal and centrist Democrats to "go after each other" and so deflecting, however momentarily, their criticism of his regime. This strategy not only destabilized the party, but damaged its public ethos with the electorate and, particularly important for the then president, detracted Democrats from going after him.

PRESIDENT ELECT

Intraparty breaches may poison public life and personal relationships and consume public space within which electoral politics, including discussion and compromise, are situated. Significantly, when a discourse that defaults to such embeds in the political culture, the organic democratic process of deliberation withers to partisan and unproductive conflict. The end game is that polarization and its manifestation in tribalism are "self-reinforcing and will likely continue to accelerate" (Hawkins et al. 2018, 4).

Within days after Joe Biden had become president-elect, tribalistic animosity was on full display within his party, with both major Democratic blocs accusing the other of slander. As a case in point, centrist Virginia Representative Abigail Spanberger voiced concern that a potentially lethal rhetorical trope successfully deployed against congressional Democratic moderates by Republicans had been inspired by progressives within her own party. She argued the party "need to not ever use the word 'socialist' again," admonishing that "we lost good members because of that." Conversely, the liberal segment of the party attributed election losses to moderates' poorly run congressional races and a blanket failure to adapt progressive campaigning strategies. To illustrate, New York Representative Alexandria Ocasio-Cortez scolded that "not a single one of these [moderate] campaigns were firing on all cylinders" (Dionne, Jr. 2020a).

Matt Bennett, executive vice president and co-founder of the center-left think tank Third Way, commended Joe Biden's "masterful job" as a candidate of "suppressing tensions between the left and center" but cautioned whether he could "succeed in doing the same as president" (Tepperman 2020). As president-elect, Biden appeared to recognize the challenge to his administration posed by Democratic intraparty tribalism. A tiered agenda took shape within which Biden rhetorically signaled his support for progressive causes. As a case in point, his transition website prioritized racial justice and mitigating climate change (Biden 2020). His choices generally reflected attempts to balance moderate policies of cabinet choices with diverse backgrounds. Notably, these included Lloyd Austin, Marcia Fudge, Xavier Becerra, Alejandro Mayorkas, Katherine Tai, and Linda Thomas-Greenfield. He also chose prominent progressives, such as Janet Yellen, Cecilia Rouse, and Heather Boushey, for key economic roles (Tepperman 2020).

A Bigger Tent

The 2020 election mirrored the distinction between Democratic inclusion and Republican exclusion ("National Election Pool . . ." 2020; "National Exit Polls . . ." 2020; Dionne Jr. 2020a). Those under Joe Biden's "big tent" included self-described liberals (42 percent), moderates (48 percent), and conservatives (10 percent). Contrary to Republican's assertions that the Democratic nominee was a dupe of "raging leftists," a majority of Biden's electorate was non-liberal. By contrast, Trump voters were 68 percent conservative, 27 percent moderate, and 5 percent liberal (Dionne Jr. 2020a).

Racially, 53 percent of Biden's voters were White, while 82 percent of Trump's were; 21 percent of Biden's were Black, while only 3 percent of Trump's were. The Hispanic vote was still crucial for Democrats: 16 percent of their support was Latino, compared with 9 percent of Trump's. The contrast is especially striking when race and religion are looked at in tandem: 67 percent of Trump's voters were White Christians; only 30 percent of Biden's were.

In addition, Democrats' diversity more accurately reflects US demographics because the GOP's coalition is aging. Among Trump's voters, 65 percent were 45 or older; only 56 percent of Biden's were—and Biden captured voters under 30 by a better than 3-to-2 margin. Although the electoral college privileges White and conservative voters (and so the Republican Party), the GOP has won the popular vote in only one of the past eight elections (Dionne Jr. 2020a).

A Matter of Time

Joe Biden's centrism and strong preference for moderation among the electorate "seems destined to alienate his short-term allies on the left before long" in that "a vengeful Democratic left could also try to make Biden's life difficult in Congress." While progressives would most likely not be able to pass any actual laws the new President Biden opposed, they could act as spoilers, blocking bills the White House favors—in particular compromise deals with the Republicans (Tepperman 2020).

As Joe Biden moved into his position as president-elect, he directly encountered the tribalism within his own party. Roadblocks from both Democratic progressives and centrists emerged as competing factions hoping to be part of his inner circle. Beyond the conundrum of how to bring the tribes within his own party somehow together, he also faced a sharply polarized

Congress that would challenge and frustrate centrist and liberal contingents. This was true to such an extent that not only were policy ambitions of even the most moderate Democrats beyond what a Biden Congress would likely pass but there could be "no gain in responding to frustration by nursing grievances over a fake sense of betrayal." Joe Biden would do the job Democrats hired him to do to such an extent that "the most valuable commodity" in Washington's new order would not be "leverage" but "viable ideas" (Shear and Martin 2020).

POST-ELECTION TRIBALISM

Nancy Pelosi's 2018 promise to step aside as top party leader after 2022—to allow for a new generation of leadership—may have enhanced rather than ameliorated tribal divisions within the party and leadership squabbles in 2020. The first volleys in that conflict began shortly after the election. Abigail Spanberger, who won a close election to defend her Republican-leaning Virginia district, was among the swing district Democrats who criticized progressive colleagues for defending socialism and calling for defunding the police, messages which energized her Republican competitor's base. In addition, other representatives from swing districts including Pennsylvania's Conor Lamb squared off against progressives led by New York's Alexandria Ocasio-Cortez (House 2020). While party voters had already rejected some of the costlier "left" initiatives, such as Medicare for all and the Green New Deal, by choosing Biden in the primaries, progressives nonetheless slightly expanded in the 2021 Congress. Wins included those in "safe" Democratic districts, including New York's Jamaal Bowman and Mondaire Jones as well as Missouri's Cori Bush. In a sense a quid pro quo existed from the progressives' point-of-view; they had supported Biden and he owed them. Ocasio-Cortez suggested their agenda was not "just about pushing" Biden but involved making "plays" in Congress to win more progressive legislation "even before it reaches the president's desk" (House 2020).

Co-chair of the Congressional Progressive Caucus, Washington State's Pramila Jayapal, suggested disagreements among House Democrats were "OK," as was trying to "get as far as we possibly can" in order to win such tribal conflicts. Although Pelosi argued that Democrats needed to be "respectful of the thinking of all members" and "advocate to unify," the House Speaker's post-election ability to build consensus behind Joe Biden's agenda nonetheless continued to be tested by competing sectors within the Democratic party (House 2020).

Progressives Demand Inclusion

After Biden was declared the winner, Ocasio-Cortez made clear the divisions within the party that animated the primaries still existed. While she had been a "good soldier" for Joe Biden and the party in his quest to defeat Trump, she dismissed criticism from party moderates and blamed down-ticket losses on weak candidates who were "sitting ducks." In this view, progressive policies "do not hurt" Democrats. For example, all candidates who co-sponsored Medicare for all in swing districts kept their seats. Furthermore, "even before" data was gathered in many of the moderates' congressional races, "there was already finger-pointing" blaming progressives and the Black Lives Matter Movement. Ocasio-Cortez's personal experience suggested additional mitigating factors in the losses:

> I've been unseating Democrats for two years. I have been defeating D.C.C.C.-run campaigns for two years. That's how I got to Congress. That's how we elected Ayanna Pressley. That's how Jamaal Bowman won. That's how Cori Bush won. And so we know about extreme vulnerabilities in how Democrats run campaigns. (Herndon 2020b)

She argued that some moderate Democrats' behavior was malpractice, "even criminal," suggesting that "these folks" (centrists who lost elections) were already vulnerable. For example:

> Conor Lamb spent $2,000 on Facebook the week before the election. I don't think anybody who is not on the internet in a real way in . . . 2020 and loses an election can blame anyone else when you're not even really on the internet . . . the fact of the matter is if you're not spending $200,000 on Facebook with fund-raising, persuasion, volunteer recruitment, get-out-the-vote the week before the election, you are not firing on all cylinders. (Herndon 2020b)

Furthermore, moderates were easily defeated by Republican counter-campaigning not because of progressive policy but because of outdated and insufficient strategies based on television and mail that resulted in failed campaigns. Moderates were why "our party isn't even online" at least "not in a real way that exhibits competency":

> If I lost my election, and I went out and I said: "This is moderates' fault. This is because you didn't let us have a floor vote on Medicare for all." And they opened the hood on my campaign, and they found that I only spent $5,000 on TV ads the week before the election? They would laugh. And that's what they look like right now trying to blame the [Progressive] Movement for Black Lives for their loss. (Herndon 2020b)

When queried about whether Joe Biden and Mitch McConnell, with a history of shared deal-making, could accomplish any significant legislation, she responded that the "leadership and elements of the party" including those in "some of the most important decision-making positions" expressed such "anti-activist sentiment" that they were "blinding themselves to the very assets that they offer." While insisting "we are not the enemy," that "it's not a personal thing" and that she was not trying to win an argument, Ocasio-Cortez nonetheless clearly warned party moderates they were "going after the wrong thing" and "just setting up their own obsolescence," doomed to fail if they did not follow her advice. Rather than defaming and blaming progressives for losses in the 2020 election, the party needed to finally accept help and, most importantly, advice from liberals in the party. Specifically, this should come from Ocasio-Cortez who insisted she had "been begging the party to let me help" to make "every single swing district Democratic":

> That's also the damn thing of it. Every single one of them, but five, refused my help. And all five of the vulnerable or swing district people that I helped secured victory or are on a path to secure victory. And every single one that rejected my help is losing. And now they're blaming us for their loss. (Herndon 2020b)

The "Squad," made up of four "progressive" Democratic women elected to the House of Representatives in 2018, supported erasing $30,000 from all student loan debts, a plan introduced in their March 2020 Student Debt Emergency Relief. That support was already in play shortly after the November election, as evidenced by Ocasio-Cortez's tweet that criticized arguments against dismissing college student debt in which she insisted that the moderates' argument that "things were bad for me" so they "should stay bad for everyone else" was not sustainable against debt cancellation "student, medical or otherwise." Massachusetts's Ayanna Pressley tweeted "Cancel rent. Cancel mortgage. Cancel student debt" while Ocasio-Cortez tweeted support for the progressive Democratic tribe's long-term goal of having tuition-free public colleges to avoid a huge debt in the first place, insisting that the nation's current education system is "financially decimating [people in] every generation" (Bradner 2020).

Both Pressley and Omar insisted the legislation would provide debt relief for 45 million workers and families, who are "being crushed by student debt during the COVID-19 pandemic." Pressley asserted that, because of that crisis, "no one should have to choose between paying their student loan payment, putting food on the table or keeping themselves and their families safe and healthy" (Bradner 2020). Progressives were uncertain about their influence on a Biden administration to support their agenda as well as the degree to which the president would be able to accomplish major platform goals.

Elizabeth Warren and New York Senate Minority Leader Chuck Schumer, along with eleven other Senate Democrats, called for Biden to, on his first day in office, instruct his secretary of education to forgive billions of dollars worth of student debt on his first day in office. Doing so would amount to up to $50,000 per borrower and provide some relief from COVID-19 incurred debt (Robillard and Bobic 2020). In addition, Bernie Sanders sought the support of top labor leaders in his campaign for the labor secretary post in the Biden administration. Sanders spoke about his desire to push from within the Senate to send progressive legislation to Biden (Krieg 2020).

Moderates Demand Allegiance

As president-elect, Biden was challenged with not only appeasing Republicans but placating the liberal component of his own party. To that end, he demonstrated early the intention to carry through on his campaign pledge to ameliorate partisan tensions in and around the Beltway. His transition team reached out to congressional Republicans to indicate an awareness of the difficulty they faced in assessing the potential backlash from Trump's base if they acknowledged Biden's win. *New York Times* reporter Charles Blow headlined his column written shortly after Biden won the presidency as a "third term of the Obama presidency," because the president-elect embraced many of the centrist policies of Obama and "because of the public nostalgia for the normalcy and decency" provided during his two terms of office. In this view, Biden would be a "restoration president," chosen by a beleaguered electorate, wary of another Trump term, to "right the ship and save the system" as a "reversion" agent, elected to "Make America Able to Sleep Again" (2020).

Concerns that Joe Biden would be under pressure to abandon his moderate position if elected president were not without merit. Such overtures, indicative of Biden's determination to govern from a position of conciliator rather than partisanship, were perceived by some in his party's polarized left cohort as weakness as well as a signal of giving up "before we've had one fight." From this perspective, Joe Biden's stance was naïve, a "fantasyland" belief that American politics still functioned as it did during the three-plus decades he had served in the Senate. Rhode Island's Democratic Senator Sheldon Whitehouse countered with a call for partisanship from a "position of strength" rather than paltry "begging Republicans to confer bipartisanship upon us if we do things their way" (Linskey and Sullivan 2020).

Additionally, on the eve of the election, some liberal Democrats expressed disappointment that their hope for a post-Trump presidency which mirrored the agendas of Bernie Sanders and Alexandria Ocasio-Cortez would likely be instead Joe Biden's feeble and far "less charismatic reprise of the Obama administration" (Linskey and Sullivan 2020).

Biden's credentials as a moderate are more substantial than most, which further alienated him from party progressives once he became president. As a consummate "Washington survivor," he was first and foremost a "creature of the Capital" (Wolf 2020). In this view, voting for Joe Biden was most likely a symptom of "Trump fatigue," only "an exercise in political hygiene." Accordingly, his tenure as president should be as brief as possible and as soon as his "usefulness" was over, "mercy would suggest" an "honorable discharge" be granted in favor of an "ideologically reliable Kamala Harris" (Gitz 2020).

After the election, positions solidified. Ocasio-Cortez speculated that the Biden administration was in danger of failing in the same way as Obama's in 2010 when progressives were generally shut out of governance positions. Opting for the "icing-out approach" rather than the "more open and collaborative approach" set up a trajectory for House losses. Decisions were the results of putting unqualified persons into leadership positions that weakened governance. If Biden decided to go that way, it was clear "we're going to lose." His transition appointments became part of a narrative, clearly revealing who Joe Biden had credited for his victory. Ocasio-Cortez again:

> And so it's going be really hard after immigrant youth activists helped potentially deliver Arizona and Nevada . . . after Detroit and Rashida Tlaib ran up the numbers in her district . . . to turn out nonvoters when they feel like nothing changes for them. When they feel like people don't see them, or even acknowledge their turnout. If the party believes after 94 percent of Detroit went to Biden, after Black organizers just doubled and tripled turnout down in Georgia, after so many people organized Philadelphia, the signal from the Democratic Party is that John Kasich won us this election? . . . I can't even describe how dangerous that is. (Herndon 2020a)

In response to Ocasio-Cortez's "sitting ducks" comment, Pennsylvania's Conor Lamb indicated to the New York representative that, while he respected her election success, particularly since she won in a such a low-turnout primary, her attacks against Democrats within their own Republican-leaning districts were of consequence. Rather than "a question of door knocking, or Facebook," the "policies you stand for, and which ones you don't" should be priorities for all Democrats if the party and its ideology was to survive:

> The American people just showed us in massive numbers, generally, which side of these issues that they are on. They sent us a Republican Senate and a Democratic president; we're going have to do things that we can compromise over. (Herndon 2020a)

Lamb also argued that while Representative Ocasio-Cortez might add credibility to issues she publicly embraced, "tweeting out that fracking is bad in the middle of a presidential debate when we're trying to win western Pennsylvania" is not being a "team player." In addition, doing so "gives false hope to constituents which makes it very difficult for Democrats to win the areas where President Trump is most popular in campaigns" (Herndon, 2020b; Herndon and Ember 2020).

WHY TRUMP LOST

Representative Lamb's concerns were a prescient warning that unless progressive Democrats establish and willingly traverse a rhetorical common ground with centrists within their larger political tribe, factionalized animosity will disadvantage any efforts, regardless of faction, to govern. This is of particular concern, considering Joe Biden's administration, while Democratic, must govern within the populist and demagogic juggernaut that the Republican Party has become. Another mitigating constraint is that, perhaps ironically, the Democrats—again regardless of intraparty identities—have as a unified body failed to address and so democratically manage the hyper-partisan tribalism that has taken root within their own party.

It is possible that Joe Biden won a presidential election that a more liberal Democrat may have lost. To illustrate, the former vice president outran many House Democrats in pivotal electoral-vote states. As a case in point, Republican candidates for the House won more votes than their Democratic, and in many cases progressive, counterparts in all of these states, including Arizona, Georgia, Pennsylvania, and Wisconsin. The pattern of Biden doing better than Democratic House candidates was seen in the national House and presidential popular vote, as well. This matched pre-election polling in which Biden's lead over Trump was larger than the Democratic advantage on the generic congressional ballot (Galson 2020).

It is unusual for a challenger in a presidential race to run ahead of their party in the race for House control when the party controls the House. In 2020, for example, expectations were that Trump and House Democrats would generally have an incumbency advantage. It is also difficult to deconstruct why Joe Biden ran ahead of so many congressional Democrats. For example, the reason could be that Donald Trump was unusually weak as a presidential candidate or Biden unusually strong, perhaps both. Regardless, Biden was overwhelmingly liked by the electorate, taking the vast majority (94 percent) who viewed him favorably (Dovere 2020).

In 2016, Hillary Clinton's unfavorable rating was above her favorable rating in the exit polls with only 43 percent of voters viewing her positively.

While beyond Trump's (38 percent), it nonetheless left 18 percent of the electorate with an unfavorable rating of both Clinton and Trump. Trump won those voters by 17 points. Enten (2020) suggests ideology may have been a major reason Biden was better liked than Clinton four years later. Compared with Trump, who was viewed as more moderate than Clinton in 2016, Joe Biden, who ran as a mainstream Democrat, was perceived as more moderate than Trump by voters in pre-election polling 2020. Biden utilized his centrist ideological position from which to argue for his candidacy during the primary season when he ran a few points stronger than progressives Bernie Sanders and Elizabeth Warren in general election polling. His assertion that, as a moderate Democrat, he would do better in the general election than a liberal is confirmed by research that suggests candidates on either end of the ideological spectrum tend to do worse than those positioned in the middle (Hall and Thompson 2018). This was displayed in races such as that for Nebraska's 2nd Congressional District. Joe Biden easily took the district by nearly seven points and earned himself an extra electoral vote in a state that awards an electoral vote to the winner of each of its congressional districts.

The Nebraska Democratic candidate for the House, Kara Eastman, was not so fortunate, losing by six points to Republican Representative Don Bacon. Enten (2020) argues that there was such a strong difference between the House and presidential voting patterns in an age of "tremendous polarization" is significant since Eastman was backed by the liberal groups Justice Democrats and stood for Medicare for all:

> That distinction between Biden and the left may have made all the difference in what ended up being a presidential race that took four days to call. Without Biden at the top of the ticket, Trump may very well have stunned the world again and earned a second term in the White House.

DISSENSION OVER THE CABINET

In mid-November, president-elect Biden released his list of advisers to help oversee the transition at the White House's Office of Management and Budget, which oversees the $5 trillion federal budget and shapes regulations ranging from labor standards to air pollution. Advisers included executives from Amazon Web Services, Lyft, Airbnb as well as vice president of WestExec Advisors, a Washington consulting firm whose secretive list of clients includes financial services, technology, and pharmaceutical companies. Jeff Hauser, of the Revolving Door Project, a liberal group that had asked that Biden avoid lobbyists and "corporatists" in general, warned that Biden's choices "puts us at a state of high alarm" (Lipton and Vogel 2020).

Hauser's concerns mirrored a broader clash between the progressive wing of the Democratic Party and the more establishment members of Biden's core team over the role of corporate executives, lobbyists, and consultants in administration. Liberal members of the Party were also anticipating Joe Biden's post-inaugural announcement about ethics rules for his government hoping to persuade the new president to adopt hiring practices that went far beyond policies embraced by Barack Obama, who barred officials in his administration from working on issues on which they had lobbied in the past two years (Lipton and Vogel 2020).

Progressives Take Issue

However, within hours after the election, liberals registered their disappointments with and disapproval of Biden's staff and cabinet choices. To illustrate, they had composed an "extensive blacklist" of possible appointees. Larry Cohen, chair of the liberal group Our Revolution, described his organization as focused on "who we don't want" rather than a "dismal rubber stamp of the unacceptable status quo." Conversely, they called for the elevation of allies to executive positions including Senators Bernie Sanders and Elizabeth Warren as well as Sarah Bloom Raskin, who served as deputy secretary of the Treasury under Obama, and Janet Yellen, the former chair of the Federal Reserve. Waleed Shahid, speaking for the Justice Democrats, noted progressives had committed substantial efforts to "push on the executive" and warned that it was "critical" for Joe Biden to govern only as a president who has won a majority of the popular vote rather than one who also seeks to "appease" Republicans (Ember 2020b).

When he announced that Louisiana's Representative Cedric Richmond, one of his campaign co-chairs, would serve as director of the White House Office of Public Engagement, the climate group Sunrise Movement tweeted that Richmond "has taken big money from the fossil fuel industry, cozied up w/oil and gas, and stayed silent while polluters poisoned his own community." Justice Democrats' Shahid denounced incoming presidential counselor Steve Ricchetti as a "former pharma lobbyist" who "has represented groups vociferously opposed to Medicare for all and the public manufacturing of prescription drugs." Antony Blinken, the designated Secretary of State, while well-regarded by national security professionals across the board, was a foreign policy hawk (Yglesias 2020). Bernie Sanders, despite campaigning for Biden in the latter portion of the general election, also expressed concern that attempting an "outreach to the right [of center moderates] ignored the party's left" and demanded progressive views be included in a Biden administration:

It would be . . . enormously insulting if Biden put together a "team of rivals"—and there's some discussion that that's what he intends to do—which might include Republicans and conservative Democrats—but which ignored the progressive community. (Linskey and Sullivan 2020)

Moderates Stay the Course

While frustration was "understandable" there was little reason for liberal's disappointment since Joe Biden had argued in the primaries that moderation was the way to defeat President Trump, and "it worked":

Incumbents don't often lose, and for Trump to do so while a majority of voters told Gallup they were better off than they were four years ago is extraordinary. . . . Biden scored a larger share of the popular vote than any challenger since Franklin D. Roosevelt facing down Herbert Hoover, and his moderation was almost certainly key to that success. (Yglesias 2020)

In addition, centrists were hesitant to consider demands for left-of-center cabinet appointments such as those of Elizabeth Warren or Bernie Sanders because doing so could complicate the president-elect's ability to govern early in his presidency. Both Senators represented states led by Republican governors and there would be no guarantee that replacements would be appointed to caucus with the Democrats in order to keep the relative balance of the Senate intact (Ember 2020b).

Tensions emerged, too, during the push-and-pull between left-leaning and moderate Democrats over consideration of Ohio's Marcia L. Fudge for Secretary of Agriculture. Fudge was vigorously endorsed by South Carolina's James E. Clyburn, the highest-ranking Black member of Congress, as someone who would revolutionize the DOA into the "kind of department it purports to be," one which "deals with consumer issues and nutrition and things that affect people's day-to-day lives." Clyburn insisted that the Agriculture Department had historically favored "big farming interests" over less wealthy people, whether they be "little farmers in Clarendon County, S.C. or food stamp recipients in Cleveland, Ohio," Marica Fudge's hometown. However, more traditional Democrats insisted the department should be a voice for rural America and favored moderates including former Iowa governor Tom Vilsack or Heidi Heitkamp, who was defeated in 2018 after serving as North Dakota attorney general and then senator in one of the most sparsely populated states in the country. In Heitkamp's view the choice was one "that only Joe Biden can make" once he understood the "unique challenges of rural America and what needs to happen in rural America" (Martin 2020a).

The CIA Director

There was also considerable tension over who Joe Biden would choose as Director of the CIA. Speculation over this appointment provoked tribal tensions not only within his own party but with Republicans as well. Liberals in his own party pressured him to choose a female or nonwhite candidate not without connections to the agency's post-9/11 history. Conversely, Democratic moderates, as well as many national security veterans, were concerned that the president-elect, under pressure from the party's progressive segment, would fail to promote the most qualified candidate, one who would rebuild trust after the intelligence community's demoralizing experience under Donald Trump.

Michael Morell, a former CIA acting director who had been one of Biden's leading contenders for the appointment, was dismissed by liberals for past actions, which included destroying video tapes of torture as well as support of drone strikes. Daniel Jones, the lead author of a comprehensive report by Senate Democrats of CIA documents that reflected Morell's support for such activities, said he had hoped anyone who had defended such programs would have been excluded from Biden's consideration but "unfortunately, this may not be the case" (McLaughlin 2020). Progressive Democratic senators including Vermont's Patrick Leahy, New Mexico's Martin Heinrich, and Oregon's Ron Wyden privately expressed concerns to Biden's transition team about the consideration of Morell to lead the intelligence agency, citing his defense of CIA interrogation tactics after September 11, 2001. Ultimately, William Burns—the deputy secretary of state in the Obama administration—was appointed to the directorship (Cohen et al. 2021; Volz et al. 2020).

WARNING THE PARTY

Alexandria Ocasio-Cortez in particular made it clear that whether or not she remained with the Democratic Party depended on how much the leadership and members who were not liberals paid attention to her ideas and what she thought needed to be done. Furthermore, she was personally disturbed by the anger directed toward her as well as other progressives in the party. As a result, she warned that her future with the Democratic Party depended on how "we get through transition," and "how the party responds" to her "approach and what I think is going to be necessary." Ocasio-Cortez further complained that even though it seemed "we've [progressives] been winning" and there is "a ton of support," the truth is that the moderates within the Democratic Party have "been extremely hostile to anything that even smells progressive." She concluded by informing Democrats, in no uncertain terms, that if their party did not support her ideas more aggressively and continued to refuse to "use the assets from everyone," preferring instead to "double down" on their "smothering approach," Ocasio-Cortez's own political future may be in jeopardy to such an extent that she did not "even know" if she wanted to "be in politics" or was going to run for re-election "this year," complaining that "it's the stress" and "the violence" and "it's your own party thinking you're the enemy.

In sum, Ocasio-Cortez believed she had been harassed and under-valued by centrists within her own party who doubted her and so undermined her dreams of a political career:

> When your own colleagues talk anonymously in the press and then turn around and say you're bad because you actually append your name to your opinion. I chose to run for re-election because I felt like I had to prove that this is real. That this movement was real. That I wasn't a fluke. That people really want guaranteed health care and that people really want the Democratic Party to fight for them. But . . . the odds of me running for higher office and the odds of me just going off trying to start a homestead somewhere—they're probably the same. (Herndon 2020a; Relman and Hickey 2019)

TWO PARTIES: FOUR TRIBAL STORIES

Of the two major parties, Democrats tend to configure Republicans as the party that has radicalized, a "self-flattering but false narrative." In truth, while the Republican Party may have become more conservative, "in the last two decades the Democratic Party has moved substantially further to the left than the Republican Party has shifted to the right" (Wehner 2015; Cillizza 2019a; Boone 2020). Some have warned that any significant reconciliation between the two major discordant tribes within the modern Democratic Party is likely futile. Interestingly, the left wing/liberal alliance within the party has itself been historically and further splintered between "those who want reform and those who want revolution" (Wehner 2015; Beinart 2018).

An "Exhausted Majority"

The More in Common 2018 study of seven distinct American political tribes reported that the "Moderates," a faction within the "Exhausted Majority" which makes up 15 percent of the electorate, embraced attitudes and beliefs that were aligned with the center of public opinion. While the "Politically Disengaged" were "at risk" of being drawn into divisive "us-versus-them" narratives, two-thirds of this contingent—"Traditional Liberals" and "Moderates"—were more likely to "instinctively support compromise" (Hawkins et al. 2018, 14). Such a liberal/moderate merger could be part of a solution to the discord between and within American political tribes.

However, reconciliation at virtually any level will be minimal at best, more likely stalled, unless simultaneous and mindful efforts are directed toward language discursively bridging the ideological, if not the partisan-driven and emotionally configured "anger at 'Other,'" which so often substitutes for productive dialogue in American party politics. Ultimately, it would be a mistake to think of this elusive cohort simplistically, as merely a midpoint from which to determine political centrism within the warring tribal segments of the Democratic Party. Such an amalgamation would likely be thwarted by the status quo as well as the celebrity enactment of American politics and public debate. Regardless and notably, the "Exhausted Majority" is nonetheless clearly highly motivated and overwhelmingly wishes to bring about change (Hawkins et al. 2018, 14).

DIVERGENT PARTY ENACTMENT

Vox editor Ezra Klein (2020) maintains Donald Trump's enactment of tribalism is singular in that the former president has not broken with the Republican Party; rather he has "become the most authentic expression of its modern psychology." The assimilation was evidenced during Trump's relentless rehashing of unsubstantiated allegations of fraud and Democratic radicalism in order to rhetorically inflame his base during a crucial early December 2020 Georgia run-off rally. Senators David Perdue and Kelly Loeffler were attempting to defeat Democrats Jon Ossoff and Raphael Warnock and keep the Senate under Republican control. Republicans had falsely labeled both Ossoff and Warnock as "socialists" who were "too liberal for Georgia," accusing the Democrats of embracing policies such as defunding the police (Jarvie and Haberkorn, 2020). This, despite the reality that both Democrats running in Georgia did not share most goals of their party's "left flank" such as single-payer health care, expanding the Supreme Court, or the Green New Deal (Ember 2020a; Herndon and Corasaniti 2020). Regardless, Trump warned rallygoers "Let them steal Georgia again, you'll never be able to look yourself in the mirror." At another point, Trump teed up a video for his base, attacking the incumbent Georgia Senators' Democratic opponents as "extreme leftists" ("The Latest: Trump Urges . . ." 2020 . . .).

Despite moving ideologically left, the Democratic Party has remained tethered to traditional institutions and behavior. As an example, despite "all the rage" the party felt toward George W. Bush in 2006 and Trump in 2018,

Nancy Pelosi resisted calls to defund the Iraq War; nor did Democrats ever attempt to gain leverage by endangering the global financial system. From this perspective, it is not that members of the Democratic Party never wanted to seek revenge against Republicans. Rather, it was that elected Democrats were able to "resist their demand."

Historical Precedents for Presidents

Although both national political parties have been affected by the same malady, while the polarization that manifests as tribalism has "given the Democratic Party the flu" the "Republican Party has caught pneumonia" (Cummings 2020). To extend the metaphor, while most cases of influenza never lead to pneumonia, those that do tend to be more deadly ("What Is the Connection?" 2021). The Democratic Party has been infected before. Until now, however, their political immune systems were robust enough to fend off any variation of the virus that might prove fatal to democracy. Notably, following World War I, social democrats split from their "revolution-minded" cohorts, with the latter joining other like-minded emerging communist parties throughout the world. Similarly, progressive Democrats ruptured in 1948, which might have threatened incumbent President Harry Truman's chance to win. In both cases, the bifurcation worked to the "center-left's" favor. Olsen (2020) argues Richard Nixon's 1968 victory is "unthinkable" without the backdrop of years of urban riots in Democrat-controlled cities. Ronald Reagan won his first race for governor in part because of the failure of the Democratic incumbent, Pat Brown, to deal with the Watts riot of 1965. Crime continued to rise throughout the 1970s, to fuel public discontent to which Bill Clinton finally responded in 1992.

Mindful post-Trump Democrats should perhaps revisit their own party's history as they reflect on how, traditionally, both cohorts of liberal and moderate coalitions apparently "mended fences" as they unified behind centrist candidates such as Joe Biden. Consequently, rather than imaging themselves as the "big tent party," twenty-first century Democrats might be better served by first acknowledging and addressing intraparty tribalism, including ruptures within their own liberal sector (Bade and Werner 2020; Sach and Yuan 2019). Furthermore, because such political tension is likely to continue to play out in the nation's streets, developing and enacting strategies of reconciliation should be practiced within their own party as well as with Republicans.

Chapter 9

Tribalism as a Rhetorical Form

Contemporary rhetorical scholarship has recommitted itself to a centuries-old pedagogical practice linking rhetorical education with civic engagement. Historically, this link has been forged in a classroom, but other forums have been prioritized within which this symbiosis may be situated, not the least of which is the American political sphere, the discursive space in which governing take place. Rhetorical forms that emerge in such forums, including tribalistic discourse, may be analyzed as language-in-use in order to "better prepare for meaningful civic public life" (Enoch 2010, 65).

Commenting on the new president-elect, *New York Times* columnist Bret Stephens cautioned that Joe Biden's "too close for comfort" win should serve as a warning that "too much of the Democratic Party has moved leftward in a way that turns off too many middle-of-the-road voters and not just a few Never-Trump columnists" (Collins and Stephens 2020). Alexandria Ocasio-Cortez countered that House losses were the result of outdated campaign techniques rather than her coalition's progressive goals, insisting that "we cannot let Republican narratives" alienate Democrat's emerging core base of "young, Black, Brown, and working class people and social movements who are the present and future of the party" (House 2020).

"Breakout liberal stars" Jamaal Bowman and Cori Bush, who defeated moderate House Democrats on the way to winning their congressional seats in the 2020 election, joined "much of the left" in immediately trying to influence their party and their country by pressuring "avowed centrist" Democrats as well as "their" president Joe Biden. Bowman insisted that Biden should consider specific left-leaning Cabinet appointments while Bush conversed with House Majority Whip South Carolina's James E. Clyburn and Biden ally to complain about the phrase "defund the police," a rallying cry that Bowman insisted was alienating but Bush had embraced.

Such efforts continued to face pushback. After an election in which the nation "opted for a reset, not a revolution," moderate Democrats rather than progressives centered their power in the party. Sullivan and Bade (2020) believe many in the party argue the polarizing and often extreme themes championed by progressives to be responsible for Democrat's House majority and Senate losses despite their party's candidate winning the presidency. As a result, recrimination from Democratic leaders, along with skepticism from some Biden allies, moved some moderates to limit liberal's influence (Sullivan and Bade 2020).

MODERATES AS THE TRIBE OF CHOICE

In general, moderate candidates tend to perform better in American elections. Also, intraparty divisions driven by hyper-partisan extremism tend to decrease turnout in general elections, skewing the electorate towards their opponent's party. Therefore, while election turnout appears to be the dominant force in determining election outcomes, it advantages ideologically moderate candidates because extremists appear to activate the opposing party's base more than their own. This was the case when Republicans, often successfully, campaigned against "any Democrat" because "all Democrats" had the potential to evolve into "socialists" (Hall and Thompson 2018). After the results of the 2020 election, Democrats' expectations of continuing the momentum of the 2018 midterms, which delivered the party control of the House of Representatives, "fell flat." Although they maintained a narrow majority, the Democrats failed to gain ground in key state legislatures, and lost ground in others. In addition, Senate races, including marquee battles in Maine and North Carolina were lost.

Conflicting Narratives

However, while Democrats were generally disappointed in the Senate and House campaigns, the party support of Joe Biden's centrist appeal facilitated reclamation of the industrial states' "blue wall" in 2020 and the defeat of Donald Trump. In particular, they did so by mobilizing voters in historic turnout levels (Riccardi and Kastanis 2020; Daniller and Gilberstadt 2020; Schaul et al. 2020). Victory in the national election had been foreshadowed by party primary voters who chose Biden over more progressive candidates and "young emerging stars" because they believed he "represented their best shot at winning" in a national campaign.

Ultimately, the national election proved bittersweet for Democrats, "thrilled" that they had coalesced to elect Joe Biden but thwarted by the task of "sifting through the wreckage of their failures down-ballot." In the aftermath of their unexpected losses, Democrats argued that they needed to come to terms with a bigger problem: Republicans had successfully cast the most vulnerable Democrats as "socialists" and tied them to liberal ideas, including Medicare for all, the Green New Deal, and cutting police budgets (Bade and Werner 2020). As a case in point, it did not matter that Biden, House Democratic leadership, and most members rejected calls to "defund the police," a position that got lost in attack ads. Consequently, while the 2020 election reclaimed a presidency, it also facilitated Democrats' splintering into mutually reactive progressive and moderate tribal sectors from which members of each could again vent their frustration at the other (Bradner 2020).

Contrasting and Conflicting Cases

While Joe Biden and the majority of the Democratic Congress, including Bernie Sanders and Elizabeth Warren, did not support defunding the police, the issue nonetheless became a controversy during the 2020 general election and contributed to both moderate Democrats and Republicans in general turning away from endorsing a straight Democratic ticket. Representative Conor Lamb contends the party, moving into the 2020s, must address tribalism and so unify through messages of good law enforcement and keeping Americans safe while simultaneously calling out systemic racism and inequities. Lamb, a Democrat from a conservative Pennsylvania House district, recalls that "when we were passing that [legislation] at the time," those with whom he was on the phone "were not the freshmen members who are criticizing us today" and that the crucial difference was that "we listened, we compromised, and we got something done . . . that's what this job is really about" (Herndon 2020b).

By contrast, centrists in the party maintain that, as reflected in the 2018 decisive defeat of liberal candidate Cynthia Nixon by New York Governor Andrew Cuomo, while a liberal agenda may "excite" young progressives, such a game plan may not resonate for older, working class communities of color. Representative Hakeem Jeffries, chair of the House Democratic Caucus, who represents parts of Brooklyn and Queens, is concerned about the ascension of the socialist left, particularly in Black and Latino neighborhoods that are "being gentrified out of existence" (Glueck and Rubinstein 2020).

Tiffany L. Cabán, a progressive candidate who ran a close but unsuccessful campaign in 2019 for the Queens district attorney race, advised progressives against taking a more cautious and conservative stance during the 2021 campaign for mayor. Cabán maintained that an opportunity to "really radicalize" must be exploited in order to elect a mayor who is not worried about "safe, small, incremental changes that tinkers around the edges" (Glueck and Rubinstein 2020). Two years after her loss in Queens, backed by an endorsement from the Democratic Socialists of America, Tiffany Cabán won the Democratic primary to represent the 22nd Council District in New York City (Songalia and Murray 2021). Conversely, the progressive cohort within the

Democratic Party did not fare as well in an early test in the 2021 New York City mayoral race, a wide-open contest billed as the "city's most momentous in decades" (Glueck and Rubinstein 2020). Moderates Eric Adams, a former police officer, and Kathryn Garcia, a former sanitation commissioner, finished first and second in their party's primary while progressive candidate Maya Wily, "a favorite of younger left-wing voters" finished third (Glueck 2021; "2021 New York City . . ." 2021).

INSURRECTION AS POLITICAL ACTION

Intransigent tribal divisions within the two major American political parties may ultimately produce potentially lethal outcomes for democracy. One post-election event that occurred as retaliation against the 2020 presidential campaign stands out as potentially unprecedented in American history. *The New York Times* columnist Ezra Klein, commented on the severity of polarization in American politics immediately after the attempt to overthrow the presidential election in January 2021. While the insurgents who attacked the Capitol needed to be "held accountable" and "punished to the fullest extent of the law," they were also victims, "conned" by elected Republican leaders, aided by a complicit media, targeted as "marks" and so intentionally manipulated through false flag and groundless discourse (Klein 2020). Rhetorical actors included an American president who successfully demanded that his audience participate in his vision of a stolen election as the "Big Lie," a phrase Trump appropriated to use against journalists who had legitimately called him out for his discourses of "fake news" (Woodward 2021). This vision became more compelling as it was shared by leadership in the Republican Party including the House Minority Leader, multiple US senators, and dozens of US congressional members, as well major conservative talk radio hosts and, essentially, the entire prime lineup of *Fox News* (Sargent 2021a).

A Distorted Rhetorical Vision

Ultimately, many of the thousands who attempted a violent coup against Congress that afternoon in Washington, DC were participating in a rhetorically created and compelling vision of America. Their violence, in thought and action, was a response to what their president and their party leadership convincingly framed as a "tremendous crime," the resolution of which could only be mass action by "patriots." As inaccurate as that belief was, and as crucial as it is to hold those who perpetrated the attempted coup, both through symbolic and literal action, accountable, the follow-through may be indiscriminate at best. It is likely that only "those we can hit with the law" will be held accountable while party leadership will "get off because it would be too divisive to do anything in terms of their accountability" (Zakaria 2021; Anwar 2021; Friedman 2021; Gillman and Benning 2021; Rubin 2021).

Shortly after the attack on the Capitol, Berkeley political scientist Steven Weber commented on how "tenuous our collective hold on civility is right now, in politics and in other aspects of American life" and argued that "democracy without civility isn't worth it." He defined political civility as the "simple practice of treating disagreement (and the people who represent it) with the respect that it deserves" (Anwar 2021). As a case in point, an initial and crucial strategy for managing the acute exigence of divisions between and within political tribes is to rhetorically engage Americans situated within these factions, to "bring down the level of conversation" in order to talk about "real issues" (Zakaria 2021; Nguyen and Scott 2021; Avlon 2021; Fisher 2021; Folkenflik 2021).

THE REPUBLICAN PARTY AS AN ALLEGORY

It is useful at this juncture to briefly consider the implications of Republican intraparty tribalism, significantly foreshadowed by a majority membership in what was known as the "Tea Party." This loose federation of conservative-to-right leaning groups initially coalesced in protest to federal government plans for economic recovery, combined with opposition to President Obama's election. Nationwide protests were organized, with congressional placement in the 2010 midterm elections (Pullum 2014; Courser 2012). Candidates backed by the Tea Party scored major victories from South Carolina to Wisconsin to Kentucky including the elections of Nikki Haley, Ron Johnson, and Rand Paul (Srikrishnan et al. 2010). When only four of the sixteen Senate Tea Party-endorsed candidates won in 2012, Matt Kibbe, president of FreedomWorks, a Tea Party-linked group, previewed the trajectory of their party's vitriolic evolution when he warned Republicans they were "going to see a continuation of the fight between the old guard and all of the new blood that has come in since 2010" (Gray 2012).

The Tea Party Legacy: The Tribe of Trump

Years later, in early January 2021, insurgents ransacked the American Capitol while both Houses were in session, in an attempt to prevent congressional confirmation of Joe Biden's presidential election and so keep Donald Trump and the Republican Party in the White House (Wolf 2020; Graham 2021; Taub 2021). These anti-democratic riots were the endgame of a decade's worth of tribalistic animosity within the Republican Party. Trump's refusal to accept that he was no longer president was propagated by relentless social mediated and cable networked messaging that reinforced his baseless assertion. In addition, Republican leadership along with the Trump base, save for a very few attempts at counter-messaging, fell into lockstep as a unified and single-minded mass with the former president. Combined, these factors discursively neutralized any intraparty opposition so that within weeks of the election, Tribe Trump and the Republican Party were the same entity.

Donald Trump's "cult of personality" leadership evidenced the power of his tribe in dominating the Republican Party, regardless of his loss of the presidency. The strength of his presence and public ethos alone within the Republican Party became a default rhetorical proof for persuading more millions of the party to embrace him as a charismatic populist. And with this leadership came deeper and hostile conflicts between Republicans and Democrats, the two dominant American political tribes. In addition, the unexpected extent of Democratic losses in the 2020 congressional races reflected the strength of Donald Trump's appeal with rural, white voters likely to "outlast his leadership" well into the next decade. The 2020 presidential election also suggested the possibility that the schism within the Republican Party that had emerged in 2009 as intraparty competition between "moderates" and "Tea Party" Republicans had organically transformed into a single entity of "Trumpism" (Tucker 2020; Kabaservice 2020). By the time that President Joe Biden was finally, safely, and officially inaugurated as President of the United States, the insurrection had already been recast as a noble act of resistance, and allegiance to a lie had become a litmus test for loyalty to Donald Trump as well as a means of self-preservation for Republicans (Woodward 2021).

Politicians Not Interested in Politics

It follows that fissures within the Republican Party, unlike those within the Democratic Party, are not ideological. To illustrate, the tribalism no longer manifests as "left wing" versus "right wing" or liberal versus conservative. Rather, each segment consolidated into discrete factions, but not in any ideological or traditional sense. Instead, while one (albeit very small) segment is "still dedicated to reality, to using politics to solve problems," the other has "done a deal with the devil and decided that politics is about lying." As a result, this bloc of the Republican Party has discursively mutated and expanded into an alternative vision of reality within which only "certain kinds of voters" and elected leaders live. Specifically, those who are attracted to, inhabit, and rhetorically perpetuate this world of abject failed, fraudulent, and stolen elections are the "particularly gullible, particularly angry" voters as well as "those politicians not interested anymore in politics" (Zakaria 2021). Sargent (2021b) argues that the Republican Party's solidification into "One

Tribe" reflects not only a fealty to (or a fear of) Donald Trump but an abandonment of democracy.

Journalist and historian Anne Applebaum maintains that the domestic terrorism of January 6, 2021 by "members of Donald Trump's party" was encouraged by and in collusion with the president, congressional allies, and "far-right propagandists." This attempt to violently interrupt the process of validating the next president evidenced a strategically executed, grave, and globally significant endgame to ultimately interrupt the American democratic process (2021). While there is clearly not a direct line between the rhetorical evolution of Republicans from a party of discrete "moderate" and "conservative" members and generally communicative tribes into a single and singular entity that openly embraced a violent insurrection in 2021, this consolidation might well be an allegory for the Democratic Party as it addresses and engages in rhetorical behavior to mitigate tribalism within its own ranks.

A Closer Look

The assumption that the United States can be divided neatly along "50–50" lines, with half of over 300 million adults supporting Democrats and the other half endorsing Republicans is likely anachronistic. As a case in point, five dominant (instead of the traditional two) American political "tribes" were identified in a 2020 public opinion survey conducted by RealClear Opinion Research, a service offered by RealClearPolitics (Cannon 2020). Slightly more than one-fourth of registered voters in the United States comprise the "Resistance Camp," with political views and social attitudes placing them on one of the far sides of the spectrum, in an anti-Trump and the Trump-era Republican Party group. On the other side of the spectrum are two "tribes" of Trump voters, roughly evenly divided, which together make up another quarter of the electorate. One of these groups (12 percent) is the "Make America Great Again" Trump base that "idolizes" his brand of conservative populism. The other (14 percent) consists of traditional Republicans with "less edgy views" on issues ranging from trade to immigration to race relations.

A fourth group, "The Detached," represents 24 percent of the electorate and is mostly male and the youngest of the five factions. Its members tend to range from being disillusioned to disgusted with traditional party politics. The "Independent Blues," the last and "most pivotal" contingent, supported Hillary Clinton by 12 percentage points and are characterized by a skepticism of Republicans that continues to grow:

> Political professionals from both major parties, along with the news media, spend far too much time focusing on reactions from the far left and far right of American politics. Among those too often forgotten are those in the middle, the

tribes we call the Detached and the Independent Blues—fully half of America's registered voters. (Cannon 2020)

Regardless of the "binary ballot choices" presented during elections, catastrophized by cable news, and echo-chambered through social media, the two most recent national American elections evidence widespread dissatisfaction with and dysfunction of the American "two-party duopoly." While a country configured as "all Federalists" or "all Democrats" may have facilitated national political engagement in a Jeffersonian America, the visceral and diverse political attitudes of the twenty-first century suggest a tribal perspective would be a more accurate, pragmatic, and useful configuration, both for the theory and practice of public life in the United States.

COMMUNICATION ACROSS DIVISION

A 2018 joint European and American study of tribalistic tendencies in the United States concluded that American public argument is increasingly focused less on issue substance and more on the "language used to discuss it." The resulting "chilling effect" dissuades Americans "away from public debate" leaving the "conversation to the loudest, most extreme voices. The polarization, generally expressed by "talking heads" in the media, has made tribalism increasingly between and within both political parties. Consequently, a remedy for such rhetorical pathologies lies in "shifting the tone of public debate," empowering the electorate to communicate more freely, essentially a deal breaker if they are to reach across their divisions.

Innovative rhetorical behaviors are crucial to mitigate, mediate, and neutralize the misrepresentations that convince so many to argue and believe that their extreme and polarizing positions represent everyone in the country. Developing discursive habits centered on common ground would be a wise and practical starting point. To illustrate, Americans who belong to conservative tribes need exposure to the patriotism of progressives and liberals just as those blocs need to hear how a majority of conservatives agree that all citizens are anchored in and answer to the rights and, importantly, own the responsibilities inherent in belonging to a constitutional democratic government. Doing so will not diminish or devalue the need to address legitimate differences over substantive ideological and effective issues. Instead, by spotlighting shared realities—including those directly related to "being Americans"—the electorate will be better equipped to "enable progress on those issues" (Hawkins et al. 2018, 125, 128). In brief, rather than denigrating the legitimacy of such differences, rhetorical engagement constitutes the spaces within which such strategic discourses of democratic governing germinate and take root.

Mass Mediated and Poorly Vetted Political Talk

It may be that what appears to be the preferred method of discursive engagement between and within the two dominant political parties in the United States is, at its core, unproductive. Political talk has transfigured into a rhetorical pathology whereby dissension and discord are privileged over consensus and compromise. The Dunning-Kruger Effect, a cognitive bias in which individuals who are incompetent at something are unable to recognize their own lack of skill, may be informative. This "metacognitive phenomenon of illusory superiority" manifests in individuals who perform poorly on a task believing they performed better than others. Specifically, not only do such individuals fail to consider their own ineptitude, but they also tend to believe they are higher achievers at a specific activity or more knowledgeable in a particular area than they actually are (Kruger and Dunning 1999; Muller et al. 2020).

This framework suggests ignorance is often invisible to most individuals. It follows that a "meta-ignorance" (or ignorance of ignorance) results because this lack of expertise is located within "unknown unknowns" area. Or it may be insufficient information disguised by erroneous beliefs and background data that only appear to be "sufficient to conclude a right answer." In this way, "poor performers" in multiple social and intellectual domains seem largely unaware of precisely how deficient their expertise is, which leaves them with a "double burden." Not only does incomplete and misguided knowledge result in mistakes but those "exact same deficits" also prevent individuals "from recognizing when they are making mistakes" and, significantly, that others are "choosing more wisely" (Dunning 2011). This confirmation bias affects citizens' perceptions of political knowledgeability. In particular, individuals with moderately low political expertise generally rate themselves as increasingly politically knowledgeable particularly when partisan identities are made salient. As a case in point, such strong often uncritical endorsement of a party's policies facilitates a reluctance to compromise with political opponents. In addition, such voters are more inclined to rely on primarily partisan source cues to evaluate the political knowledge of peers (Anson 2018).

It is often daunting, without consulting other more informed individuals, for one to surmise what one does not know. Doing so is an inherently difficult task and one that people "fail repeatedly" (Carter and Dunning 2008). While some may infrequently recognize aspects of their own incompetence, such as the absolute superiority of the group to which one belongs, they are "far from perfect in identifying all of them." Conversely, such people often believe they act with "adequate if not excellent expertise, when instead they misstep out of misunderstanding and miscalculation that they fail to recognize as such." This is often the case about tribal affiliations, including perceptions of others within one's own party, about which citizens "display remarkable misbeliefs" with those who are "most wrong" often "expressing the greatest confidence in their beliefs" (Dunning 2011; Murphy 2017).

Rhetorical Interventions for Errors of Omission

There are circumstances that lend themselves to accurate self-judgment. To illustrate, if an individual is in circumstances where they are able to be competent, can receive and comprehend information about errors of omission in their own views, can receive and comprehend feedback, and are working to complete a clearly identified task, self-judgment and perceptual acuity can be very accurate. Furthermore, it is important to avoid blaming constituents—including those who belong to the "wrong" faction within a political party. This is especially important for errors in self-judgment that foreground an absolute certainty in the "truths" of the tribe with which an individual identifies to the exclusion of the "other's" perspective. Consequently, people required to make self-judgments regarding their own knowledge in poorly vetted and insufficient mass mediated Internet and cable-news cultures are often ill prepared to accomplish the task. Instead, information environments surrounding individuals anchored in and dependent on such limited knowledge perspectives should be assessed. How does the Democratic Party leadership address intraparty discord? What kinds of rhetorical responses would be most beneficial to the values and goals of the entire party? Of the entire nation?

Withholding or skewing feedback regarding such judgments in general as well as specifically to those caught making mistakes perpetuates the impoverished information environment responsible for others' inaccurate judgments. From this perspective, flawed self-assessments that basically distort and discourage self-awareness, such as those demonstrated by the Dunning-Kruger effect, are frequently a function of poorly developed information cultures rather than "wishful thinking, or foolishness" on the part of the individuals.

To counter such cognitive biases, suggestions could be offered to encourage more cautious and critical self-assessment. As an illustration, rhetorical interventions in the form of constructive feedback might introduce perspectives such individuals lack or of which they are unaware, empowering them to make more accurate assessments of their own information regarding the assumptions that undergird, justify, and reinforce uncritical, if not unexamined allegiance to one political faction within another political faction. The polarizing division between self-identified "progressives" and "moderates" within the Democratic Party may be a paradigmatic example of uncritical compliance. So too would the Republicans' appropriation of and obedience to inaccurate meanings of redefined terms such as "socialist" and "liberal" or even "the (Big) lie." Engaging in dialogic and strategic public talk "may prove to be a task that is well worth the effort, making each of us a little bit less of a mystery to ourselves" (Carter and Dunning 2008) and perhaps more effective and proactive members of a representative democratic republic.

RECONCILIATION

A dominant theme of the 2020 campaign was "mobilization politics," galvanizing voters whose minds were already made up rather than expanding the electorate pool through discursive appeals to Americans who had yet to commit to a candidate or even a party. An unintended outcome of this strategy is that successful mobilization of one side often moves the other to do the same. This was the case when Donald Trump's win of the "second-most votes" in an American presidential election helped Joe Biden "win the first-most." Furthermore, the support for Joe Biden was not mirrored in the House and Senate as there were "still some ticket-splitters out there" (Harris 2020).

So, while "mobilization" has motivated an unprecedented number of American voters to elect (or reject) a president or serve as the dominant (and not quite so successful) rhetorical ploy to direct a younger cohort of thinkers and movers into Congress, it also produced results that were the antithesis of those originally intended. Harris (2020) suggests successful political persuasion cannot occur without "engaging consistently—in both political and substantive terms—people whose views overlap only in part with your own." This perspective informs an intraparty tribalism that may be as prescient for the twenty-first century Democratic Party as its traditional and more familiar manifestation within the Republican Party. As a result, the rhetorical resolution of tension between the politics of mobilization and coalition-centric persuasion is more likely central to the Democrats' future than the increasingly stale debate over whether moderates are too tepid to drive meaningful change or progressives are too radical to win (Harris 2020).

Constraints and Opportunities

Both progressive and moderate Democrats would do well to acknowledge that there are cities, counties, and districts throughout the United States where an impending crisis of tribalism mandates that better arguments be rhetorically invented, constructed, and delivered that reach the portion of Democrats who don't currently support party (or faction) goals. Regardless, there are both constraints and opportunities available for such a realignment of a modern, diverse, and united Democratic Party. As a case in point, cohorts within the party might acknowledge the validity of what their internal rivals say. The left does energize the party, particularly young voters and those in urban centers. Yet, the centrists are correct in arguing that Democrats must embrace middle-of-the-road voters, particularly from swing districts who are essential to building a congressional majority. Progressives encourage the party to vigorously occupy the moral high ground of asserting racial justice should not be compromised, an electoral asset as 85 percent of Biden voters told the exit pollsters in 2020 that the criminal justice system treated Blacks unfairly. And moderates are right that slogans like "defund the police" can bring down center and center-left lawmakers. In addition, while the word "socialist" may engage younger progressives, it also impacts negatively with older voters who associate the term with the Soviet Union and repressive Communist regimes.

At its core, the Democratic Party appears grounded in a shared truth that despite tribal quarrels, the membership wants the nation to move in the same direction. Doing so would likely mandate decent, affordable health insurance for every American (79 percent of Biden's voters supported the Affordable Care Act), rigorous programs to combat climate change (which 90 percent of Biden voters saw as a serious problem), and guarantees to redress economic inequality (Dionne Jr. 2020a).

RHETORICAL FIREWALLS AND DEFENSE STRATEGIES

Rhetorical Education

A destabilizing ethos of self-destructive communication has exploded within and between contemporary Democratic and Republican Parties. This has accelerated to such an extent that activist agendas in both are now singularly laser-focused on consolidating, extending, and maintaining any and all means of power within members' own factions and keeping it away from "the other." Approaching partisan political tribalism from a heuristic of rhetorical education may be an immediate and doable first solution to the behavior.

Creating a grounded sensibility within which the rationale for and skills to enact a participatory problem-solving rhetoric is essential to the well-being, survivability, and purpose of American political parties. Such a pedagogy could begin with informing the politically active groups, and the members therein, of the disciplines' twenty-five-hundred-year history. Next, this legacy could be reimagined into contemporary party-centric contexts that constitute rhetoric as both the delivery system of and the primary mechanism for enacting the political and so public culture through meaningful intraparty civic engagement, specifically in this instance for Democrats. As an example, centrist criticism of progressives' self-identification as "socialists" could be better understood, on both counts, if the situations that provoked the varied responses were deconstructed by determining the exigences, constraints, and audiences that "called forth" the different rhetorical acts (Bitzer 1968). This general framework of educating public organizations such as political parties to "take up rhetorical practices" they consider "relevant and effectual" authorizes them to start with the question of civic engagement and work backwards. Such groups (factions/cohorts) are then already working to enact change in the world; the rhetorical education each espouses is contingent upon the bloc's political agenda and specific to the contemporary moment in which it works (Enoch 2010, 167).

The Possibility of Political Tribalism as a Genre

Determining whether political tribalism could be configured as a rhetorical genre could be useful in managing its emergence within the nations' dominant political organizations. Genre criticism initially deconstructs examples of multiple emergent discourses within similar contexts or environments in order to discover if shared attributes—exigences, forms, arguments, audiences—have presented within these discrete communication events. A rhetorical genre, then, coalesces when similar rhetorical situations (typically managed through "language-in-action") are discovered to have produced similar responses (artifacts) from similar audiences (Campbell and Hall 1978; Miller and Devitt 2018; Davidson 2018). It follows that once a discursive artifact such as a political speech, blog, online narrative, or series of tweets, is recognized as belonging to a discrete genre, it may be facilitated, diminished, replicated, modified, or even anticipated in a future form.

While conclusively identifying tribalism and its variations as a distinct rhetorical genre is beyond the scope of *Democratic Disunity*, tribalism has clearly presented through traditional rhetorical forms as political discourse within both major parties. An essentially dysfunctional modification of such discourse, paradigmatically polarized hyper-partisan language-in-use, has evolved into a viral default rhetorical form within the Republican Party. Importantly, it is also germinating within the Democratic Party.

Discursive Interventions

Configuring tribalistic political communication and its intraparty variations as a rhetorical genre could facilitate discourse-based firewalls. Such rhetorical interventions might then be introduced on digital platforms or interpersonally as first lines of defense at junctures where democracy enabling discourses of argument and division are vulnerable to being weaponized into destabilizing discourses of division and hyper-partisanship. To illustrate, "firewalls" for the algorithms and confirmation bias driven "echo chambers" and the polarization effects of social media may be simple to initiate. One may like "everything" (or nothing) on their social media feeds or read and interact with diverse prestige media or create spaces for fresh perspectives by muting celebrities or BFFs to "make room for the rest of your efforts to break through" (Seneca 2020). Other discursive devices could be a personal or institutional "talk" intervention beginning with the questions such as "Why do so many Americans say 'yes' to compromise, but 'no' to compromises?" followed by suggesting consideration that the latter position undermines the mutual respect that is essential for a robust democratic process legislation (Gutman and Thompson 2013). These and other defense or mediation strategies may become more sophisticated, pervasive, and effective as recognition of toxic tribalism's impact becomes more obvious. In this way, political rhetoric (itself a firewall) foregrounds the American system of governing, regardless of party or polarization, as dependent on healthy democratic discourses for its survival.

STRATEGIC DISCOURSE

In his investigation of whether Donald Trump's rhetoric caused the January 2021 insurrection at the Capitol, Cherwitz (2021) suggests that because much communication "operates through implicature and inference" even through Trump did not directly order the riots to violently disrupt Congress, his words implied that action:

> Basic speech act theory explains this: the seeming question, "Do you have the salt?" implies that you should pass me the salt. In Trump's case, phrases such as "let's get wild" implied that the insurrectionists should commit insurrection. They understood precisely what Trump was asking them to do. (Austin 1975; Bach and Harnish 1979)

Words Matter

The rhetorical concept of language-in-use suggests strategies for discursive intervention in intraparty tribalism before it coalesces into uncivil and anti-democratic political action. This construct is anchored in the knowledge that "words matter" (Tyler et al. 2005). Audiences or receivers of public communication internalize, mindfully or not, the values and beliefs implied by the words of a speaker. In this way, implied premises are completed, and behavior generally aligns with words. This includes the speech acts that are situated in and essential for maintaining the public space within which American politics take place. Such a language-in-use frame could empower Democratic leaders, through counternarratives, to mediate discordant factions within their party before it ruptures entirely and succumbs to the same fate as its Republican counterpart.

That many who participate in tribalism are unaware of its effects on healthy public deliberation or refuse to counter those effects when they do become informed contributes to a cycle of ignorance and neglect (Kruger and Dunning 1999). Both of these outcomes are counterintuitive to healthy democratic dialogue. The focus on factions within and between American political parties has foregrounded demonization of the "other," much as ethnic and national groups have historically experienced. Even so, a "tribe" is not, by default, either violent or culturally narcissistic. Instead, tribalism is premised on a change from a social organization based on egalitarian kinship to one structured by hierarchical administration in a defined territory. This theory became the frame within which the concept of "tribe" developed. Anthropologist Jan Abbink of the Netherlands's Leiden University maintains that tribal rules governing cases of intergroup violence often involve "culturally sanctioned reconciliation, with elders and ritual leaders of the local ethnic communities involved, and an appeal to traditional moral values of co-operation, reciprocal exchange and compromise" (Mungai 2019).

Rapprochement

In this way, "the other" is rarely discursively recast as "inhuman," despite the violence that sometimes presents with ruptures between and within discrete tribes, such as those occurring within American political alliances. That authorized rapprochement strategies could become integral to political tribal culture and so function as innate mediatory responses to intraparty conflict is of consequence, particularly with regard to strategic political discourse.

As Burke (1969) suggests, an understanding and combination of identification and division, when individuals are not certain where one ends and the other begins, is the essence of substance and a "characteristic invitation to rhetoric" (Burke 1969; Meadows 1957). Therefore, identification functions to rhetorically intervene in at least the mechanism of "othering," which allows "mindlessness" (made concrete as objectification) to substitute for reconnecting with "others," the sharing of the substance of humanity if not citizenship within (and between) American political tribes.

RHETORICAL STRATEGIES

Public discourse is intended to foreground or resolve shared concerns or issues within a democratic system, including the antecedents of tribalism. Nonetheless, inflammatory rhetoric and other divisive communication strategies have fractured the cultures both between and within American political parties.

Productive Discourse

Specifically, elected leaders who choose to "market their own platforms" or ideas rather than focus on the "hard work of compromise" weaken the public sphere, the space in which relationships are built by community members. So too does a public "hesitant to become involved in public affairs" or who "too often mimic" the combativeness, dogmatic, and dichotomous thinking and speech of such political actors (Abbot et al. 2016, 31–35). Language-in-use communicative behaviors that counter these tendencies are grounded in essential democratic principles, characterized by attributes such as deliberation, inclusiveness, learning imagination, and empowerment (375). Using such productive discourse may encourage civic participation and so equip citizens—including leaders—who engage in political culture at any level to share public space fully and effectively, including that occupied by Democrats (and Republicans).

Invitational Rhetoric

An additional discursive arbitration strategy for mediating breaches between moderate and progressive tribes within the Democratic Party is suggested within the invitational rhetoric framework of Foss and Griffin (1995). An invitation approach "can and does occur" in various communicative situations including political speeches and discussions:

> In an era in which violence, war, and overt hostility are frequently seen as the "best" options for communicating a disagreement, and in which a binary of "for or against" prevails, a continued exploration of the role of invitational rhetoric in negotiating complex exchanges seems imperative. (Bone et al. 2008, 457)

As with essentially all forms of argument (which are neither entirely persuasive nor informative), invitational rhetoric is fundamentally available as a discursive choice. As a case in point, invitational rhetoric may facilitate productive conflict resolution or constructive civic participation. The outcome of such discourse is respect for the audience (the "other") and an understanding anchored in civility even if the argument is resolved as mutual disagreement. Such a perspective seems tailored for ameliorating intragroup tensions—such as those within the Democratic Party—before they do irreparable damage to the fabric of American public life.

Constitutional Patriotism and Other Lessons

Amy Chua and Jed Rubenfeld, both professors of constitutional law and comparative politics, argue the United States serves as the best model for how to overcome its own political tribal divisions. The United States is clearly equipped to unite a diverse and divided society; conceptualized and created by revolution, the nation has served as the prototype of modern democracy from day one:

> Alone among the world powers, America has succeeded in forging a strong group-transcending national identity without requiring its citizens to shed or suppress their subgroup identities. Its citizens don't have to choose between a national identity and multiculturalism. Americans can have both. But the key is constitutional patriotism. [Americans must] remain united by and through the Constitution, regardless of our ideological disagreements. (Chua and Rubenfeld 2018)

Democratic tribal members, by right of membership, possess the agency to mediate conflict within their party before it becomes pathological. A pivotal lesson, then, is that leadership matters. Generally, conflict-affected states have found it "nearly impossible" to overcome tribal divisions without their respective leadership agreeing to do so. In addition, strong and principled leaders may facilitate and guide tribal factions toward more united futures. The "conditions need to be ripe for leaders to move their supporters from hostility to comity with long-established adversaries," but a willingness to renounce violence and contribute effort across tribal divides is crucial, establishing a line of demarcation between perpetual conflict and durable peace (Brigety 2021).

Effective communication skills through which to facilitate civic engagement of the electorate (the voting public) are consequential in that, because "serving leaders" are constrained by politics including their constituents, groups and individuals dedicated to reconciliation and mediation may be called on to make compromise and deliberate discourse possible. This may be an easier fix than might be expected, considering the historical connection between such strategic discourse in the United States beyond that of rhetoric, civility, and a robust democracy. Additionally, legal systems and constitutions can either encourage or discourage co-operation. Americans are "proud of the durability of their country's constitution," which was "designed to stifle factionalism," although its rationale and connection to American citizens' "lived lives" is often poorly understood and so tenuous. It follows that the basic road map for a free society with a rigorous and vigorous public life and platforms for participation is still articulated in the US Constitution. Brigety (2021) argues that demands will be put on Democrats to personally assume the responsibility of bridging their own intratribal divisions, noting "the task will not be easy" primarily because those on whom the burden of addressing the crisis falls are themselves caught up in the tribalism."

The mechanism of rhetorical discourse and its antecedents of civic and civil public interaction have been in place since the nation's inception in the eighteenth century. So too have the problems of democracy, including its exigences and constraints. *Democratic Disunity: Rhetorical Tribalism in 2020* makes the argument that the time is right for considering intraparty tribalism as a rhetorical form, albeit situated within the twenty-first century. It is likely that the state of American democracy, as well as the nation's position in the global environment, depends in large measure on whether its citizens can meet the tribalism challenge. To that point, progressives and moderates appear, at best, reluctant to any kind of deconstructive deep dive into normative problem behaviors that might ameliorate their own, as well as "the others,'" dysfunctional talk. To that end, members of both Democratic tribes could (re)discover "words-in-use" and "substance-sharing" strategies through which they might regularly and meaningfully interact with those "other" Democrats. The goal is not to eliminate differences but to learn how to share governance because of them.

Conclusion

RHETORICAL TRIBAL RECONCILIATION

Tribalism between Democrats and Republicans has been a ubiquitous presence in American politics (Hobfoll 2018; Kornacki 2018; Chua 2018b). However, contemporary sectarian and embedded intratribal hostility has so far anchored primarily within only one of these political parties, congealing into an ideologically insulated and so fundamentally closed political system. Republicans' solidification reflects fealty to (or fear of) Donald Trump as well as an abandonment of democracy (Sargent 2021b). The other is following a similar trajectory.

Despite evidence of latent intraparty division, both moderate and progressive Democrats united to propel Joe Biden into the presidency, more or less expelling Trump from the White House, if not presidential politics. Both returned to "old habits and an old rule" that "Republicans fight Democrats while Democrats battle each other." Until recently Democrats have generally affiliated under an inclusive "big tent" assembly, with occasional spats, while Republicans began solidifying into one ideologically, racially, and religiously "rigid, radical, unified bloc." In short, "as the Republicans cast off free-thinkers, Democrats took them in" (Dionne, Jr. 2020a).

A CIRCULAR FIRING SQUAD

Democrats have internalized a management challenge in that coalition-based politics requires substantial work and inevitably produce clashes. That discord over ideology and policy as well as divisive and ongoing battle over party identity has emerged from this challenge is a major theme of *Democratic Disunity: Rhetorical Tribalism in 2020*. It follows that maintaining the integrity of inclusion while sharing a unifying ideology has become one of the prescient challenges for the modern Democratic Party, progressives and centrists alike. Without internal arbitration and realignment, these issues are likely to shadow and so diminish the party as Democrats move into the rest of the century.

In particular, as the Biden presidency evolves and positions itself within a national and global context, tribalism threatens both moderate and liberal Democrats. Each of these factions is crucial to the party's ability to hold even a simple majority in Congress while simultaneously provoking center-left members, increasingly the mechanism for enacting a Democratic agenda in urban areas (Dionne, Jr. 2020a). Barack Obama maintained the very "idea of purity" with its assumptions that "you're never compromised, and you're always politically woke" was something that Democrats needed to "get over that quickly" (Osnos 2020a). It is also reasonable to guess that one of the two dominant tribal factions within the post-2020 Democratic Party will ignore the former president's advice because the tribal cohort to which Barak Obama belongs is not "woke"—or at least "awake enough."

Tribes and Party Structure

Shortly after the 2020 election, moderate Democrat Representative Conor Lamb suggested that Democrats should try to have a discussion about "policy, not personality" and that, while he respected how hard progressive House Democrats worked to get elected and represent their constituencies, "the fact is that they and others" were advocating policies that were "unworkable and extremely unpopular" (Herndon 2020b). In addition, David Carlucci, a former state senator from New York's Rockland County who lost a House primary in 2018 to progressive Mondaire Jones, argued that "any politician that's part of the old guard" must be "very concerned about a potential primary." He warned that while the majority leader "appears relatively secure, no Democrat should feel immune" (Burns 2021).

As post-inaugural and former president Donald Trump further consolidates not only his base but the entire Republican Party into his movement to take back the presidency in 2024 (or sooner), President Biden faces twin rhetorical assaults. The first is a demagogic-driven unprecedented Republican populism (which by itself mandates heavy lifting for a Democratic president), and the second is a re-emergent, vocal, and contentious tribalistic sparring between progressives and moderates within his own party. It is within this environment and despite these constraints that Joe Biden, who campaigned on a platform of unity, as president must somehow appeal to the entire country, including Trump's acolytes, all 70-plus million of them (Lockhart 2020).

The absence of cross-party coalitions means that members of Congress no longer see their colleagues across the aisle as potential resources for advancing their political and policy goals. This is even true of the few remaining moderates in both parties, who, in a less centralized, more entrepreneurial legislative environment, would be allies in creative lawmaking.

MITIGATING DISCORD

It has been suggested that if Independent Bernie Sanders had not run as a Democrat in 2016, most Americans would never have heard of him and, accordingly, he and other left-leaning members of the Democratic Party, would not have been in the power-brokering position they secured in 2020. This leverage was evident after democratic socialist India B. Walton's June 2021 defeat of a four-time incumbent mayor Byron Brown. Claiming the victory as "ours" and "the first of many," Walton warned other Democratic moderates that her victory was only "the first of many, warning that "if you are in elected office right now, you are being put on notice. We are coming" (Lerer 2021). Historian Michael Kazin maintains that tribes cannot "just be a movement outside the party structure" without engaging with the party by being "both radical and Democratic with a capital D" (Levitz 2019).

Decline of Moderates

While Teles and Saldin (2021) argue that moderates have been an "endangered species" in the Republican Party for essential two decades, they foreground Joe Biden's victory in the primaries and achieving the presidency as a "last gap of an exhausted tradition" of political moderation and compromise as well, for Democrats. After a final but likely futile effort, Democrats will "hand over the reins" to their party's left and are likely to be absorbed into the dominant progressive or liberal political tribe, mirroring a similar outcome of intraparty division within the Republican Party.

Negative partisanship—party attachment driven by fear and loathing of the other side more than a genuine commitment to that party's ideology—has damaged much of the nation's ability to participate in a bipartisan government through demonization of the "other faction," whether outside or within one's own party. The stability of Joe Biden's presidency and his administration's ability to enact that office is contingent to a large extent on how the tribal factions within the Democratic Party mitigate their mutual discord. Obstruction from progressive organizations and members of Congress could extend well into his presidency and so impact the United States well beyond his tenure.

As a case in point, liberals within his party took issue with Biden's willingness to compromise on progressive's priorities, rejecting the President's consideration of nuanced narratives regarding the nation's collective history of systematic racism. He reminded the party that because a "blanket condemning" of the United States as a "force for repression" failed for Democrats during the Republican presidencies of Richard Nixon and Ronald Reagan, doing so again would not work against Donald Trump but instead "lead Democrats to ruin" in the midterms. In brief, if Democrats "hold their own in 2022" it will "be because the president told his American story . . . not theirs" (Bai 2021).

In this view, the decline of political moderates has bifurcated the two-party American system to such an extent that both Democrats and Republicans have become dominated by their ideological extremes. As a result, spaces within which rhetorical discourse may emerge and thrive and so facilitate cross-party coalition-building and governance have diminished. It follows that, with centrists so devalued, the interparty coalitions they once forged have essentially given way to congressional gridlock. Furthermore, leadership increasingly depends on single-party separatism rather than interparty alliances integral to a proactive and healthy national governance. This has occurred to such an extent that a discourse of negative partisanship grounded in an antipathy of outsiders has silenced deliberative discussion as a conduit of deliberative democracy. In the short term, if tribalism persists within the party, a lack of grassroots support for Biden could produce rigorous primary challenges from liberals going in the 2022 midterm elections (Bade and Werner 2020).

Shifting and Accommodating

Challenges to centrist Democrats surfaced in the last two election primary cycles, including during the races of Joseph P. Crowley and Eliot L. Engel, two senior New York House members who were successfully primaried by progressive candidates. Senate Democratic Leader Chuck Schumer indicated he was trying to "do the best job for my constituents and for my country" and acknowledged a shift in the direction and scope of his governing goals. To illustrate, regular meetings with national liberal advocacy groups began intensifying when he spent time with an alliance of New York progressives elected in 2020. In December, he met with State Senator Jabari Brisport, a 33-year-old newly elected self-described Democratic socialist, to stress his support for addressing climate change. "We joked about me being a socialist in Brooklyn," Brisport said, recalling that Schumer emphasized he "works well with Bernie Sanders," also a socialist from Brooklyn (Burns 2021).

It would appear that with Chuck Schumer at the helm of the Senate, the prospect of progressive tribal-inspired challenge in 2022 could factor into legislation that comes out of a Biden administration with a Democratic majority (albeit razor thin) in Congress. While potential challengers to Schumer have not yet committed to running against the majority leader in a primary battle for his Senate seat, members of that cohort have not been timid about the possibility. Specifically Representative Alexandria Ocasio-Cortez has not ruled out challenging Schumer, indicating in January 2021 that she was "still very much in a place where I'm trying to decide what is the most effective thing I can do" (Goldiner 2021). Others have encouraged members of the Democratic left to openly threaten Schumer with a potential primary challenge. Waleed Shahid, communications director for Justice Democrats, the alliance that recruited Ocasio-Cortez to run for Congress in 2018, warned that during the run-up to his campaign to retain his Senate seat, the Speaker will have to justify himself and his actions, particularly attempts to "make nice" with the Senate Minority Leader:

> Schumer will have to explain every one of his decisions to one of the most progressive primary electorates in the country, and if voters think he's capitulating to Mitch McConnell and not organizing his caucus to deliver for working families, then he's going to be in some trouble. (Otterbein 2021)

Nonetheless, Chuck Schumer has initially been proactive in protecting his own tribe of Democrats. Specifically, he has engaged with social media such as Twitter as well as cable-news interviews to call for President Biden to take executive actions on student debt and climate change. Furthermore, as House Majority Leader, Schumer has called on "old and new alliances" to help him govern. He has discussed concerns including pandemic relief plans with some of the "big policy minds of the Democratic Party," including centrists such as former Treasury Department official Antonio Weiss. Others have included progressive economists Felicia Wong of the Roosevelt Institute and Stephanie Kelton of Stony Brook University as well as "liberal think-tank" members Heather Boushey and Michael Linden. Since unresolved intratribal conflicts could lower voter turnout, which quite possibly could hurt the entire party during the 2022 midterms and beyond, Schumer's efforts may be a wise, if temporary, attempt to address partisan tribalism within the Democratic Party (Tepperman 2020).

Chuck Schumer is not the only established Democratic member of the Senate to experience attacks originating within his own party. West Virginia's Joe Manchin, elected as a moderate conservative Democrat in one of the most Republican majority states in the nation, was accused by Representative Jamaal Bowman of "doing everything in his power to stop democracy." Furthermore, Bowman insisted that the West Virginia Senator was "stopping our work for the people," was "doing the work of the Republicans by being an obstructionist" and so had become the "new Mitch McConnell" (Bernstein 2021). Jamaal Bowman joined Ocasio-Cortez and other liberals within the Democratic Party angry at Manchin as well as other Democratic moderates, including Arizona's Kyrsten Sinema, for exerting what they perceived to be outsized power within an evenly divided Senate. In choosing to publicly mediate their intraparty conflicts through such unproductive discourse rather than deliberative discussion, Bowman and others may have, albeit unintentionally, further destabilized their own party. And in so doing, they may have also provided more fodder for the intertribal hostilities between the Democratic and Republican Parties.

TRANSCENDENT REASONING

In Klein's (2020) view, the "power identity holds"—whether that identity is as a Democrat or progressive or Republican or "Christian" or "curious" or "New Yorker"—can be managed ("harnessed"). Consequently, constituents must "become more aware of the ways that politicians and media manipulate" voters as well as a willful ignorance of such manipulation. Because such organized identities, including those promoted by polarized and polarizing coalitions within the major parties, are supported by massive "defining, politicking, and activating" apparatus (263), their "superstructure" must be recognized, addressed, and possibly reconfigured, if not deconstructed.

A Novel Rhetorical Form

Democratic Disunity: Rhetorical Tribalism in 2020 posits a benchmark for negotiating tribalism as a rhetorical form. Once recognized and understood as such, the public may develop discursive skills with which to transcend the compelling and powerful ultra-partisan binaries entrenched in American partisan intraparty tribes. Deliberative discourse can be rediscovered as the original delivery system for democracy and platforms constructed from which to engage with and in a representative, constitutional, and decidedly democratic system of governing.

A second benchmark derives from recognizing that while intraparty divisions between Democratic factions are primarily driven by genuine ideological and fundamental values differences between the "moderate"/"liberal"/"p rogressive"/"conservative" alliances, evidence also suggests that "treaties" may be negotiated, if initially only short term for immediate goals.

Finally, the most pressing rhetorical challenge for mediating polarized tribalism within the Democratic Party becomes introducing and then reattaching party members to the nation's political system, enacted through productive discourse.

Language-in-Action as Politics

A deconstruction of specific behaviors or policies or programs that might re-create cultures within American political parties with moderate or centrist factions as their epicenters is beyond the scope of this study. However, a necessary and pivotal criterion for any such reform is singularly germane: that such governing innovations be grounded in the rhetorically configured election of more moderate legislators, at state and federal levels. Furthermore, even with "optimal institutional rules," there are "few shortcuts around the hard work of organization, mobilization, and engagement" necessary for such to occur.

Consequently, any sustainable constitutive strategy to counter the suppression of moderates' voices by those at the ideological extremes of their respective parties must persuade centrists within those organizations to actively engage in the language-in-action that is politics. Doing so would empower moderates to communicatively counter those occupying the ideological poles by finding leverage within the two major parties. To accomplish this, centrists will need to speak and act as a synergized entity to recruit capable, if not charismatic, candidates, mobilize their constituents in each party to join in the conversation of partisan politics, and so rhetorically move them to action. Without such a robust discourse-driven tribal center, moderates, possibly even entire state parties, will be unable to emerge from the shadows of their respective national brands or "fight for leverage in national politics." In brief, this requires the "showing up, organizing, and devoting themselves to building durable institutions for political and intellectual combat" (Teles and Saldin 2021).

Securing a healthy public infrastructure within which deliberate discourse may be nurtured and thrive is therefore crucial. To accomplish this, the invention, enactment, and integration of such rhetorical communication must become organic within sustainable environments. As an example, preparing (or reminding) Americans to participate in public life as citizens could spotlight civic literacy. In so doing, proactive interest in and responsibility for government could be routinely encouraged (or reimagined) as communicative interaction, specifically civil person-to-person dialogues with differently opinioned others (Adler and Goggin 2005).

Moreover, a pedagogical heuristic that foregrounds the symbiotic and necessary relationship between twenty-first-century American democracy and rhetoric could be useful. This could occur formally within public education or more casually, perhaps introduced through various digital media platforms and other social media venues. As a case in point, cultivating an understanding of the interdependence of rhetorical practices (including deliberative discourse) and the civic engagement of governing could dissuade political parties from resorting to divisive and destructive responses to conflict (Enoch 2010).

"Priming," discussing, and evoking "civic duty" also tends to reduce the effect of partisanship on decision making in general. In part, this occurs because reminding the electorate (including that portion affiliated with political parties) of the civic ideas of impartiality, framing evidence "even-handedly," and "triggering" facilitates the "desire to form accurate opinions." In this way, American citizens may take into account that their politics have "norms of respecting opinions from both sides of the aisle" (or polarized corners of one's own party), and so listen more carefully. As a result, compromise may legitimately be considered without fear of reprisal from one's own tribe or faction. It follows that being "open" to compromise reduces animosity toward the "other" party or faction within one's own cohort with whom conflict is occurring (Levendusky and Stecula 2021a).

POLITICAL TRIBES BEYOND 2020

Joe Biden's centrist "cross-party" discourse validated the Democrat's ethos among moderate and conservative constituencies, regardless of political affiliation, to such an extent that he won the presidency in 2020 (Igielnik et al. 2021; Cohn 2021). That said, immediate and obvious melioration strategies of the hyper-partisan tribalism enacted within and between both parties examined in *Democratic Disunity: Rhetorical Tribalism in 2020* may initially yield only incremental adjustments of the electorate within either organization in the near future.

Deconstructing Division

Regardless, there are relatively straightforward discursive interventions for the political overconfidence and resulting intractable perspectives responsible for such tribal pathologies. These include discussing unresolved issues in terms of "probabilities" rather than "certainties," being "a little bit more careful about what pops out of your head" or "out of your mouth" when engaging in such discussions, and "if the situation is important" or "fractious" taking a "time out" to reclaim an emotional frame conducive to dialogue rather than diatribe. Also, since members of the electorate "not only author their own opinions" but "their factual beliefs about the world" (as evidenced by how both parties as well as factions within each differ "wildly" in terms of what they think is factually true), become comfortable saying "I don't know."

Moreover, internalizing a cognitive frame within which to "think about what you don't know" and from which to "check your assumptions" would be useful. Finally, engage those with whom "disagreement" is the most common bond through dialogue, mindful of one's own "cognitive blind spots" and so enacted as "skeptical, humble and aware" deliberative discourse (Resnik 2019). In brief, cultivating a sense of civic duty through rhetorically anchoring the rhetoric of governing in a mindful, deliberative dialogue diminishes the effect of American political partisanship, including its toxic variations both between and within American political parties.

Privileging Deliberative Discussion

Astor (2017) suggests that the two dominant political parties provide the most effective environment within which to organize and influence the public policies of the United States. Rather than endangering democracy they provide rhetorical spaces within which the business of government is enacted in its most basic form as healthy democratic rivalries. However, dueling narratives of divisive polarization between and within the Democratic and Republican Parties are increasingly sabotaging the process. As each party's 2020 campaign platforms suggest (Republicans rolled over their 2016 version), each is anchored by distinct and often conflicting ideologies and positions ("2020 Democratic Party Platform" 2020; "Resolution Regarding . . ." 2020; Epstein and Karni 2020).

Rosenbluth and Shapiro (2019) argue that decentralized political decision making has made political parties less effective and so less able to address constituents' long-term interests. Specifically, the relegation of majority political power to a grassroots base has eroded trust in elected leaders, parties, and democratic institutions, provoking divisive, populist politics. The result is that parties are directly compromised as they internalize a mutual dependence with "unrepresentative voters on their fringes and those who fund them" demand (Cummings 2020).

Defaulting to discursive strategies such as those championed in this text would enable deliberative discussions of any salient issues that mutually affect voters regardless of tribal affiliations within or between groups. These could range from debating economic recovery to combating the coronavirus to establishing a unified and universal plan for health care to discovering solutions for problems that have yet to materialize. Doing so would also mitigate as well as inoculate against hyper-tribalistic discourse and so simultaneously begin to establish and maintain a mutual and robust rhetoric, launched from socially responsible platforms. It would be from these structures and through this discourse that an electorate rediscovers how to "speak their truths" within the constraints and opportunities of a system of government in place for well over two centuries. It is within this shared rhetorical culture that political civility, compromise, and dialogue rather than diatribe, all crucial to the health of the Democratic Party as well as American constitutional democracy, will most likely recover, emerge, and thrive.

Bibliography

Abbot, Jennifer Y., Todd F. McDorman, David M. Timmerman, and L. Jill Lamberton. *Public Speaking and Democratic Participation: Speech, Deliberation, and Analysis in the Civic Realm.* New York, NY: Oxford University Press, 2016.

"About the FCC." *Federal Communications Commission* (June 15, 2021). https://www.fcc.gov/about/overview.

"About Justice Democrats." *Justice Democrats* (February 15, 2020). https://justicedemocrats.com/about/.

Accetti, Carlo Invernizzi. "Joe Biden Isn't a Liberal or a Moderate. He's a Christian Democrat." *Foreign Policy*(March 16, 2020). https://foreignpolicy.com/2020/03/16/joe-biden-election-liberal-moderate-christian-democrat/

Adler, Richard P., and Judy Goggin. "What Do We Mean By 'Civic Engagement'?" *Journal of Transformative Education* 3, no. 3 (July 2005): 236–253. https://www.unomaha.edu/international-studies-and-programs/_files/docs/adler-goggin-civic-engagement.pdf.

Aistrope, Tim. "Social Media and Counterterrorism Strategy." *Australian Journal of International Affairs* 70, no. 2 (2016): 121–138. https://doi.org/10.1080/10357718.2015.1113230.

Alberta, Tim. "The Democrat's Dilemma. *Politico* (March 8, 2019). https://www.politico.com/magazine/story/2019/03/08/ilhan-omar-dean-phillips-minnesota-democratic-party-225696/.

Alcindor, Yamiche. "Bernie Sanders Refuses to Concede Nomination to Hillary Clinton." *The New York Times*(June 12, 2016). https://www.nytimes.com/2016/06/13/us/politics/bernie-sanders-campaign.html.

Anderson, Christopher L. "Which Party Elites Choose to Lead the Nomination Process?" *Political Research Quarterly* 66, no 1 (2013): 61–76. https://www.jstor.org/stable/23563589.

Andersen, Michael C., and Mary Hoekstra. *Tribalism: The Curse of 21st Century America.* Morrow, GA: Simms Books Publishing, 2019.

Anderton, Kevin. "This Is the Reason American Politics Are so Polarized [Infographic]." *Forbes* (October 27, 2020). https://www.forbes.com/sites/kevinanderton/2020/10/27/this-is-the-reason-american-politics-are-so-polarized-infographic/?sh=33476492187b.

Ansolabehere, Stephen, and Brian Schaffner. "CCES Common Content, 2016." *Harvard Dataverse* (2017). https://doi.org/10.7910/DVN/GDF6Z0.

Anson, Ian G. "Partisanship, Political Knowledge, and the Dunning-Kruger Effect." *Political Psychology* 39, no. 5 (2018): 1173–1192. https://doi.org/10.1111/pops.12490.

Antholis, William. "The Road to a Four Party System." *U.S. News and World Report* (November 6, 2017). https://www.usnews.com/opinion/articles/2017-11-06/intra-party-war-could-lead-to-a-four-party-system.

Anwar, Yasmin. "Berkeley Scholars' Outrage, Reflections on U.S. Capitol Mob Siege." *Berkeley News* (January 7, 2021). https://news.berkeley.edu/2021/01/07/berkeley-scholars-outrage-reflections-on-u-s-capitol-mob-siege/.

"AOC, Omar, Pressley, Tlaib: Who Are 'The Squad' of Congresswomen?" BBC News (July 18, 2019). https://www.bbc.com/news/world-us-canada-48994931.

Applebaum, Anne. "What Trump and His Mob Taught the World About America." *The Atlantic* (January 7, 2021). https://www.anneapplebaum.com/2021/01/07/what-trump-and-his-mob-taught-the-world-about-america/.

"Applying Private Sector Media Strategies to Fight Terrorism." The Office of the Director of National Intelligence (2016). https://www.odni.gov/files/PE/Documents/Media-Strategies.pdf.

Ashford, Emma. "Biden Wants to Return to a 'Normal' Foreign Policy. That's the Problem." *The New York Times* (August 25, 2020). https://www.nytimes.com/2020/08/25/opinion/biden-foreign-policy.html?referringSource=articleShare&fbclid=IwAR2gqDzDLvDAzlwdY8-r7y4gC9fTOnh2khJJmGqy7eI11Vd4547LsNDcOzQ.

Astor, Aaron. "Partisanship Is an American Tradition—And Good For Democracy." *The Washington Post* (July 12, 2017). https://www.washingtonpost.com/news/made-by-history/wp/2017/07/12/partisanship-is-an-american-tradition-and-good-for-democracy/.

Austin, John L. *How to Do Things with Words.* 2nd ed. James O. Urmson and Marina Sbisa (eds.). Oxford: Oxford University Press, 1975.

Avlon, John. "Donald Trump's American Carnage Ends With a Coup Attempt." CNN (January 6, 2021). https://www.cnn.com/2021/01/06/opinions/trumps-american-carnage-ends-with-a-coup-attempt-avlon/index.html.

Bach, Kent, and Robert M. Harnish. *Linguistic Communication and Speech Acts.* Cambridge: MIT Press, 1979.

Bacon, Jr., Perry. "The Six Wings of the Democratic Party." FiveThirtyEight (March 11, 2019). https://fivethirtyeight.com/features/the-six-wings-of-the-democratic-party/.

———. "The Trumpiest Republicans Are at the State and Local Levels—Not in D.C." FiveThirtyEight, (February 16, 2021). https://fivethirtyeight.com/features/the-trumpiest-republicans-are-at-the-state-and-local-levels-not-in-d-c/.

Bade, Rachael. "Rep. Ocasio-Cortez's Convention Speech Serves as a Warning to Democratic Establishment and Biden." *The Washington Post* (August 18, 2020). https://www.washingtonpost.com/politics/rep-ocasio-cortezs-convention-speech-to-serve-as-warning-to-democratic-establishment-and-biden/2020/08/18/28c3d34a-e155-11ea-8dd2-d07812bf00f7_story.html?fbclid=IwAR0VL6jmha5M0DBdVTwwo4LY-CiCYIshH5odorbatZpBuETmE_hPwMQRs8o.

Bade, Rachael. and Erica Werner. "Centrist House Democrats Lash Out at Liberal Colleagues, Blame Far-Left Views for Costing the Party Seat." *The Washington Post* (November 5, 2020). https://www.washingtonpost.com/politics/house-democrats-pelosi-election/2020/11/05/1ddae5ca-1f6e-11eb-90dd-abd0f7086a91_story.html?outputType=amp&fbclid=IwAR15BQLPMMDsNe_Owj7S-51qmXeY_2HQEyrVJugh0KZklj5yDLl_kqzobQM.

Bai, Matt. "Opinion: Can Biden Save the Democrats From Themselves?" *The Washington Post* (June 20, 2021). https://www.washingtonpost.com/opinions/2021/06/20/can-biden-save-democrats-themselves/.

Ball, Molly. "Moderates: Who Are They, and What Do They Want?" *The Atlantic* (May 15, 2014). https://www.theatlantic.com/politics/archive/2014/05/moderates-who-are-they-and-what-do-they-want/370904/.

———. "What Do Democrats Stand For? Inside a Fight Over America's Future." *Time* (July 25, 2019). https://time.com/5634769/future-of-the-democratic-party/.

Ballacci, Giuseppe. *Political Theory Between Philosophy and Rhetoric: Politics as Transcendence and Contingency*. London, UK: Palgrave Macmillan Publishers, 2018.

Balz, Dan. "A Republican Party at War With Itself Hits the Wall on Health Care." *The Washington Post* (July 18, 2017). https://www.washingtonpost.com/politics/a-republican-party-at-war-with-itself-hits-the-wall-on-health-care/2017/07/18/3c3c1002-6bd0-11e7-b9e2-2056e768a7e5_story.html.

———. "Democrats Head to Convention United Against Trump, But Expecting Conflict Once the Election is Over." *The Washington Post* (August 16, 2020a). https://www.washingtonpost.com/politics/democrats-head-to-convention-united-against-trump-but-expecting-conflict-once-the-election-is-over/2020/08/15/a6754a88-de41-11ea-809e-b8be57ba616e_story.html?fbclid=IwAR34hH5NNydmbyFf3ppl_RF1_Mp4BXq31lHt2DgC935QUDtJyph-uYPflq8.

———. "For Most of the Night, Biden Weathers a Volley of Attacks." *The Washington Post* (September 12, 2019). https://www.washingtonpost.com/politics/biden-delivers-the-debate-performance-he-needed-despite-occasional-missteps/2019/09/12/824e0b30-d55b-11e9-9610-fb56c5522e1c_story.html?fbclid=IwAR2VxNv9vTGCx04ADqey1uZ6ZLhcpn3RLMlrKBTKxaCncS0YfYD9GSxI-QU.

———. "It's a Critical Moment in the Democratic Race. The Debate Made That Clear." *The Washington Post* (February 20, 2020b). https://www.washingtonpost.com/politics/its-a-critical-moment-in-the-democratic-race-the-debate-made-that-clear/2020/02/20/093fff18-532e-11ea-929a-64efa7482a77_story.html?fbclid=IwAR2QAThAHBw_xGND6j3iyi9KDrPl6SFt_Ni02LOOHKPF8npBH8qasOV1K2o.

———. "Sanders vs. Warren and the State of the Progressive Movement." *The Washington Post* (January 18, 2020c). https://www.washingtonpost.com/politics/

sanders-vs-warren-and-the-state-of-the-progressive-movement/2020/01/18/62b79 2f0-3a0f-11ea-9541-9107303481a4_story.html?fbclid=IwAR3hqvc3TDPuIExSX TuUalXaLySp2DS0b__JWGCyvmPCnsQ78htVH5nQoqo.

Barber, Benjamin. *Strong Democracy.* Berkeley, CA: University of California Press, 1984.

———. The Ambiguous Effects of Digital Technology on Democracy in a Globalizing World." Talk Given to Heinrich Boll Stiftung, September 7, 2002.

Barrett, Harrold. *Rhetoric and Civility: Human Development, Narcissism, and the Good Audience.* New York, NY: SUNY Press, 1991.

Barrow, Bill. "Biden's Top 2020 Democratic Rivals Avoid Rush to Defend Him." *AP News* (September 27, 2019). https://apnews.com/68f19fffdbdf4-638ab94117b83f5c8f1?fbclid=IwAR1YdBydnb8XO2WO0ft7Rvc x1y-x9t-86J1PlwcWsbIBVcTcrqliFYhZC_E.

———. "Republicans Press Democratic Caricatures in Georgia Races." *AP News* (November 11, 2020). https://apnews.com/article/republicans-leftism-georgia-senate-races-592bcb75f3d0f57ff259cb342681f0a8.

Barrett, William. "Capitalism, Socialism, and Democracy: A Symposium." *Commentary* (April 1978). https://www.commentarymagazine.com/articles/william-barrett-2/capitalism-socialism-and-democracy/.

Batton, Hannah. "Rhetoric of the Far Right: A Rhetorical Analysis of Donald Trump and Viktor Orbán." *The Review: A Journal of Undergraduate Student Research* 20 (2019): 1–11. https://fisherpub.sjfc.edu/ur/vol20/iss1/6.

Beauchamp, Zack. "Identity Politics Isn't Hurting Liberalism. It's Saving It." *VOX* (February 20, 2020). https://www.vox.com/2020/2/20/20954059/liberalism-identity-politics-defense.

Behl, Manka. "Change Is Coming Whether You Like It or Not: Greta." *Times of India* (September 22, 2019). https://timesofindia.indiatimes.com/world/us/change-is-coming-whether-you-like-it-or-not greta/articleshow/71240450.cms?utm_source=contentofinterest&utm_medium=text&utm_campaign=cppst.

Beinart, Peter. "The Electoral College Was Meant to Stop Men Like Trump From Being President." *The Atlantic* (November 21, 2016). https://www.theatlantic.com/politics/archive/2016/11/the-electoral-college-was-meant-to-stop-men-like-trump-from-being-president/508310/.

———. "Will the Left Go Too Far?" *The Atlantic* (December 2018). https://www.theatlantic.com/magazine/archive/2018/12/democratic-party-moves-left/573946/.

Berkowitz, Peter. "A Madisonian Remedy to the Social Media Revolution." *RealClearPolitics* (June 22, 2019). https://www.realclearpolitics.com/articles/2019/06/22/a_madisonian_remedy_to_the_social_media_revolution_140619.html.

"Bernie Sanders 2020 DNC Speech Transcript." *REV* (2020). https://www.rev.com/blog/transcripts/bernie-sanders-dnc-speech-transcript.

"Bernie Sanders's Permanent Revolution." *The Economist* (August 15, 2019). https://www.economist.com/united-states/2019/08/15/bernie-sanderss-permanent-revolution.

Bernstein, Brittany. "Progressive Rep. Calls Manchin 'The New Mitch McConnell' Over H.R. 1 Dissent." *The New Republican* (June 7, 2021). https://www.nationalreview.com/news/progressive-rep-calls-manchin-the-new-mitch-mcconnell-over-h-r-1-dissent/.

"Beyond Red vs Blue: The Political Typology." *Pew Research Center* (June 26, 2014).

Bialik, Carl. "How the Republican Field Dwindled From 17 to Donald Trump." FiveThirtyEight (May 5, 2016). https://fivethirtyeight.com/features/how-the-republican-field-dwindled-from-17-to-donald-trump/.

Bibby, John E. *Politics, Parties, and Elections in America*. Chicago: Nelson-Hall, 1996.

Biden, Joe. "President-Elect Joe Biden Transition Website." *Restoring American Leadership* (December 14, 2020). https://buildbackbetter.gov/.

Bilansky, Alan. "Rhetoric, Democracy and the Deliberative Horizon" in *Rhetoric, The Polis, and the Global Village*, ed. C. Jan Swearingen and Dave Pruett. Mahway, NJ: Lawrence Erlbaum Associates, 1999, 221–229.

Bitzer, Lloyd. "The Rhetorical Situation." *Philosophy and Rhetoric* 1 (June 1968): 1–14.

Black, Eric. "Gallup Poll: Majority of Democrats Want More Moderate Party." *MINNPOST* (January 25, 2019). https://www.minnpost.com/eric-black-ink/2019/01/gallup-poll-majority-of-democrats-want-more-moderate-party/.

Blake, Aaron. "Roy Blunt's Senate Exit Highlights Big Opportunity for GOP's Trump Wing in 2022." *The Washington Post* (March 8, 2021). https://www.washingtonpost.com/politics/2021/03/08/roy-blunts-exit-highlights-trump-wing-gops-big-opportunity-2022//exit highlights big opportunity for GOP's Trump wing in 2022.

———. "Winners and Losers From Night 1 of the Second Democratic Debate." *The Washington Post* (July 30, 2019). https://www.washingtonpost.com/politics/2019/07/31/winners-losers-night-one-second-democratic-debate/?fbclid=IwAR0XfIvlazCWk4XuH3dSchGwqrldl4ECrakGkRgASycYSjhNWUDTPQvRyng.

———. "Winners and Losers From the Nevada Democratic Debate." *The Washington Post* (February 19, 2020). https://www.washingtonpost.com/politics/2020/02/19/takeaways-nevada-debate/?fbclid=IwAR144AUMlM-ikDRK12klWPkQOoETIB-I0YZCnvUvMljXGkqevjYIpXD3I4NQ.

Blow, Charles. "Third Term of the Obama Presidency." *The New York Times* (November 8, 2020). https://www.nytimes.com/2020/11/08/opinion/biden-obama-presidency.html?referringSource=articleShare&fbclid=IwAR0gqqezPbw7WNtFExOees4JORMfMG7DaWg5U5RaixmQbB572NdsWHZaapY.

Blanco, Oscar. "Bernie Sanders and Donald Trump Are Speaking for the Same Voters—Which Should Worry Joe Biden." *The Washington Post* (April 9, 2020). https://www.washingtonpost.com/outlook/2020/04/09/bernie-sanders-donald-trump-are-speaking-same-voters-which-should-worry-joe-biden/.

Bone, Jennifer Emerling, Cindy L. Griffin, amd T. M. Linda Scholz. "Beyond Traditional Conceptualizations of Rhetoric: Invitational Rhetoric and a Move Toward Civility." *Western Journal of Communication* 70 no.4 (2008): 434–462.

Boone, Ronald P. "The Democratic Party Is Often Violent, Divisive and Hypocritical; If It Doesn't Change, Trump Will Be Back." *The Baltimore Sun* (November 29, 2020). https://www.baltimoresun.com/opinion/op-ed/bs-ed-op-1122-democrats-their-own-worst-enemy-20201120-tybsvfh2vfcaxoua2xmqy6p27y-story.html.

Boot, Max. "Opinion: Once Again, Republicans Put Tribalism Over Patriotism." *The Washington Post* (February 11, 2021). https://www.washingtonpost.com/opinions/2021/02/11/once-again-republicans-put-tribalism-over-patriotism/.

———. "Vote Against All Republicans. Every Single One." *The Washington Post* (October 31, 2018). https://www.washingtonpost.com › opinions › global-opinions › 2018/10/31.

Bordo, Susan. *The Destruction of Hillary Clinton.* London: Melville House, 2017.

Bouie, Jamelle. "Why the 'Wokest' Candidates Are the Weakest." *The New York Times* (December 6 2019). https://www.nytimes.com/2019/12/06/opinion/woke-democrats-harris.html.

Bowles, Nellie. "The Pied Pipers of the Dirtbag Left Want to Lead Everyone to Bernie Sanders." *The New York Times* (February 29, 2020). https://www.nytimes.com/2020/02/29/us/politics/bernie-sanders-chapo-trap-house.html.

Bradner, Eric. "7 Takeaways From Biden's Win in the 2020 Presidential Race." CNN (November 8, 2020). https://www.cnn.com/2020/11/07/politics/takeaways-2020-presidential-race/index.html?fbclid=IwAR3K68zVMjuxsU9bxcCyU_NJ1PjLhIcqpHW7GNgIrn1kVLzJleSweAOC2bc.

Breuninger, Kevin. "Trump Tells Capitol Rioters to 'Go Home' But Repeatedly Pushes False Claim That Election Was Stolen." CNBC (January 6, 2021). https://www.cnbc.com/2021/01/06/trump-tells-capitol-rioters-to-go-home-now-but-still-calls-the-election-stolen.html.

Brick, Cameron, and Sander van der Linden. "How Identity, Not Issues, Explains Partisan Divide." Scientific American (June 19, 2018). https://www.scientificamerican.com/article/how-identity-not-issues-explains-the-partisan-divide/?fbclid=IwAR2_f4IOJ_NOrNBxBqsV4s3529nhz2EKIWlsyZJjvdxPVj7g3PKvF89xWFQ.

Brigety II, Reuben. "The Fractured Power: How to Overcome Tribalism." Foreign Affairs (March/April 2021). https://www.foreignaffairs.com/articles/united-states/2021-02-16/fractured-power.

Britton-Purdy, Jedediah. "Populism's Two Paths." The Nation (October 31, 2016). https://www.thenation.com/article/archive/the-rage-of-white-folks/.

Brooke, Collin Gifford. "Cybercommunities and McLuhan: A Retrospect" in *Rhetoric, the Polis, and the Global Village,* eds. C. Jan Swearingen and Dave Pruett. Mahwah, NJ: Lawrence Erlbaum, 1999, 23–25.

Brooks, David. "Dems, Please Don't Drive Me Away." *The New York Times* (June 27, 2019a). https://www.nytimes.com/2019/06/27/opinion/democratic-debate-2020.html.

———. "If It's Trump vs. Warren, Then What?" *The New York Times* (October 17, 2019b). https://www.nytimes.com/2019/10/17/opinion/trump-warren-2020.html.

———. "Moderates Have a Better Story." *The New York Times* (July 1, 2019c). https://www.nytimes.com/2019/07/01/opinion/moderates-progressives-warren.html.

Brooks, Anthony. "Markey Releases His Travel Records, Defends His Time Away From Massachusetts." WBUR (July 28, 2020). https://www.wbur.org/news/2020/07/28/sen-ed-markey-travel-records.

Brownstein, Ronald. "The GOP's Demographic Doom." *The Atlantic* (October 23, 2020a). https://www.theatlantic.com/politics/archive/2020/10/millennials-and-gen-z-will-soon-dominate-us-elections/616818/.

———. "The 2020 Democrats All Have the Same Problem." *The Atlantic* (February 10, 2020b). https://www.reuters.com/article/us-usa-election-2020-candidates-factbox/12-democrats-still-in-u-s-presidential-race-days-before-iowa-caucusesi-dUSKBN1ZN278.

Bruni, Frank. "Why Democrats Are Bound for Disaster." *The New York Times* (February 21, 2020). https://www.nytimes.com/2020/02/21/opinion/sunday/brokered-convention-democrats-2020.html.

Buchanan, Allen. *Our Moral Fate: Evolution and the Escape From Tribalism.* Cambridge, MA: MIT Press, 2020.

Bump, Philip. "The Ideological Tension Between Pelosi and Outspoken Democratic Freshmen." *The Washington Post* (July 11, 2019). https://www.washingtonpost.com/politics/2019/07/11/ideological-tension-between-pelosi-outspoken-democratic-freshmen/?fbclid=IwAR3MBjL7_bsfmWZ5LG6E5qqWpHeEY3XSaXGu2AT5u-wrWmwCyIfNNpUuKk0I.

Buncombe, Andrew. "Donald Trump One Year On: How the Twitter President Changed Social Media and the Country's Top Office." *Independent* (January 17, 2018). https://www.independent.co.uk/news/world/americas/us-politics/the-twitter-president-how-potus-changed-social-media-and-the-presidency-a8164161.html.

Burgis, Ben. "No Honeymoon for Joe Biden." *Jacobin* (November 7, 2020). https://jacobinmag.com/2020/11/joe-biden-administration-opposition-push-left.

Burke, Kenneth. *Language as Symbolic Action.* Berkeley: University of California Press, 1966.

———. *Permanance and Change.* 3rd ed. Berkeley: University of California Press, 1984.

———. *A Rhetoric of Motives*. Berkeley: University of California Press, 1969.

Burns, Alexander. "Biden Wants to Work With 'the Other Side.' This Supreme Court Battle Explains Why." *The New York Times* (September 7, 2019a). https://www.nytimes.com/2019/09/07/us/politics/joe-biden-bork-supreme-court.html?smid=nytcore-ios-share&fbclid=IwAR1bvfTkvdzFfkRso7MjqLpomnlUFxDi3W7a-aUieOus_kzkxFPLTr-T354.

———. "Why America's Politics Are Stubbornly Fixed, Despite Momentous Changes." *The New York Times* (July 4, 2021). https://www.nytimes.com/2021/07/04/us/politics/biden-infrastructure-trump-republicans-democrats.html.

———. "Why Populist Democrats Have Gained the Upper Hand in the 2020 Race." *The New York Times,*(October 11, 2019b). https://www.nytimes.com/2019/10/11/us/politics/2020-democrats-primary-polls.html?fbclid=IwAR1gGAroJq24ulnr5SQibUKsPvTXPFOGHq-ZJaXT1u9UylrdClw5ApujD6s.

———. "Why Chuck Schumer Is Cozying Up to the A.O.C. Wing of His Party." *The New York Times* (February 7, 2021). https://www.nytimes.com/2021/02/07/us/politics/schumer-impeachment-new-york.html.

Burns, Alexander, and Jonathan Martin. "Biden Under Fire From All Sides as Rivals Attack His Record." *The New York Times* (July 31, 2019). https://www.nytimes.com/2019/07/31/us/politics/democratic-presidential-debate-recap.html?smid=nytcore-ios-share&fbclid=IwAR3JVtAjzr3DNbkG8HynhsG8moGbl2yPB_uYXhFrUzUqdyRw1b_ZjC8i_Uo.

———, and Jonathan Martin. "Alarmed by Sanders, Moderate Democrats Can't Agree on an Alternative." *The New York Times* (February 12, 2020a). www.nytimes.com/2020/02/12/us/politics/democrats-new-hampshire-sanders.html.

———. "Trump, Impeachment Trial: Is US Politics Beyond the Point of Repair?" BBC (February 9, 2020b). https://www.bbc.com/news/world-us-canada-51417722?fbclid=IwAR3EPICtkFu-DNLgwy9yonklp1HJLXTCG3CVKl-2caE2L83v3hzWJmIbJmhQ#.

———. "Virus Takes Center Stage as Pence and Harris Skirmish in Debate." *The New York Times* (October 7, 2020c). https://www.nytimes.com/2020/10/07/us/politics/vice-presidential-debate.html?referringSource=articleShare&fbclid=IwAR2eBGwx9u3B4V6BF1m9dWeB3faiLyxHAqVKtAhlYOSjx3yvgVG0l_itXx8.

Burns, Alexander Matt Flegenheimer, Jasmine Lee, Lisa Lerer, and Jonathan Martin. "Who's Running for President in 2020?" *The New York Times* (April 8, 2020). https://www.nytimes.com/interactive/2019/us/politics/2020-presidential-candidates.html.

Burns, Alexander, and Shane Goldmacher. "Iowa Democrats Release Partial Caucus Results, but No Winner Yet." *The Washington Post*, (February 4, 2020). https://www.washingtonpost.com/politics/sanders-declares-very-strong-victory-in-iowa-caucuses-pointing-to-popular-count/2020/02/06/76c0ec88-490a-11ea-9475-535736e48788_story.html.

Bycoffe, Aaron, Sarah Frostenson, and Julie Wolfe. "Who Won The Fourth Democratic Debate?" *FiveThirtyEight* (October 16, 2019). https://projects.fivethirtyeight.com/democratic-debate-october-poll/.

Campbell, Karlyn Kohrs, and Kathleen Hall Jamieson. *Form and Genre: Shaping Rhetorical Action*. Falls Church VA: Speech Communication Association, 1978.

———. "Rhetorical Hybrids: Fusions of Generic Elements." *Quarterly Journal of Speech*, 68 (1982): 146–157.

Cannon, Carl M. "Five Tribes of American Voters." *RealClearPolitics* (October 18, 2020). https://www.realclearpolitics.com/articles/2018/10/18/five_tribes_of_american_voters_138390.html#!.

Carlisle, Madeleine. "What to Know About the Origins of 'Left' and 'Right' in Politics, From the French Revolution to the 2020 Presidential Race." *Time* (September 14, 2019). https://time.com/5673239/left-right-politics-origins/.

Carpenter, Michael. "Tribalism Is Killing Liberalism: Why We Are Succumbing to the Politics of Division." Foreign Affairs (March 5, 2020). https://www.foreignaffairs.com/articles/2020-03-05/tribalism-killing-liberalism.

Carter, Travis, and David Dunning. "Faulty Self-Assessment: Why Evaluating One's Own Competence Is an Intrinsically Difficult Task." *Social and Personality Psychology Compass* 2, no.1 (2008): 346–360. http://10.1111/j.1751□9004.2007.00031.x.

Cathey, Libby. "Rep. Jaime Herrera Beutler's Written Testimony Admitted Into Evidence in Impeachment Trial." ABC News (February 13, 2021). https://abcnews.go.com/Politics/democrats-call-subpoenaing-gop-rep-jaime-herrera-beutler/story?id=75873161.

Caygle, Heather, and Sarah Ferris. "Pelosi Endorses Kennedy Over Markey in Contentious Primary." POLITICO (August 20, 2020). https://www.politico.com/news/2020/08/20/nancy-pelosi-endorses-joe-kennedy-senate-race-399447.

Cherwitz, Richard A. "Did President Trump Incite Resurrection? The Causal Connection Between Words and Deeds." *Spectra* (February 4, 2021). https://www.natcom.org/spectra/did-president-trump-incite-insurrection-causal-connection-between-words-and-deeds.

Chinoy, Sahil. "What Happened to America's Political Center of Gravity?" *The New York Times* (June 26, 2019). https://www.nytimes.com/interactive/2019/06/26/opinion/sunday/republican-platform-far-right.html.

Chotiner, Isaac. "How Socialist Is Bernie Sanders?" *The New Yorker* (March 2, 2020). https://www.newyorker.com/news/q-and-a/how-socialist-is-bernie-sanders.

Chua, Amy. "The Destructive Dynamics of Political Tribalism." *The New York Times* (February 20, 2018a). https://www.nytimes.com/2018/02/20/opinion/destructive-political-tribalism.html?fbclid=IwAR1YwM1JV-brCKiisIHJKm3abvTA-blk-zlQqQB7BYY1AeQf_nXchjyRiL4.

———. *Political Tribes: Group Instinct and the Fate of Nations*. New York: Penguin Press, 2018b.

Chua, Amy, and Jeb Rubenfeld. "The Threat of Tribalism." *The Atlantic* (October 2018). https://amp.theatlantic.com/amp/article/568342/?fbclid=IwAR3ukF2GVem2VDp_p5MVhhlGeiqdq1MnqiO2q4fiWD9V9lZ9JHtVwyOu7sQ.

Cillizza, Chris. "Do Republicans Really Want a 'Bigger Tent' Party?" CNN (July 13, 2020). https://www.cnn.com/2020/07/13/politics/larry-hogan-gop-big-tend-2024-donald-trump/index.html.

———. "Half of Americans Think the Democratic Party Has Moved Too Far Left." CNN (October 24, 2019a). https://www.cnn.com/2019/10/24/politics/democratic-party-left-liberal-q-poll/index.html.

———. "The 5 Candidates With the Most to Lose in This Week's Debates." CNN (July 28, 2019b). https://amp.cnn.com/cnn/2019/07/28/politics/debate-stakes-cnn-detroit/index.html?fbclid=IwAR01YnDIhGNEE1_PnW8LhqiskULZTPoPditVY6iug7dmUCmt-xU2P-nJrZY.

Cinelli, Matteo, Gianmarco De Francisci Morales, Alessandro Galeazzii, Walter Quettro Ciocchia, and Michele Starnini. "The Echo Chamber Effect on Social Media." *PNAS* 118, no.9 (March 2, 2021). https://doi.org/10.1073/pnas.2023301118.

Clark, Andrew. "Populism Is Back in the US Election, But Not as You Know It." *Foreign Affairs* (August 21, 2020). https://www.afr.com/policy/foreign-affairs/populism-is-back-in-the-us-election-but-not-as-you-know-it-20200817-p55mfb.

Coglianese, Cary. "Democracy and Its Critics." *Faculty Scholarship at Penn Law* (May 1990). https://scholarship.law.upenn.edu/faculty_scholarship/1241.

Cohen, Zachary, Alex Marquardt, and Jennifer Hansler. "Biden's CIA Director Pick Skates Through Confirmation Hearing and Receives Bipartisan Praise." CNN (February 24, 2021). https://www.cnn.com/2021/02/24/politics/burns-cia-director-confirmation-hearing/index.html.

Cohn, Nate. "Biden Gained with Moderate and Conservative Voting Groups, New Data Shows." *The New York Times* (June 30, 2021). https://www.nytimes.com/2021/06/30/us/politics/pew-election-2020.html.

———. "Trump's Electoral College Edge Could Grow in 2020, Rewarding Polarizing Campaign." *The New York Times* (July 19, 2019). https://www.nytimes.com/2019/07/19/upshot/trump-electoral-college-edge-.html?smid=nytcore-ios-share&fbclid=IwAR08PVku4X4NNSH8beuJaytlOq4bp8kwfTOn89QoB5oIGPOlN1FCOvaIpfg.

Colarossi, Jessica. "Banning Trump from Social Media Makes Sense. But Beware the Downside." *Boston University* (January 8, 2021). https://www.bu.edu/articles/2021/trump-banned-from-twitter-facebook/.

Cole, Devin. "AOC Isn't Concerned Biden's Opposition to Fracking Ban Will Hurt Young Voter Turnout." CNN (October 25, 2020). https://www.msn.com/en-us/news/politics/aoc-isnt-concerned-bidens-opposition-to-fracking-ban-will-hurt-young-voter-turnout/ar-BB1anlen?ocid=msedgdhp.

Coleman, Justine. "Ocasio-Cortez Says Democrats Must Focus on Winning White House for Biden." *The Hill* (October 15, 2020). https://www.msn.com/en-us/news/politics/ocasio-cortez-says-democrats-must-focus-on-winning-white-house-for-biden/ar-BB1amUQj?ocid=msedgdhpOc.

Coleman, Peter. "The Invisible Escalation of Hate—Is Political Violence in Our Future?" *The Hill* (March 17, 2020). https://thehill.com/opinion/national-security/488021-the-invisible-escalation-of-hate-is-political-violence-in-our.

Collins, Gail, and Bret Stephens. "Elizabeth Warren Divides the Room." *The New York Times* (October 15, 2019a). https://www.nytimes.com/2019/10/15/opinion/elizabeth-warren-trump.html.

———. "Hell Hath No Fury Like a Trump Scorned." *The New York Times* (November 9, 2020). https://www.nytimes.com/2020/11/09/opinion/biden-harris-trump-2020.html?referringSource=articleShare&fbclid=IwAR3dyiht9jpMm-e_mhNG0KAf5SltUKPC7ruBIcgOOzJOV0Tx6CbPNuLiWKY.

———. "The Democrats Should Stop Doing Trump's Work for Him." *The New York Times* (July 30, 2019b). https://www.nytimes.com/2019/07/30/opinion/democratic-debate-detroit.html?smid=nytcore-ios-share&fbclid=IwAR0aZeEVBMzGpoCv90PvFIwKkeMRR72K3bqVB0Kp4NMlNivUdaCh2OHavlY.

Collins, Sean. "Biden Is Now the Presumptive Democratic Nominee." *VOX* (July 9, 2020). https://www.vox.com/policy-and-politics/2020/4/9/21213793/biden-presumptive-democratic-nominee-trump-2020-polls-swing-state.

Conger, Kate, and Mike Issac. "Twitter Permanently Bans Trump, Capping Online Revolt." *The New York Times* (January 12, 2021). https://www.nytimes.com/2021/01/08/technology/twitter-trump-suspended.html.

Conger, Kate, Mike Isaac and Sheera Frankel. "Twitter and Facebook Lock Trump's Accounts After Violence on Capitol Hill." *The New York Times* (January 14, 2021). https://www.nytimes.com/2021/01/06/technology/capitol-twitter-facebook-trump.html.

Cooper, Martha. *Analyzing Public Discourse*. Prospect Heights, IL: Waveland Press, 1989.

Corasaniti, Nick. "Tulsi Gabbard Criticizes Democrats in Democratic Debate, and Kamala Harris Fires Back." *The New York Times* (November 20, 2019). https://www.nytimes.com/2019/11/20/us/politics/tulsi-gabbard-harris-debate.html?smid=nytcore-ios-share&fbclid=IwAR30-PvrpBZwBTAELwDLF-UddevR8y52Rm4uvJCweNRV2b8aSQe49UyGJ0.

Costa, Robert, Phillip Rucker, and Ashley Parker. "A 'Pressure Cooker': Trump's Frustration and Fury Rupture Alliances, Threatens Agenda." *The Washington Post* (October 9, 2017). https://www.washingtonpost.com/politics/a-pressure-cooker-trumps-frustration-and-fury-rupture-alliances-threaten-agenda/2017/10/09/41115744-ad0d-11e7-9e58-e6288544af98_story.html.

Courser, Zachary. "The Tea 'Party' as a Conservative Social Movement." *Society* 49 (2012): 43–53. https://link.springer.com/article/10.1007/s12115-011-9501-0.

Craig, Geoffrey. *Performing Politics: Media Interviews, Debates and Press Conferences*. Cambridge: Polity Press, 2016.

Cronin, Audrey Kurth. "The Capitol Has Been Attacked Before: This Time It Was Different." *American University School of International Service* (February 9, 2021). https://www.american.edu/sis/centers/security-technology/the-capitol-has-been-attacked-before-this-time-it-was-different.cfm.

Cummings, Mike. "Polarization in U.S. Politics Starts With Weak Political Parties." *Yale News* (November 17, 2020). https://news.yale.edu/2020/11/17/polarization-us-politics-starts-weak-political-parties?fbclid=IwAR0jq-PVRHqtYy-0Rs1uzA-1vgWFr-uP_e-ryWzW8kIHzM7usyp1737tadUk.

Cupp, S.E. "Tribalism Isn't the Real Reason America is Divided." CNN (November 13, 2019). https://www.cnn.com/2019/11/13/opinions/political-tribalism-not-reason-america-divided-cupp/index.html.

Dahl, Robert A. *Democracy and Its Critics*. New Haven: Yale University Press, 1989.

———. *Dilemmas of Pluralistic Democracy*. New Haven: Yale University Press, 1982.

Daniels, Eugene and Holly Otterbein. "Progressives Prepare to Put the Squeeze on Joe Biden." *POLITICO* (August 17, 2020). https://www.politico.com/news/2020/08/17/biden-progressives-left-no-honeymoon-395778?fbclid=IwAR3HJ6bRUhxzQ0JozTejPby-zmEnraVCkn4hQO-VxB-Kj6EAPJ-MMW5JR0EI.

Daniller, Andrew, and Hannah Gilberstadt. "Key Findings About Voter Engagement in the 2020 Election." *Pew Research Center* (December

14, 2020). https://www.pewresearch.org/fact-tank/2020/12/14/key-findings-about-voter-engagement-in-the-2020-election/.

Dargis, Manohla. "'Knock Down the House' Review: Running to Win Hearts and Minds and Votes." *The New York Times* (April 30, 2019). https://www.nytimes.com/2019/04/30/movies/knock-down-the-house-review.html.

Davidson, Rachel. "Rhetorical Genre" in *The SAGE Encyclopedia of Communication Research Methods*, Ed. Mike Allen. Thousand Oaks CA: Sage, 2018, 1497—1499. doi: https://dx.doi.org/10.4135/9781483381411.

Davies, Dave. "How Ted Kennedy's '80 Challenge To President Carter 'Broke The Democratic Party.'" NPR (January 17, 2019).https://www.npr.org/2019/01/17/686186156/how-ted-kennedys-80-challenge-to-president-carter-broke-the-democratic-party.

Davis, Julie Hirschfield. "For All the Talk of a Tea Party of the Left, Moderates Emerge as a Democratic Power." *The New York Times* (June 30, 2019a). https://www.nytimes.com/2019/06/30/us/politics/left-moderate-democrats.html.

———. "Identity Politics Roil Most Diverse House Democratic Caucus Ever." *The New York Times* (August 2, 2019b). https://www.nytimes.com/2019/08/02/us/politics/democrats-identity-politics-diversity.html?smid=nytcore-ios-share&fbclid=IwAR1PQS8rcblWYXkNvB6AidSVl0h7ToXQW6GIPQFkXYwhzBsQc5b8xxaw1lQ.

Deb, Anamitra, Stacy Donahue, and Tom Glaisyer. "Is Social Media a Threat to Democracy?" *Global Investigative Journalism Network* (October 13, 2017). https://gijn.org/2017/10/31/is-social-media-a-threat-to-democracy/.

DeCosta-Klipe, Nik. "Ed Markey 'Ain't No Bernie.' But Left-Wing Groups Are Rallying Behind Him All the Same." Boston.com (July 26, 2020). https://www.boston.com/news/politics/2020/07/26/ed-markey-progressives.

deFrance, Olivier. "Brexit Has Broken the UK, but Can It Mend Europe?" *European Council on Foreign Relations,*(June 19, 2019). https://ecfr.eu/article/commentary_brexit_has_broken_the_uk_but_can_it_mend_europe/.

"Democrats Will Control the Senate Following the Presidential Inauguration, After Sweeping Both Runoff Elections in Georgia." *POLITICO* (January 6, 2021). https://www.politico.com/2020-election/results/senate/.

Denham, Hannah. "These Are the Platforms That Have Banned Trump and His Allies." *The Washington Post* (January 14, 2021). https://www.washingtonpost.com/technology/2021/01/11/trump-banned-social-media/.

DeSilver, Drew. "Partisan Polarization, in Congress and Among Public, Is Greater Than Ever." *Pew Research Center* (July 17, 2013). https://www.pewresearch.org/fact-tank/2013/07/17/partisan-polarization-in-congress-and-among-public-is-greater-than-ever/.

Detrow, Scott. "Divide Between Moderate and Progressive Democrats Comes to Fore in New Hampshire." NPR (February 10, 2020). pr.org/2020/02/10/804616708/divide-between-moderate-and-progressive-democrats-comes-to-fore-in-new-hampshire.

Diamond, Larry, Lee Drutman, Tod Lindberg, Nathan P. Kalmoe, and Lilliana Mason. "Americans Increasingly Believe Violence is Justified if the Other

Side Wins." *POLITICO* (October 1, 2020). https://www.politico.com/news/magazine/2020/10/01/political-violence-424157.

Dimonk, Michael, and John Gramlich. "How America Changed During Donald Trump's Presidency." *Pew Research Center* (January 29, 2021). https://www.pewresearch.org/2021/01/29/how-america-changed-during-donald-trumps-presidency/.

Dimonk, Michael, and Richard Wike. "America Is Exceptional in the Nature of Its Political Divide." *Pew Research Center* (November 13, 2020). https://www.pewresearch.org/fact-tank/2020/11/13/america-is-exceptional-in-the-nature-of-its-political-divide/?fbclid=IwAR0Nxa8ehcTbZl56BIf9jbOiNjgbDwZut-29H2PPsulnN17VmlTApI6zMx8.

Dionne Jr., E. J. "A Realist's Case Against Despair." *The Washington Post* (September 13, 2020a). https://www.washingtonpost.com/opinions/a-realists-case-against-despair/2020/09/11/44d6d300-f46c-11ea-999c-67ff7bf6a9d2_story.html.

———. "Why They Fight." *The Washington Post* (November 23, 2020b). https://www.washingtonpost.com/outlook/2020/11/23/democrats-moderates-progressives-fighting/?arc404=true.

DiSalvo, Daniel. *Engines of Change: Party Factions in American Politics 1868–2010.* Oxford: Oxford University Press, 2012.

"Does Biden-Harris Ticket Appeal to Progressives in the Democratic Party?" (August 18, 2020). https://www.npr.org/2020/08/18/903433818/does-biden-harris-ticket-appeal-to-progressives-in-the-democratic-party.

"Donald Trump & Joe Biden 1st Presidential Debate Transcript 2020." *REV* (September 29, 2020a). https://www.rev.com/blog/transcripts/donald-trump-joe-biden-1st-presidential-debate-transcript-2020?fbclid=IwAR2Th6g3Av5ujV4sJ93CqcFHMXZt-c4bj_KIAye2DRiOxsvtxtqnQJqmYFY.

"Donald Trump & Joe Biden Final Presidential Debate Transcript 2020." *REV* (October 22, 2020b). https://www.rev.com/blog/transcripts/donald-trump-joe-biden-final-presidential-debate-transcript-2020.

Dovere, Edward-Issac. "Why Biden Won." *The Atlantic* (November 7, 2020). https://www.theatlantic.com/politics/archive/2020/11/why-biden-won-presidency/616980/.

Dowd, Maureen. "It's Nancy Pelosi's Parade." *The New York Times* (July 6, 2019). https://pharmacy.amazon.com/?ref_=DIS_GDN_ACQ_MC_AFFNP_DK_CropBottle-Introducing_thehill.com__970x250.png_201203.

Downie, James. "Democratic Leaders Play a Ridiculous Blame Game with Progressives." *The Washington Post* (November 8, 2020). https://www.washingtonpost.com/opinions/2020/11/08/democratic-leaders-play-ridiculous-blame-game-with-progressives/.

Drutman, Lee. "America Is Now the Divided Republic the Framers Feared." *The Atlantic* (January 2, 2020). https://www.theatlantic.com/ideas/archive/2020/01/two-party-system-broke-constitution/604213.

Dunning, David. "The Dunning-Kruger Effect: On Being Ignorant of One's Own Ignorance." *Advances in Experimental Social Psychology* 44 (2011): 247–296. https://doi.org/10.1016/B978-0-12-385522-0.00005-6.

Durham, Weldon B. "Kenneth Burke's Concept of Substance." *Quarterly Journal of Speech* 66 no. 4 (1980): 351–364. https://doi.org/10.1080/00335638009383534.

Durkin, Erin. "'AOC Effect' Put to the Test in Heated New York Primaries." *POLITICO* (June 15, 2020). https://www.politico.com/states/new-york/albany/story/2020/06/05/new-york-primary-battles-struggle-to-draw-attention-in-a-shaken-city-1290875ut.

Easley, Jonathan. "Biden on if He Can Reach Trump's Base: 'Probably Not.'" *The Hill* (April 16, 2020a). https://thehill.com/homenews/campaign/493123-biden-on-if-he-can-reach-trumps-base-probably-not.

———. "Iowa Debacle Deepens Division Between Sanders, National Party." *The Hill* (February 7, 2020b). https://thehill.com/homenews/campaign/481961-iowa-debacle-deepens-division-between-sanders-national-party?fbclid=IwAR1MRiZ4qiBq2c1zMZjFTQv5h3n3wJPJhmq6hpPIzLNuU5Hc4x-h8NM1TBs.

Edsall, Thomas B. "Bernie Sanders Scares a Lot of People, and Quite a Few of Them Are Democrats." *The New York Times* (April 24, 2019a). https://www.nytimes.com/2019/04/24/opinion/sanders-2020-trump.html?smid=nytcore-ios-share&fbclid=IwAR0jVWm2oZm8WPvDfVFM6XBIpPF_q3UJbEIxNllu3nbB8O55o81_SeRDLW8.

———. "How Far Is Too Far Left for 2020 Democrats? *The New York Times* (April 10, 2019b). https://www.nytimes.com/2019/04/10/opinion/democratic-candidates-primaries.html.

———. "The Audacity of Hate." *The New York Times* (February 19, 2020a). https://www.nytimes.com/2020/02/19/opinion/trump-anger-fear.html.

———. "The Democratic Party Is Actually Three Parties." *The New York Times* (July 24, 2019c). https://www.nytimes.com/2019/07/24/opinion/2020-progressive-candidates.html.

———. "Why Trump Persists." *The New York Times* (January 22, 2020b). https://www.nytimes.com/2020/01/22/opinion/trump-voters.html.

———. "The Trump Sanders Fantasy." *The New York Times* (February 24, 2016). https://www.nytimes.com/2016/02/24/opinion/campaign-stops/the-trump-sanders-fantasy.html.

Edwards, Jason, and David Weiss. *The Rhetoric of American Exceptionalism: Critical Essays.* Jefferson, NC: McFarland and Co., 2011.

Egan, Lauren. "Marjorie Taylor Greene Warns Herrera Beutler: 'The Trump Loyal 75 Million Are Watching.'" *NBC News* (February 13, 2021). https://www.nbcnews.com/politics/donald-trump/live-blog/2021-02-13-trump-impeachment-trial-live-updates-n1257801/ncrd1257851#liveBlogHeader.

Ehlinger, J. "'That's Where I Draw the Line': How the Issue-Publics Can Overcome Partisan Tribalism." PhD dissertation. The University of North Carolina at Chapel Hill, 2019. http://search,proquest.com/docview/22583871.

Eisenstat, Yael. "How to Hold Social Media Accountable for Undermining Democracy." *Harvard Business Review* (January 11, 2021). https://hbr.org/2021/01/how-to-hold-social-media-accountable-for-undermining-democracy.

Eisenstein, Elizabeth. *The Printing Press as an Agent of Change: Communications and Cultural Transformations in Early-Modern Europe*. New York, NY: Cambridge University Press, 1979.

Emanuel, Rahm. "Why Joe Biden Needs Bipartisanship." *Wall Street Journal* (February 14, 2021). https://www.wsj.com/articles/why-joe-biden-needs-bipartisanship-11613307600.

Ember, Sydney. "Bernie Sanders Lost Again, but This Time He'll Deliver a Victory Speech." *The New York Times* (August 17, 2020a).

———. "'Georgia Is Not New York': Progressives Adapt Efforts for Senate Runoffs." *The New York Times* (December 1, 2020b). https://www.nytimes.com/2020/12/01/us/politics/georgia-senate-election-democrats.html.

———. "Sanders Urging Biden to Do More to Excite Progressives." *The New York Times* (September 12, 2020c). https://www.nytimes.com/2020/09/12/us/politics/bernie-sanders-joe-biden.html.

———. "Treasury Secretary Warren? Progressives Line Up to Press Their Agenda on Biden." *The New York Times* (November 7, 2020d). https://www.nytimes.com/2020/11/07/us/politics/progressives-biden-warren.html.

———. "Why Bernie Sanders Went on Attack Against Joe Biden. *The New York Times* (January 22, 2020e). https://www.nytimes.com/2020/01/22/us/politics/sanders-biden-democratic-polls.html.

Ember, Sydney, and Nick Corasanti. "Democrats' Attacks Get Personal Ahead of New Hampshire Primary." *The New York Times* (February 10, 2020). https://www.nytimes.com/live/2020/new-hampshire-primary-02-09?fbclid=IwAR3I2WjYzm4A-Jp_Bks0_uGNIDiGk9TuldOHswhFh8KzEQA-_7mWG5LXEYs#sanders-recanvass.

Ember, Sydney, Katie Glueck and Asteed W. Herndon. "What We Learned From the Democratic Debates." *The New York Times* (August 1, 2019). https://www.nytimes.com/2019/08/01/us/full-democratic-debate-highlights.html?smid=nytcore-ios-share&fbclid=IwAR2m1Bx42o9QUmGyZ1Ntvr13CHOYhD3sN2ejnanuyXhM4osQ_g7skDSbnO0.

Ember, Sydney, and Astead W. Herndon. "Progressives Didn't Want Harris for V.P. They're Backing Her Anyway." *The New York Times* (August 19, 2020). https://www.nytimes.com/2020/08/12/us/politics/kamala-harris-progressives-popularity.html?fbclid=IwAR39GXOe65hUQzQOi9fV6p6gzABFt1hkoPafgHK1lG79hLywMZUeps2atwk.

Enoch, Jessica. "Composing a Rhetorical Education for the Twenty-First Century: TakingITGlobal as Pedagogical Heuristic." *Rhetoric Review* 29 no. 2, (2010): 165–185. https://www.jstor.org/stable/pdf/27862421.pdf?refreqid=excelsior%3Acb958172c3ebba66d0398290bb317f6b.

Enten, Harry. "Joe Biden Won a Race Another Democrat May Have Lost." CNN (November 8, 2020). https://www.cnn.com/2020/11/08/politics/democrats-biden-election/index.html?fbclid=IwAR1jE0lNkKjbuksCSLLfj0vFLmIhW8xjrRC0R9bLoe4KIpedZK-peunxfz0.

Epstein, Reid J., and Annie Karni. "G.O.P. Platform, Rolled Over From 2016, Condemns the 'Current President.'" *The New York Times* (June 29, 2020). https://www.nytimes.com/2020/06/11/us/politics/republican-platform.html.

Epstein, Reid J., and Lisa Lerer. "Why Democrats Are So Far from Consensus in 2020." *The New York Times* (July 28, 2019). https://www.nytimes.com/2019/07/28/us/politics/democrats-2020-trump.html?smid=nytcore-ios-share&fbclid=IwAR0r5fJxb54nXLLWYN7CdhG62Dq7w4nqJcIY9gwyQyvSHaeyT4_8ka-cUxs.

Epstein, Reid J., and Shane Goldmacher. "7 Takeaways From the Democratic Debate in New Hampshire." *The New York Times* (February 7, 2020). https://www.nytimes.com/2020/02/07/us/politics/democratic-debate-tonight.html?referringSource=articleShare&fbclid=IwAR281zx8-RffKEAWYhsIcEFIw1H8gFu9vELMnxbSmwsWeLX4MtzquWlvP5w.

Epstein, Reid J., and Trip Gabriel. "Pete Buttigieg to Quit Democratic Presidential Race." *The New York Times* (March 1, 2020). https://www.nytimes.com/2020/03/01/us/politics/pete-buttigieg-drops-out.html?action=click&module=Top%20Stories&pgtype=Homepage.

Everett, Burgess, and Heather Caygle. "'I Would Tell Joe to Wait': Democrats Warn Kennedy Against Challenging Markey." *POLITICO* (September 11, 2019). https://www.politico.com/story/2019/09/11/joe-kennedy-ed-markey-challenge-1491098.

Fallows, James. "A Nation of Tribes and Members of the Tribe." *The Atlantic* (November 4, 2017). https://www.theatlantic.com/notes/2017/11/a-nation-of-tribes-and-members-of-the-tribe/544907/.

Fandos, Nicholas. "Cori Bush Defeats William Lacy Clay in a Show of Progressive Might." *The New York Times* (August 5, 2020a). https://www.nytimes.com/2020/08/05/us/politics/cori-bush-missouri-william-lacy-clay.html.

———. "Democrats, Facing Critical Supreme Court Battle, Worry Feinstein Is Not Up to the Task." *The New York Times* (October 10, 2020b). https://www.nytimes.com/2020/10/10/us/politics/dianne-feinstein-supreme-court-judiciary-committee.html?referringSource=articleShare&fbclid=IwAR1qjpPlyIwhJ6eLO8EQlg_BfjqO-T87FXix-NUFkkh4OKwfTPzVlGkYKOg.

Faragó, Laura, Anna Kende, and Peter Kreko. "We Only Believe in News That We Doctored Ourselves: The Connection Between Partisanship and Political Fake News." *Social Psychology* (September 20, 2019). doi:10.1027/1864-9335/a000391.

Felton, Lena. "Can American Survive Tribalism." *The Atlantic* (May 31, 2018). https://amp.theatlantic.com/amp/article/561662/?fbclid=IwAR2V5C62U631Eoe04jTwTj10DoCC3z6pa-pI7B02BVAuoHZPaVblotUOy3Y.

Feuer, Alan. "The Capitol Attack Aftermath." *The New York Times* (February 6, 2021). https://www.nytimes.com/live/2021/01/07/us/capitol-building-trump.

Finch, Christian. "Trump and Sanders Aren't That Different." *The Crimson White* (March 9, 2020). https://cw.ua.edu/64507/top-stories/trump-and-sanders-arent-that-different/.

Finer, Lauren. "Justice Thomas Suggests Regulating Tech Platforms Like Utilities." CNBC (April 5, 2021). https://www.cnbc.com/2021/04/05/justice-thomas-suggests-regulating-tech-platforms-like-utilities.html.

Fisher, Anthony. "Capitol Siege Is a Coup. Trump Led American Towards This for 5 Years." *Business Insider* (January 6, 2021). https://www.businessinsider.com/capitol-coup-trump-led-country-america-towards-this-5-years-2021-1.

Flegenheimer, Matt, and Katie Glueck. "Joe Biden's Non-Radical 1960s." *The New York Times* (October 17, 2020). https://www.nytimes.com/2020/10/17/us/politics/joe-biden-college-1960s.html?referringSource=articleShare&fbclid=IwAR0wZptmO0v6J4onGNjsFnTuHRLNEYzPcTlMwfn8SbUPlXiqago_5q3bhCw.

Folkenflik, David. "A Look at the Rhetoric Around the Storming of U.S. Capitol." NPR (January 6, 2021). https://www.npr.org/2021/01/06/954149242/a-look-at-the-rhetoric-around-the-storming-of-u-s-capitol.

Foran, Clare. "Another QAnon Victory and 2 Other Takeaways in Key Primary Races in Minnesota and Georgia." CNN (August 12, 2020). https://www.cnn.com/2020/08/11/politics/primary-runoff-highlights-minnesota-georgia/index.html?fbclid=IwAR2srJkxSGuxnleVF1rHZ0Epo8gC-ndjTPMJgY21T4Js8EttsphEorfokro.

Foss, Sonja K., and Cindy L. Griffin. "Beyond Persuasion: A Proposal for an Invitational Rhetoric." *Communication Monographs 62*, no. 1 (March 1995): 2–18. https://www.tandfonline.com/doi/abs/10.1080/03637759509376345.

Frenkel, Sheera. "The Storming of Capitol Hill Was Organized on Social Media." *The New York Times* (January 6, 2021). https://www.nytimes.com/2021/01/11/us/politics/republican-party-trump.html.

Friedman, Thomas. "Never Forget the Names of These Republicans Attempting a Coup." *The New York Times* (January 5, 2021). https://www.nytimes.com/2021/01/05/opinion/trump-republicans-election.html.

———. "The American Civil War, Part II." *The New York Times* (October 2, 2018). https://www.nytimes.com/2018/10/02/opinion/the-american-civil-war-part-ii.html?smid=fb-nytimes&smtyp=cur&fbclid=IwAR1eXuY-soMgpo7rLA8lt42BUpuDUJEXODaZTcgirg6HmPGD57IdsZwKQ8k.

Fritz, Angela. "What's Behind the Confidence of the Incompetent? This Suddenly Popular Psychological Phenomenon." *The Washington Post* (January 7, 2019). https://citeseerx.ist.psu.edu/viewdoc/summary?doi=10.1.1.64.2655.

Frizell, Sam. "Bernie Sanders Does Not Concede Democratic Nomination to Hillary Clinton." *Time* (June 16, 2016). https://time.com/4372644/bernie-sanders-hillary-clinton-speech-democratic-nomination/.

"From John Adams to Jonathan Jackson, 2 October 1780." *Founders Online, National Archives* (2021). https://founders.archives.gov/documents/Adams/06-10-02-0113.

Fukuyama, Francis. "Against Identity Politics: The New Tribalism and the Crisis of Democracy." *Foreign Affairs* (September/October 2018). https://www.foreignaffairs.com/articles/americas/2018-08-14/against-identity-politics-tribalism-francis-fukuyama?fbclid=IwAR3SKBM4qwauQotI_Uy32PmPO5KhZf4lpUp_yi-hqwket99JnWnv-WxtroM.

———. "Why Red and Blue American Can't Hear Each Other Anymore." *The Washington Post* (January 24, 2020). https://www.washingtonpost.com/outlook/2020/01/24/why-red-blue-america-cant-hear-each-other-anymore/?arc404=true.

Galson, William. "Why Did House Democrats Underperform Compared to Joe Biden?" *Brookings* (December 21, 2020). https://www.brookings.edu/blog/fixgov/2020/12/21/why-did-house-democrats-underperform-compared-to-joe-biden/.

Gao, George. "Public Opinion on the Economy and Obama's Handling of It." *Pew Research Center* (January 20, 2015). https://www.pewresearch.org/fact-tank/2015/01/20/us-economy/.

Garrison, Joey. "While Iowa Keeps Counting, Candidates Hit the Trail in New Hampshire to Spin Incomplete Results." *USAToday* (February 5, 2020). https://www.usatoday.com/story/news/politics/elections/2020/02/05/new-hampshire-primary-iowa-caucus-results-leave-democrats-spinning/4669512002/.

Ghitis, Frida. "Biden's Genius Move." CNN (November 30, 2020). https://www.bing.com/news/search?q=Biden%27s+Genius+Move.&qpvt=Biden%27s+genius+move.&FORM=EWRE.

Gillman, Todd J., and Tom Benning. "Biden's Victory Sealed in Wee Hours After Pro-Trump Mob Storms Capitol; Trump Vows Orderly Transition." *The Dallas Morning News* (January 6, 2021). https://www.dallasnews.com/news/politics/2021/01/06/drama-in-congress-as-trump-makes-last-ditch-effort-to-overturn-bidens-election/.

Gitz, Bradley. "Opinion/Bradley Gitz: Mysteries of Biden." *Arkansas Democrat Gazette* (November 6. 2020). https://www.arkansasonline.com/news/2020/nov/02/mysteries-of-biden/.

Glueck, Katie. "Biden Takes Credit for the Discussion of Unity in the Primary." *The New York Times* (February 9, 2020a). https://www.nytimes.com/live/2020/new-hampshire-primary-02-09?referringSource=articleShare&fbclid=IwAR1FsUEiwU793aKSZAAVAY5yV1r87w_YmES173xeuPMNo5wsHJyvHfjYETI#joe-biden-unity.

———. "Eric Adams Wins Democratic Primary for New York City Mayor." *The New York Times* (July 6, 2021). https://www.nytimes.com/2021/07/06/nyregion/eric-adams-wins.

———. "New Hampshire Live Updates: The Democrats' Attacks Get Personal Ahead of Primary." *The New York Times* (February 9, 2020b). https://www.nytimes.com/live/2020/new-hampshire-primary-02-09?referringSource=articleShare&fbclid=IwAR1FsUEiwU793aKSZAAVAY5yV1r87w_YmES173xeuPMNo5wsHJyvHfjYETI#.

———. "7 Takeaways From the Democratic National Convention." *The New York Times* (August 21, 2020c). https://www.nytimes.com/2020/08/21/us/politics/dnc-takeaways-biden-obama.html.

Glueck, Katie, and Dana Rubinstein. "They Fueled A.O.C.'s Win. Can They Shape the N.Y.C. Mayor's Race?" *The New York Times* (December 23, 2020). https://www.nytimes.com/2020/12/23/nyregion/nyc-mayors-race-progressives.html?referringSource=articleShare&fbclid=IwAR03Xn2VHoev0FhbqX1czZ3i0tR_2118B9GrkazIwGRX7eIKIHTlKnhvDhQ.

Glueck, Katie,and Lisa Lerer. "'I'm a Democrat': Biden Accuses Sanders of Not Being a Party Member." *The New York Times* (January 30, 2020). https://www.nytimes.com/2020/01/30/us/politics/pete-buttigieg-joe-biden-bernie-sanders.html?smid=nytcore-ios-share&fbclid=IwAR0H63KnvvfWSnG0xfxViztti9ByqAiJr6vEBg65CzlM_cEfrsO6MiT8G0Q.

Godfrey, Elaine. "Democrats Go to War Over Neil Gorsuch." *The Atlantic* (March 30, 2017). https://www.theatlantic.com/politics/archive/2017/03/democrats-go-to-war-over-neil-gorsuch/521268/.

Goins-Phillips, Tre. "MSNBC Anchor Asks Donald Trump Slick Trick Question—See How He Answers." *The Blaze* (February 17, 2016). https://www.theblaze.com/news/2016/02/18/msnbc-anchor-asks-donald-trump-slick-trick-question-see-how-he-answers.

Goldberg, Jonah. *Suicide of the West: How the Rebirth of Tribalism, Populism, Nationalism, and Identity Politics is Destroying American Democracy*. Manhattan, NY: Crown Forum Publishers, 2018.

Golden, James, Goodwin F. Berquist, William E. Coleman, and J. Michael Sproule, eds., *The Rhetoric of Western Thought*, Dubuque, IA: Kendall-Hunt, 2004.

Goldiner, Dave. "AOC Won't Rule Out Challenging Schumer for Senate Seat in 2022." MSN (January 4, 2021). https://www.msn.com/en-us/news/politics/aoc-wont-rule-out-challenging-schumer-for-senate-seat-in-2020/ar-BB1csKEs\.

———. "Schumer Seeks to Block Fast Track Supreme Court Replacement Before Election Day." *New York Daily News* (September 23, 2020). https://www.nydailynews.com/news/politics/ny-ruth-bader-ginsburg-rbg-schumer-20200923-5uc4q3n-6pza6pef2zcgtrsnwpq-story.html.

Goldmacher, Shane. "Alexandria Ocasio-Cortez Defeats Joseph Crowley in Major Democratic House Upset." *The New York Times* (June 26, 2018). https://www.nytimes.com/2018/06/26/nyregion/joseph-crowley-ocasio-cortez-democratic-primary.html.

———. "Fractured by Trump, the G.O.P. Can't Agree on a Way Back to Power." *The New York Times* (January 15, 2021). https://www.nytimes.com/2021/01/11/us/politics/republican-party-trump.html.

Goldmacher, Shane, and Nick Corasaniti. 'A Systemwide Disaster': How the Iowa Caucuses Melted Down." *The New York Times* (February 6, 2020). https://www.nytimes.com/2020/02/04/us/politics/what-happened-iowa-caucuses.html?smid=nytcore-ios-share&fbclid=IwAR33obW1hPmCHIR3gggMp_58qqm8JmpovRoM6AKU2MMp5KJVFlC9gThDg3s.

Goldmacher, Shane, and Reid J. Epstein. "6 Takeaways From the September Democratic Debate." *The New York Times* (September 12, 2019). https://www.nytimes.com/2019/09/12/us/politics/september-democratic-debate-live.html?smid=nytcore-ios-share&fbclid=IwAR24_BX2s623tUFZhzVYJEvYHjDJgc17Y1vbf8yx3scyyI0-UFuNNoE6ITQ.

———. "6 Takeaways From the Democratic Debate in Nevada." *The New York Times* (February 20, 2020). https://www.nytimes.com/2020/02/20/us/politics/democratic-debate-las-vegas.ht.

Goldsmith, Jack. "Will Donald Trump Destroy the Presidency?" *The Atlantic* (October 2017). https://www.theatlantic.com/magazine/archive/2017/10/will-donald-trump-destroy-the-presidency/537921/.

Golec de Zavala, Agnieszka, Karolina Kydich-Hazar, and Dorottya Lanto. "Collective Narcissism: Political Consequences of Investing Self-Worth in the Ingroup's Image." *Advances in Political Psychology* 40, Suppl.1 (March 20, 2019): 37–71. https://doi.10.1111/pops. 12569.

Gontcharova, Natalie. "'Vote Like Your Life Depends on It': Elizabeth Warren on Protecting Roe, Expanding the Court & Losing Her Brother to

COVID." MSN (November 2, 2020). https://www.msn.com/en-us/news/politics/vote-like-your-life-depends-on-it-elizabeth-warren-on-protecting-roe-expanding-the-court-losing-her-brother-to-covid/ar-BB1aCpLR.

Gordon, Michael. "Democrats Need to Get Serious About New Ideas to Transform the Supreme Court." *Business Insider* (March 7, 2021). https://www.businessinsider.com/democrats-can-transform-supreme-court-consider-packing-more-justices-2021-.

Graham, David A. "Biden Seizes Trump's Populist Mantle." *The Atlantic* (October 13, 2020). https://www.msn.com/en-us/news/opinion/biden-seizes-trumps-populist-mantle/ar-BB1ajriu.

———. "This Is a Coup." *The Atlantic* (January 6, 2021). https://www.theatlantic.com/ideas/archive/2021/01/attempted-coup/617570/.

Graham, Michael. "Markey Won the Senate Seat, But AOC Can Claim Victory." *The Boston Herald* (September 3, 2020). https://www.bostonherald.com/2020/09/03/markey-won-the-senate-seat-but-aoc-can-claim-victory/.

Gray, Ian. "Tea Party Election Results: Conservative Movement of 2010 Takes Pounding in 2012." *HuffPost* (November 7, 2012). https://www.huffpost.com/entry/tea-party-election-results_n_2084506.

Greenblatt, Alan. "Moderates Are 'Politically Homeless.' Does Either Party Want Them?" *Governing* (March 26, 2019). https://www.governing.com/archive/gov-moderate-voters-trump-centrists-2020.html.

Gregory, Elena Renee. "President Trump's Manipulation of Digital Rhetoric to Maintain His Presidential Status During the 2020 Election." *University of New Hampshire Scholar's Repository* (Spring 2020). https://scholars.unh.edu/cgi/viewcontent.cgi?article=1528&context=honors.

"Greta Thunberg Tells World Leaders 'You Are Failing Us.'" *United Nations Department of Economic and Social Affairs* (September 24, 2019). https://www.un.org/development/desa/youth/news/2019/09/greta-thunberg/.

Grieco, Elizabeth. "Americans' Main Sources for Political News Mary by Party and Age." *Pew Research Center* (April 1, 2020). https://www.pewresearch.org/fact-tank/2020/04/01/americans-main-sources-for-political-news-vary-by-party-and-age/.

Grieder, Erica. "Americans Should Be Worried About Tribalism, Not Identity Politics." *Houston Chronicle* (September 15, 2019). https://www.houstonchronicle.com/news/columnists/grieder/amp/Americans-should-be-worried-about-tribalism-not-13231209.php?fbclid=IwAR3rOhD3P9zcaHwVL7tEtsXiw46Q93a65UGfR_ZSF2X_tjJk6YoAoXS_OAA.

Griffin, Ian-Michael. "Woke Culture Destroyed the 'Blue Wave.'" *The Daily Cardinal* (November 19, 2020). https://www.dailycardinal.com/article/2020/11/woke-culture-destroyed-the-blue-wave.

Gross, Neil. "Are Americans Experiencing Collective Trauma?" *The New York Times* (December 16, 2016). https://www.nytimes.com/2016/12/16/opinion/sunday/are-americans-experiencing-collective-trauma.html?smid=fb-nytimes&smtyp=cur&fbclid=IwAR0XwvHS4_4NdWmpayAq105ewFI8ihmgONZwMx0VcTc1_5WomPt6dp57x2A.

Gutmann, Amy, and Dennis Thompson. "The Mindsets of Political Compromise," *Perspectives on Politics* 8, no. 4 (2010): 1125–1143. https://doi.org/10.1017/S1537592710003270.

———. "Valuing Compromise for the Common Good." *Daedalus* (Spring 2013). https://www.amacad.org/publication/valuing-compromise-common-good.

Guttman, A. "U.S. Advertising Revenues of Social Networks 2017–2021." *Statistica* (November 23, 2020). https://www.statista.com/statistics/271259/advertising-revenue-of-social-networks-in-the-us/#:~:text=U.S.%20advertising%20revenues%20of%20social%20networks%202017%2D2021&text=In%202019%2C%20social%20network%20advertising,by%20the%20end%20of%202021.

Hall, Andrew B., and Daniel M. Thompson. "Who Punishes Extremist Nominees? Candidate Ideology and Turning Out the Base in U.S. Elections." *American Political Sciences* 112, no. 3 (2018): 509–524. https://doi.org/10.1017/S0003055418000023.

Haltiwanger, John. "Where Biden Stands on the Most Important Issues in 2020." *Business Insider* (November 3, 2020). https://www.businessinsider.com/joe-biden-policy-positions-most-important-election-issues-2020-9.

Hamid, Shadi. "American Politics is Tribal. Are We Ready to Admit That?" *The Guardian* (April 23, 2018). https://www.theguardian.com/commentisfree/2018/apr/23/amy-chua-political-tribalism-book-overcome#img-1.

Hamilton, Alexander, James Madison, and John Jay. *The Federalist: A Collection of Essays, Written in Favor of the New Constitution As Agreed Upon by the Federal Convention* (1787, 2014). Mineola, NY: Dover.

Hansell, Saul. "A Quiet Year in the Internet Industry. Right? Right." *The New York Times* (December 28, 1998). https://www.nytimes.com/1998/12/28/business/the-markets-market-place-a-quiet-year-in-the-internet-industry-right-right.html.

Harper, Steven. "UPDATED: Insurrection Timeline—First the Coup and Then the Cover-Up." *Moyers on Democracy* (March 7, 2021). https://billmoyers.com/story/insurrection-timeline-first-the-coup-and-then-the-cover-up-updated/.

Harris, John F. "What Planet Is AOC On?" *Politico* (November 12, 2020). https://www.politico.com/news/magazine/2020/11/12/what-planet-is-aoc-on-436258?fbclid=IwAR1SEZVzm0RtKBE_sATHcm2O8t6zbEXUKfppy_1aYMkNES44P27EtTwjQpU.

Harris, Rachael L., and Lisa Tarchak. "Donald Trump, and Others, Had a Lot to Say About Friedman's Column." *The New York Times*, (July 11, 2019). https://www.nytimes.com/2019/07/19/opinion/trump-2020-democrats.html?smid=nytcore-ios-share&fbclid=IwAR2PGSRygIb_J9ilQUR4CWRxRJHFmI3bnXid_1kEkwsBurijbNEn--hbo00.

Harsany, David. "Progressivism, or Why the Culture War Is Turning in the Republicans' Favor." *The National Review* (November 5, 2020). https://www.nationalreview.com/corner/progressivism-or-why-the-culture-war-has-turned-in-the-republicans-favor/.

Harwood, John. "Democratic Sen. Elizabeth Warren: 'I Am a Capitalist'—But Markets Need to Work for More Than Just the Rich." CNBC (July 24, 2018). https://www.cnbc.com/2018/07/23/elizabeth-warren-i-am-a-capitalist-but-markets-need-rules.html.

Hauser, Gerard A. "Rhetorical Democracy and Civic Engagement" in *Rhetorical Democracy: Discursive Practices of Civic Engagement*, eds. Gerald A. Hauser and Amy Grim. Mahwah, NJ: Lawrence Erlbaum Associates, Publishers, 2004: 1–14.

Hawkins, Stephen, Daniel Yudkin, Miriam Juan-Torres, and Tim Dixon. *Hidden Tribes: A Study of America's Polarized Landscape*. New York, NY: More in Common, 2018.

Hayakawa, S.I., and Alan R. Hayakawa. *Language in Thought and Action*. 5th ed. New York, NY: Houghton Mifflin Harcourt, 1941, 1990.

Heim, Joe. "'Disinformation Can Be a Very Lucrative Business, Especially if You're Good at it,' Media Scholar Says." *The Washington Post* (January 19, 2021). https://www.washingtonpost.com/lifestyle/magazine/disinformation-can-be-a-very-lucrative-business-especially-if-youre-good-at-it-media-scholar-says/2021/01/19/4c842f06-4a04-11eb-a9d9-1e3ec4a928b9_story.html?fbclid=IwAR2gr68a602_qtTSLntnTkX9Djz2pLKtfLjCofqksGPOeIGHDN8oydpeDqs.

Henninger, Donald. "Trumpism According to Trump." *The Wall Street Journal* (March 3, 2021). https://www.wsj.com/articles/trumpism-according-to-trump-11614812815.

Herndon, Astead W. "Alexandria Ocasio-Cortez on Biden's Win, House Losses, and What's Next for the Left." *The New York Times* (November 7, 2020a). https://www.nytimes.com/2020/11/07/us/politics/aoc-biden-progressives.html?referringSource=articleShare&fbclid=IwAR18tCiMEVQcDVaeHrvhMkTTYp3djP6YQUiFwEjTfqy2rz0hi0gEtW_R4Eo.

———. "Conor Lamb, House Moderate, on Biden's Win, 'the Squad' and the Future of the Democratic Party." *The New York Times* (November 16, 2020b). https://www.nytimes.com/2020/11/08/us/politics/conor-lamb-democrats-biden.html?referringSource=articleShare&fbclid=IwAR2DoZkVuOokmrEZ98iMyLu-w10SJp3wlJM4pKB_2VAENP1JwwfzFwZPnt4.

———. "Kamala Harris." *The New York Times* (September 22, 2020c). https://www.nytimes.com/interactive/2020/us/elections/kamala-harris.html.

Herndon, Astead, and Nick Corasaniti. "Georgia Is a Purple State, But Don't Expect Centrist Politicians." *The New York Times* (November 23, 2020). https://www.nytimes.com/2020/11/23/us/politics/ossoff-perdue-loeffler-warnock.html.

Herndon, Astead, and Sydney Ember. "A Call to Rally Around Joe Biden 'Like Our Lives Depend on It.'" *The New York Times* (August 17, 2020). https://www.nytimes.com/2020/08/17/us/politics/convention-democratic-night-1.html?referringSource=articleShare&fbclid=IwAR1Wr6NydGLKGsaR426aHb_Lej6OtkCNN53sSNvnP4ZRtFnbCRV2F4Byea0.

Herrick, James A. *The History and Theory of Rhetoric: An Introduction*. 7th ed. New York, NY: Routledge, 2020.

Hertzell, Katharine. "Meme Distorts AOC's Election Vote Count." *FactCheck.org* (July 22, 2019). https://www.factcheck.org/2019/07/meme-distorts-aocs-election-vote-count/.

Hess, Abigail Johnson. "29-Year-Old Alexandria Ocasio-Cortez Makes History as the Youngest Woman Ever Elected to Congress." CNBC (November 7, 2018).

https://www.cnbc.com/2018/11/06/alexandria-ocasio-cortez-is-now-the-youngest-woman-elected-to-congress.html.

Hiatt, Steven. "Social Democrat or Democratic Socialist?" *The Eugene Register Guard* (March 16, 2020).

"Hillary Clinton Campaign Blames Leaked DNC Emails About Sanders on Russia." *The Guardian* (July 24, 2016). https://www.guardian.com/us-news/2016/jul/24/clinton-campaign-blames-russia-wikileaks-sanders-dnc-emails.

Hobfoll, Steven E. *Tribalism: The Evolutionary Origins of Fear Politics*. London, England: Palgrove Macmillan Publishers, 2018.

Hohmann, James. "Castro's Kamikaze Mission Makes Biden More Sympathetic—and Six Other Debate Takeaways." *The Washington Post* (September 13, 2019a). https://www.washingtonpost.com/news/powerpost/paloma/daily-202/2019/09/13/daily-202-castro-s-kamikaze-mission-makes-biden-more-sympathetic-and-six-other-debate-takeaways/5d7b14aa602ff171a5d735ad/?fbclid=IwAR0W4zCEgk8Qq-qswvvz1f-stqFLTSd8OeGpn0RJ_RNc4XTohSRJnrnr6cc.

———. "Counterpunching Like Trump, Biden Attacked Most of His Rivals on the Debate Stage. He Looked Weak." *The Washington Post* (August 1, 2019b). https://www.washingtonpost.com/news/powerpost/paloma/daily-202/2019/08/01/daily-202-counterpunching-like-trump-biden-attacked-most-of-his-rivals-on-the-debate-stage-he-looked-weak/5d42804c88e0fa1454f800e2/?fbclid=IwAR3JVtAjzr3DNbkG8HynhsG8moGbl2yPB_uYXhFrUzUqdyRw1b_ZjC8i_Uo.

Hook, Janet. "A Kennedy Loses in Massachusetts and a Storied Dynasty Fades." *The Los Angeles Times* (September 1, 2020). https://www.latimes.com/politics/story/2020-09-01/a-kennedy-loses-in-massachusetts-and-a-storied-dynasty-fades.

———. "The Burden of a 40-Year Career: Some of Joe Biden's Record Doesn't Age Well." *The Los Angeles Times* (March 18, 2019). https://www.latimes.com/politics/la-na-pol-biden-senate-record-controversies-20190318-story.html.

Horger, Marc. "Breaking Up Is Hard to Do: America's Love Affair with the Two-Party System." *Origins: Current Events in Historical Perspective 6, no.* 10 (July 2013). https://origins.osu.edu/article/breaking-hard-do-americas-love-affair-two-party-system.

House, Billy. "Pelosi Faces Challenges of Slim Majority and Party Divisions." *Bloomberg* (November 16, 2020). https://www.bloomberg.com/news/articles/2020-11-16/pelosi-faces-challenges-of-slim-majority-and-party-divisions?fbclid=IwAR0JtvxnUpwLpiDmfypMf_9zewR-EKwsqkkLQEaT4F3bqa8HiYZDyCQ7qYQ.

Hurt, Alyson. "2020 Presidential Candidates: Tracking Which Democrats Ran." NPR (January 31, 2019). https://www.npr.org/2019/01/31/689980506/which-democrats-are-running-in-2020-and-which-still-might.

Igielnik, Ruth, Scott Keeter and Hannah Hartig. "Behind Biden's 2020 Victory." *Pew Research Center* (June 30, 2021). https://www.pewresearch.org/politics/2021/06/30/behind-bidens-2020-victory/?utm.

"In a Politically Polarized Era, Sharp Divides in Both Partisan Coalitions." *Pew Research Center* (December 17, 2019). https://www.people-press.org/2019/12/17/in-a-politically-polarized-era-sharp-divides-in-both-partisan-coalitions/.

"Internet/Broadband Fact Sheet." *Pew Research Center* (June 12, 2019). https://www.pewresearch.org/internet/fact-sheet/internet-broadband/.

"Is It Possible to Expand The Supreme Court?" NPR (September 21, 2020). https://www.npr.org/2020/09/21/915381446/is-it-possible-to-expand-the-supreme-court.

Iyengar, Shanto, Yphtach Lelkes, Matthew Levendusky, Neil Malhotra, and Sean J. Westwood. "The Origins and Consequences of Affective Polarization in the United States." *Annual Review of Political Science* 22 (2019): 129–146. https://doi.org/10.1146/annurev-polisci-051117-073034.

Izadi, Elahe, and Kayla Epstein. "'Squad' Jumped From Pop Culture to Become the Most Politically Polarizing Word of the Year." *The Washington Post* (July 27, 2019). https://www.washingtonpost.com/lifestyle/style/squad-jumped-from-pop-culture-to-become-the-most-politically-polarizing-word-of-the-year/2019/07/27/6cfdd468-acbb-11e9-a0c9-6d2d7818f3da_story.html.

Jackson, David. "'Tribalism is a Hell of a Drug.' Trump Impeachment Trial Reopens GOP Battle Lines Even as He is Acquitted." *USA Today* (February 13, 2021). https://www.msn.com/en-us/news/politics/tribalism-is-a-hell-of-a-drug-trump-impeachment-trial-reopens-gop-battle-lines-even-as-he-is-acquitted/ar-BB1dEQIG?ocid=entnewsntp&item=flights%3Aprg-enterpriseblended-t%2C1s-ent-microsoft.

Jacobs, Ben. "Why 'Socialism' Killed Democrats in Florida." *Intelligencer* (November 17, 2020). https://nymag.com/intelligencer/2020/11/republican-socialism-attacks-haunt-democrats-in-florida.html.

Jarvie, Jenny, and Jennifer Haberkorn. "Georgia's Senate Candidates Run as Dynamic Duos. Will It Work?" *Los Angeles Times*, (November 18, 2020). https://www.latimes.com/politics/story/2020-11-18/georgia-senate-candidates-team-up-in-high-stakes-race-might-that-backfire.

Judkis, Maura. "In a Year of Political Anger, Undecided Voters Inspire a Special Kind of Scorn." *The Washington Post* (October 19, 2020). https://www.washingtonpost.com/lifestyle/style/undecided-voters-are-driving-people-crazy-they-might-decide-the-election/2020/10/16/53ebb3bc-0cac-11eb-b1e8-16b59b92b36d_story.html?fbclid=IwAR1bD9qjYFb4JZvV0xBCSBP4f5tjsj5XLyXXzmh98RuimOTTXDWCSHFW5qI.

Junger, Sebastian. *Tribe: On Homecoming and Belonging*. New York, NY: Twelve Publishing, 2016.

Jurkowitz, Mark, Amy Mitchell, Elisa Shearer, and Mason Walker. "U.S. Media Polarization and the 2020 Election: A Nation Divided." *Pew Research Center* (January 24, 2020). https://www.journalism.org/2020/01/24/u-s-media-polarization-and-the-2020-election-a-nation-divided/.

Kabaservice, Geoffrey. "The Forever Grievance." *The Washington Post* (December 4, 2020). https://www.washingtonpost.com/outlook/2020/12/04/tea-party-trumpism-conservatives-populism/?arc404=true.

Kahn, Michael. "Democrats Must Overcome the Tribalism of Their Campaigns." *The Salt Lake Tribune* (February 27, 2020). https://www.sltrib.com/opinion/commentary/2020/02/27/michael-kalm-democrats/.

"Kamala Harris & Mike Pence 2020 Vice Presidential Debate Transcript." *REV* (October 7, 2020). https://www.rev.com/blog/transcripts/kamala-harris-mike-pence-2020-vice-presidential-debate-transcri.

Kamarck, Elaine, and Alexander R. Podkul. "Political Polarization and Congressional Candidate in the 2018 Primaries." *Brookings* (October 23, 2018a). https://www.brookings.edu/multi-chapter-report/political-polarization-and-congressional-candidates-in-the-2018-primaries/?fbclid=IwAR32epoV0HnaBcZ5iV004mPaq8lX9BsChPjjlklqhCyoo7ixvm2D4GoBJsg.

———. "The 2018 Primaries Project: What are the internal divisions within each party?" *Brookings* (October 23, 2018b). https://www.brookings.edu/research/the-2018-primaries-project-what-are-the-internal-divisions-within-each-party/?fbclid=IwAR34SESBrqdc6b9-ckZ9E2Pa5dOQM8bZ7Z_2lu9RSWFv3BocmkyqHnp4fr8.

Kampf-Lassin, Miles. "They're Not Just Mad at AOC—They're Scared of Her." *Jacobin* (July 15, 2019). https://www.jacobinmag.com/2019/07/alexandria-ocasio-cortez-aoc-nancy-pelosi-democratic-party.

Kane, Tim, and Elad Yoran. "Two-Handed Bipartisanship—the Remedy for Political Tribalism." *The Hill* (February 1, 2021). https://thehill.com/opinion/white-house/536746-two-handed-bipartisanship-the-remedy-for-political-tribalism.

Kaplan, Thomas. "Bernie Sanders Rallies Progressives: 'This Election is About Preserving Our Democracy.'" *The New York Times* (August 28, 2020). https://www.nytimes.com/live/2020/08/17/us/dnc-convention?referringSource=articleShare&fbclid=IwAR2ADFJ6lwkprR7cxRzDGj3GLwSh1eTPUaHv8z5KPbDtqT3-7OhoEYZmWf4#bernie-sanders-rallies-progressives-this-election-is-about-preserving-our-democracy.

Kappes, Andreas, Ann H. Harvey, Terry Lohrenz, P. Read Montague, and Tali Sharot. "Confirmation Bias in the Utlilization of Others' Opinion Strength." *Nature Neuroscience* 23 (December 16, 2012): 130–137.

Kapur, Sahil. "'Bernie or Bust' Voters Create Predicament for Democrats in 2020." *Bloomberg* (April 17, 2019). https://www.bloomberg.com/news/articles/2019-04-17/-bernie-or-bust-voters-create-predicament-for-democrats-in-2020.

———. "'I Am Not Upset With Biden': Progressives Dismiss Trump's Effort To Splinter Democrats." NBC News (September 30, 2020). https://www.nbcnews.com/politics/2020-election/i-am-not-upset-biden-progressives-dismiss-trump-s-effort-n1241597.

Karim, Sameena. "The Co-Existence of Globalism and Tribalism: A Review of the Literature." *Journal of Research in International Education 11, no. 2 (2012)*: 137–151.

Karni, Annie. "The Crowded, Competitive World of Anti-Trump G.O.P. Groups." *The New York Times* (October 12, 2020). https://www.nytimes.com/2020/10/12/us/politics/never-trump-republicans.html?referringSource=articleShare&fbclid=IwAR01DY6SfT1KszeXqXMPY_OdVF9sem30MQu6YjRm2AtJd7MIW3nuDPMb4oU.

Kass, John. "Ginsburg's Death Puts Rule of Law and the Constitution on November Ballot." *Townhall.com* (April 16, 2020). https://townhall.com/columnists/johnkass/2020/09/24/ginsburgs-death-puts-rule-of-law-and-the-constitution-on-november-ballot-n2576758.

Kaufman, Alexander. "As Kamala Harris Defended Fracking, Mike Pence Painted Her As A Green Radical." *HUFFPOST* (October 8, 2020). https://www.huffpost.com/entry/vice-presidential-debate-climate-fracking_n_5f7e8129c5b6a9322e22bc0d?fbclid=IwAR0FRIXUH8D8wc6stcd_dVVymSnSaoTRVnimBXfHcEvkC8xWESfgJ1Jd62o.

Keeter, Scott. "How We Know the Drop in Trump's Approval Rating in January Reflected a Real Shift in Public Opinion." *The Pew Research Center* (January 20, 2021). https://www.pewresearch.org/fact-tank/2021/01/20/how-we-know-the-drop-in-trumps-approval-rating-in-january-reflected-a-real-shift-in-public-opinion.

Keith, Tamara. "Research Challenges Assumptions on Why Voters Support Trump." NPR (August 22, 2016). https://www.npr.org/2016/08/22/490895567/research-challenges-assumptions-on-why-voters-support-trump.

Kelley, Colleen E. *A Rhetoric of Divisive Partisanship: The 2016 American Presidential Campaign Discourse of Bernie Sanders and Donald Trump.* New York: Lexington, 2018.

Kelly, Casey Ryan. "Donald J. Trump and the Rhetoric of Ressentiment." *Quarterly Journal of Speech,* 106, no. 1 (December 20, 2020): 2–24. https://doi.org/10.1080/00335630.2019.1698756.

Kemp, Simon. "Digital 2020: The United States of America." *DataReportal* (February 11, 2020). https://datareportal.com/reports/digital-2020-united-states-of-america#:~:text=There%20were%20288.1%20million%20internet,at%2087%25%20in%20January%202020.

Khalid, Asma. "Joe Biden Won The Primary. Now He's Trying To Win Over Progressive Groups." NPR (April 10, 2020). https://www.npr.org/2020/04/10/830853819/joe-biden-won-the-primary-now-hes-trying-to-win-over-progressive-groups?fbclid=IwAR0LiEm6bbdBgnekt1JFIg17oXweV9tJBQ7IUsMD5AxtFvQHo0xF2XLRbvMBooks.

King, Colbert I. "Democrats Must Support Each Other Before It's Too Late." *The Washington Post* (July 19, 2019). https://www.washingtonpost.com/opinions/democrats-must-support-each-other-before-its-too-late/2019/07/19/dc142840-a99e-11e9-86dd-d7f0e60391e9_story.html?fbclid=IwAR3j2I3tJ8uUbK6Y9YUFqOetkSIhl5eI_aN4kvLSEFNCc63XeaenuBi8P6A.

Klein, Ezra. *Why We're Polarized.* New York, NY: Avid Reader Press, 2020.

Kornacki, Steve. "No Collusion Won't Re-elect Trump." *THE WEEK* (April 19, 2019): 1.

———. *The Red and the Blue: The 1990s and the Birth of Political Tribalism.* New York: Harper Collins Publishers, 2018.

Kraybill, Jeanine. *Unconventional, Partisan, and Polarizing Rhetoric: How the 2016 Election Shaped the Way Candidate Strategize, Engage and Communicate.* Lanham, MD: Lexington, 2018.

Krieg, Gregory. "Bernie Sanders seeks support from allies in push to lead Biden's Labor Department." CNN (November 10, 2020). https://www.cnn.com/2020/11/10/politics/bernie-sanaders-joe-biden-labor-department/index.html?fbclid=IwAR2TeMQjWbKHNakv6bwrpL74dLtJqAPDf53r5yqR4F3ynSKGYVp2c5jg32U.

Krippendorff, Klaus, and Nour Halabi. *Discourses in Action: What Language Enables Us to Do.* New York, NY: Routledge, 2020.

Kruger, Justin, and David Dunning. "Unskilled and Unaware of It: How Difficulties in Recognizing One's Own Incompetence Lead to Inflated Self-Assessment." *Journal of Personality and Social Psychology* 77, no. 6 (1999): 1121–1134. https://citeseerx.ist.psu.edu/viewdoc/summary?doi=10.1.1.64.2655.

Krugman, Paul. "Bernie Sanders Isn't a Socialist." *The New York Times* (February 13, 2020). https://www.nytimes.com/2020/02/13/opinion/bernie-sanders-socialism.html.

Kuhn, David Paul. "Woke-Lash: Should the Cultural Left Check its Privilege?" *Newsweek* (December 15, 2020). https://www.newsweek.com/woke-lash-should-cultural-left-check-its-privilege-opinion-1553944.

Kurtzleben, Danielle. "Supporters Ultimately Voted For Trump." NPR (August 24, 2017). https://www.npr.org/2017/08/24/545812242/1-in-10-sanders-primary-voters-ended-up-supporting-trump-survey-finds.

Kurtzleben, Danielle, and Kenny Malone. "What You Need To Know About The Democratic Socialists Of America." *NPR* (June 26, 2018). https://www.npr.org/2018/07/26/630960719/what-you-need-to-know-about-the-democratic-socialists-of-america.

Lai, K.K. Rebecca, and Karen Yourish. "The Insults Trump Has Hurled at 2020 Democrats." *The New York Times* (May 26, 2019). https://www.nytimes.com/interactive/2019/05/26/us/politics/trump-tweets-democrats.html?smid=nytcore-ios-share&fbclid=IwAR3aTQVB-6AnZvW9Eg2t5N_Q_BNPGaYPtpRfsSZq4goU_DutMb-7Vv_9vL8.

Leader, Lauren. "Why Dems Have a Duty to Consider Backing Sanders." *USA Today* (October 17, 2019). https://amp.usatoday.com/amp/3997594002?fbclid=IwAR1Cj_PZmv0ExazW2LEjhCP4Cnf_LpmTDnqFWOQ40AiH2IcWfAAcshvKOA4.

Leatherby, Lauren, Arielle Ray, Anjeli Singhvi, Christiaan Tribert, Derek Watkins, and Haley Willis. "How a Presidential Rally Turned Into a Capitol Rampage." *The New York Times* (January 12, 2021). https://www.nytimes.com/interactive/2021/01/12/us/capitol-mob-timeline.html.

LeBlanc, Steve. "Kennedy Loses Senate Bid; Race for His House Seat is Tight." *AP News* (September 2, 2020). https://apnews.com/article/virus-outbreak-ri-state-wire-ap-top-news-politics-ma-state-wire-482019e7f5449dc6efb22fb7178c8ec0.

Le Miere, Jason. "Bernie Sanders Voters Helped Trump Win and Here's Proof." *Newsweek* (August 23, 2017). https://www.newsweek.com/bernie-sanders-trump-2016-election-654320.

Lepore, Jill. "The Party Crashers: Is the New Populism About the Medium or the Message?" *The New Yorker* (February 14, 2016). https://www.newyorker.com/magazine/2016/02/22/did-social-media-produce-the-new-populism?irclickid=38NWTjVV1xyOWpmwUx0Mo38LUkByvAyn0yEy380&irgwc=1&source=affiliate_impactpmx_12f6tote_desktop_Bing%20Rebates%20by%20Microsoft&utm_source=impact-affiliate&utm_medium=2003851&utm_campaign=impact&utm_content=Logo&utm_brand=tny.

Lerer, Lisa. "Amy Klobuchar's Big Idea: Bipartisan Appeal Can Beat Trump." *The New York Times* (April 22, 2019). https://www.nytimes.com/2019/04/22/us/politics/amy-klobuchar-2020-president.html?smid=nytcore-ios-share&fbclid=IwAR291E8CQnQk4oAZMz1II5ciSyTnUK4tq_7Fm7Pj01gbwHD3NPIJvUFLdqE.

———. "Liberals Are Furious. Their Standard-Bearer Wants to Hold Back." *The New York Times* (September 29, 2020a). https://www.nytimes.com/2020/09/29/us/politics/supreme-court-joe-biden.html?fbclid=IwAR2Qi-zM8MZvHqn7WIlZn-3P0cmX56dPfEyOYtuajSDntHQ7tP42hpRrCtKw.

———. "On Politics: We Could Be Here Awhile." *The New York Times* (February 12, 2020b). https://www.nytimes.com/2020/02/1/us/politics/on-politics-primary-slog.html.

———. "What Did New York's Primaries Mean for Progressives? It's Complicated." *The New York Times* (June 24, 2021). https://www.nytimes.com/2021/06/24/nyregion/maya-wiley-progressive-nyc-primary.html?searchResultPosition=3.

——— and Sydney Ember. "'Nobody Likes Him': Hillary Clinton Risks a Party Split Over Bernie Sanders." *The New York Times* (January 21, 2020). https://www.nytimes.com/2020/01/21/us/politics/hillary-clinton-bernie-sanders.html.

Levendusky, Matthew, and Dominik Stecula. *We Need to Talk: How Cross-Party Dialogue Reduces Affective Polarization.* Cambridge UK: Cambridge University Press, 2021a. https://doi.org/10.7910/DVN/K0YKHD.

———. "Why There's Hope for Joe Biden's Quest to Unify America Will Work." *USA Today* (January 21, 2021b).

Levitz, Eric. "Moderate Democrats 'Delusions' of 'Prudence' Will Kill Us All." *The New Yorker* (May 22, 2019). http://nymag.com/intelligencer/2019/05/moderate-democrats-delusions-2020-senate-climate-democracy-crisis.html.

Li, Roland, and Chase DiFeliciantonio. "Trump Resumes Tweeting as Facebook, Twitch, You Tube Threaten Permanent Bans." *The San Francisco Chronicle* (January 7, 2021). https://www.sfchronicle.com/business/article/Facebook-suspends-Trump-until-at-least-Jan-20-15853125.

Liasson, Mara. "Is Joe Biden Too Centrist For Today's Democratic Party?" NPR (April 22, 2019). https://www.npr.org/2019/04/22/715875291/is-joe-biden-too-centrist-for-todays-democratic-party.

Linskey, Annie. "Biden's Flexibility on Policy Could Mean Fierce Fights If He Wins." *The Washington Post* (September 7, 2020b). https://www.washingtonpost.com/politics/bidens-flexibility-on-policy-could-mean-bloody-fights-if-he-wins/2020/09/06/b8d66c3c-e622-11ea-bc79-834454439a44_story.html.

———. "Two Liberal Groups Offer Tempered Endorsements of Joe Biden." *The Washington Post* (August 13, 2020c). https://www.washingtonpost.com/elections/2020/08/13/trump-biden-live-updates/?p9w22b2p=b2p22p9w00098&no_nav=true&fbclid=IwAR1qDxQjJy7_6NDR-uYPcM30B9yYWShnHRUL-2sxdUB_Y7rRqdaKpuTm2WPI#link-YAANEVA53RDDPP6AO7QYC6B6BY.

Linskey, Annie, and Matt Viser. "Biden's Moderation Contrasts With Democratic Rage as Court Fight Looms." *The Washington Post* (September 21, 2020). https://www.washingtonpost.com/politics/

biden-trump-supreme-court-ginsburg/2020/09/21/140f205a-fc1a-11ea-8d05-9beaaa91c71f_story.html?fbclid=IwAR3RGojoOvuAYaEJn3oYx5KB8HjYgvZ90rHz4F3s7FlenZKgF8Mvp2FtPuQ.

Linskey, Annie, and Sean Sullivan. "Biden Tries To Spread Calm, As Some Democrats Worry About His Willingness to Fight." *The Washington Post* (November 26, 2020). https://www.washingtonpost.com/politics/biden-transition-conciliatory-tone/2020/11/25/aacd4ed6-29bf-11eb-8fa2-06e7cbb145c0_story.html?fbclid=IwAR0JUpcVTDCZ1sJFDB85VNk1Mv-J9driP_0YVujbH2HaZYkWmpvYAnnxf_Y.

Lipton, Eric, and Kenneth P. Vogel. "Progressives Are Pressing Biden to Limit Corporate Influences in His Administration." *The New York Times* (November 12, 2020). https://www.nytimes.com/live/2020/11/12/us/joe-biden-trump?fbclid=IwAR1ADdIu7Dg__QLPAqEceaAKBgR7LuJCkELFD9KYNH5wRuquqJxXfIexBqs#progressives-are-pressing-biden-to-limit-corporate-influence-in-his-administration.

Lizza, Ryan, Laura Barron-Lopez, and Holly Otterbein. "Why Biden Is Rejecting Black Lives Matter's Boldest Proposals." *Politico* (June 26, 2020). https://www.politico.com/news/magazine/2020/06/26/joe-biden-refuses-get-woke-will-the-democratic-base-still-embrace-him-340753.

Lockhart, Joe. "Democrats' All-out Battle Over Who Deserves Credit for Biden Win." CNN (November 10, 2020). https://www.cnn.com/2020/11/10/opinions/democrats-battle-credit-biden-election-win-lockhart/index.html?fbclid=IwAR2fAZYllULVm9k4aqCUGxsKehkSIIQotjLheAWDxMmuXEXAYNd5UVNgVtc.

Lockie, Alex. "Trump Rails Against 'Radical Socialist' Democrats in Blistering Op-Ed." *Business Insider* (October 10, 2018). http://businessinsider.com/trump-oped-usa-today-radical-socialist-democrats-2018-10.

Lorenz, Taylor. "James Madison Would Be Horrified by a Tweeting President." *The Atlantic* (June 25, 2018). https://www.theatlantic.com/technology/archive/2018/06/james-madison-jeffrey-rosen-national-constitution-center/563675/.

Lorenzo-Reich, Nina M., and Dana Cloud. "The Uncivil Tongue: Invitational Rhetoric and the Problem of Inequality." *Western Journal of Speech* Communication 73, no. 2 (2009): 220-226.

Lybrand, Holmes, and Tara Subramaniam. "Fact Check: Is Kamala Harris the Most Liberal Member of the Senate?" CNN (August 17, 2020). https://www.cnn.com/2020/08/17/politics/kamala-harris-most-liberal-senator-fact-check/index.html.

Lynch, Michael. "Bernie Sanders Channels Donald Trump With His Green New Deal." *Forbes* (August 23, 2019). https://www.forbes.com/sites/michaellynch/2019/08/23/bernie-sanders-channels-donald-trump-with-his-green-new-deal/amp/?fbclid=IwAR3sDWgvet63E7gr7ESOYN5zjM2cJDGIG6RV6oGLDR-888ARGgKh0h4xbTM.

Lynch, Suzanne. "Joe Biden May Be More Left-Wing as President Than Expected." *The Irish Times* (November 9, 2020). https://www.irishtimes.com/opinion/joe-biden-may-be-more-left-wing-as-president-than-expected-1.4403814?mode=sample&auth-failed=1&pw-origin=https%3A%2F%2F.

Madden, Heather. "The Outsiders: Public Discontent and a New Class of Presidential Hopefuls." *The American Spectator* (September 28, 2015). https://www.iwv.org/

detail.php?c=2798293&t=The-Outsiders%3A-Public-discontent-and-a-new-class-of-Presidential-hopefuls.

Madison, James. "Excerpts from *Federalist #10.*" The Bill of Rights Institute (November 22, 1787). https://docs-of-freedom.s3.amazonaws.com/uploads/document/attachment/448/Federalist_No_10_Excerpts_Annotated_proof_3__1_.pdf.

Mahdawi, Arwa. "Nancy Pelosi's Renewed Attacks on AOC Aren't Just Disrespectful, They're Dangerous." *The Guardian* (July 12, 2019). https://www.theguardian.com/commentisfree/2019/jul/12/nancy-pelosis-renewed-attacks-on-aoc-arent-just-disrespectful-theyre-dangerous.

Malone, Clare. "The Young Left's Anti-Capitalist Manifesto." *FiveThirtyEight* (January 22, 2019). https://fivethirtyeight.com/features/the-young-lefts-anti-capitalist-manifesto.

Manium, Shiva, and Samantha Smith. "A Wider Partisan and Ideological Gap Between Younger, Older Generations." *Pew Research Center* (March 20, 2017). https://www.pewresearch.org/fact-tank/2017/03/20/a-wider-partisan-and-ideological-gap-between-younger-older-generations/.

Marsh, Sarah. "'I Never Thought Trump Would Win': Meet the Americans Who Chose Not to Vote." *The Guardian* (2016). https://www.theguardian.com/commentisfree/2016/nov/18/donald-trump-win-americans-not-vote.

Martin, James. *Politics and Rhetoric: A Critical Introduction*. London: Routledge, 2013.

Martin, Jonathan. "A Fight Over Agriculture Secretary Could Decide the Direction of Hunger Policy." *The New York Times,* (November 26, 2020a).

———. "A Major Fear for Democrats: Will the Party Come Together by November?" *The New York Times* (January 24, 2020b). https://www.nytimes.com/2020/01/24/us/politics/democratic-party-unity-primary.html?fbclid=IwAR3Qsbv0x6EwRXGwomXjQzLbGIcWX4VZ-ituxgSn_QzIrw0wXw0_qe0eLPw.

———. "Trumpism Grips a Post-Policy G.O.P. as Traditional Conservatism Fades." *The New York Times* (March 1, 2021). https://www.nytimes.com/2021/03/01/us/politics/trump-republicans-policy.htm.

Martin, Jonathan, and Alexander Burns. "Biden Comes Under Attack From All Sides in Democratic Debate." *The New York Times* (June 27, 2019). https://www.nytimes.com/2019/06/27/us/politics/democratic-debate-recap.html?smid=nytcore-ios-share&fbclid=IwAR289XCB-XHZlxyXkBU2-nLEy4jrpzHqdaLPfhXs8v1j-AkiBVr7RoE8SV4.

———. "Biden Revives Campaign, Winning Nine States, But Sanders Takes California." *The New York Times* (March 3, 2020). https://www.nytimes.com/2020/03/03/us/politics/super-tuesday-primary-winners.html.

Martin, Jonathan, and Katie Glueck. "Biden Slashes Into Buttigieg: 'This Guy's Not a Barack Obama!'" *The New York Times* (February 8, 2020). https://www.nytimes.com/2020/02/08/us/politics/biden-buttigieg-sanders-new-hampshire.html?referringSource=articleShare&fbclid=IwAR1TibcBN-p8Al2zs7hzp3n1-HEi0OJIeBsLEWyTEXQbG8zYdCrMeOKBaFo.

Martin, Jonathan, and Sydney Ember. "Bernie Sanders-Style Politics Are Defining 2020 Race, Unnerving Moderates." *The New York Times* (March 9, 2019). https://

www.nytimes.com/2019/03/09/us/politics/bernie-sanders-2020-election-democrats.html.

Martina, Michael, and John Whitesides. "Sanders to Discuss Campaign After Sweeping Biden Victories." *Reuters* (March 11, 2020). https://news.trust.org/item/20200311160540-5w8qw.

Masket, Seth. "The GOP Doesn't Seem To Be Cracking Up In Down-Ballot Races." FiveThirtyEight (May 9, 2016). https://fivethirtyeight.com/features/the-gop-doesnt-seem-to-be-cracking-up-in-down-ballot-races/.

Mason, Lilliana. *Uncivil Agreement: How Politics Became Our Identity.* Chicago, IL: University of Chicago Press, 2018.

Mason, Melanie. "Biden and Harris Play Defense: Five Takeaways From Night 2 of the Democratic Debate." *Los Angeles Times* (July 31, 2019). https://www.latimes.com/politics/story/2019-07-31/democratic-debate-harris-biden-takeaways-night-two?fbclid=IwAR240_30-5uy8_7-RDw7C7Barrds6q0NKNak5HhklTBHzthaEGMi9RXrc20.

Matthews, Chris. "The Anti-Trump Coalition Biden Must Hold Together." *The San Francisco Chronicle* (December 12, 2020). https://www.sfchronicle.com/opinion/openforum/article/The-anti-Trump-coalition-Biden-must-hold-together-15795791.php.

Mayhew, David. "Robert A. Dahl: Questions, Concepts, Proving It." Department of Political Science, Yale University, (2015). https://politicalscience.yale.edu/sites/default/files/2015-02-25_-_dahl_-_questions_concepts_proving_it.pdf.

McCarthy, Daniel. "Why Trump Holds a Grip on the G.O.P." *The New York Times* (March 1, 2021). https://www.nytimes.com/2021/03/01/opinion/donald-trump-republican-party.htm.

McCarthy, Tom. "Alexandria Ocasio-Cortez Ends Truce By Warning 'Incompetent' Democratic Party." *The Guardian* (November 8, 2020). https://www.theguardian.com/us-news/2020/nov/08/alexandria-ocasio-cortez-ends-truce-by-warning-incompetent-democratic-party.

McChesney, Robert W. *Rich Media, Poor Democracy.* Urbana, IL: University of Chicago Press, 1999.

McEvoy, Jemima. "Gab CEO Denies Responsibility For Capitol Attack Amid Increased Scrutiny." *Forbes* (January 14, 2021). https://www.forbes.com/sites/jemimamcevoy/2021/01/14/gab-ceo-denies-responsibility-for-capitol-attack-amid-increased-scrutiny/?sh=2b3c10d6c845.

McLaughlin, Jenna. "Biden Caught Between Progressives and National Security Veterans on CIA Pick." *Yahoo!News* (December 2, 2020). https://news.yahoo.com/biden-caught-between-progressives-and-national-security-veterans-on-cia-pick-163707860.html.

McLuhan, Marshall and Q. Fiore. *The Medium is the Massage: An Inventory of Effects.* San Francisco, CA: HardWired, 1996.

McManus, Doyle. "Column: Ignore Trump's Warnings—Biden and Harris Are Not Radicals." *Los Angeles Times* (August 16, 2020). https://www.latimes.com/politics/story/2020-08-16/ignore-trumps-warnings-biden-and-harris-are-no-radicals?fbclid=IwAR0HRmhqVpTjg6_0dZK8mN4QCVpBXMG8wQlLo_.

McNally, Katie. "The Third-Party Impact on American Politics." *UVA Today* (August 3, 2016). https://news.virginia.edu/content/third-party-impact-american-politics.

Meadows, Paul. "The Semiotic of Kenneth Burke." *Philosophy and Phenomenological Research* 18 no. 1 (September 1957): 80–87.

Medhurst, Martin, and James Arnt Aune. *American Political Rhetoric: Essential Speeches and Writings On Founding Principles and Contemporary Controversies.* Lanham, MD: Rowman and Littlefield, 2010.

———. *The Prospect of Presidential Rhetoric.* College Station, TX: Texas A&M University Press, 2008.

Medina, Jennifer. "Obama Urges Democrats to 'Chill Out' About 2020 Presidential Field." *The New York Times* (November 21, 2019). https://www.nytimes.com/2019/11/21/us/politics/obama-2020-democrats.html?smid=nytcore-ios-share&fbclid=IwAR3aRTtmWmlIgP0ivALPFQO4rMu7oy1zvyH6jklZvauOT9CtmQqyvuEk64c.

Megerian, Chris. "Conservative Media Provide Soft Landing for Trump's Election Lies." *Los Angeles Times* (February 17, 2021). https://www.latimes.com/politics/story/2021-02-17/trump-reemerges-with-flurry-of-on-conservative-tv-and-repeats-election-lies.

Mendenhall, Allen. "Tribalism By Any Other Name." *Academic Questions 31, no. 3* (2018): 360–367. doi: 10.1007/s12129-018-9712-6.

"Mike Capuano: Senior Urban Leadership Fellow." Boston University Initiative on Cities (February 2. 2021). https://www.bu.edu/ioc/profile/rep-mike-capuano/.

Milbank, Dana. "Bernie Sanders Has Emerged as the Donald Trump of the Left." *The Washington Post* (April 2, 2019a). https://www.washingtonpost.com › opinions › 2019/04/02.

———. "The Racism Stops When Trump Goes Back to the Place From Which He Came." *The Washington Post* (July 15, 2019b). https://www.washingtonpost.com/opinions/trump-has-done-the-impossible-he-has-united-the-democrats/2019/07/15/58da67aa-a741-11e9-86dd-d7f0e60391e9_story.

———. "Why the Democratic Establishment Fears Bernie Sanders." *The Washington Post* (February 19, 2016). https://www.washingtonpost.com/opinions/why-the-democratic-establishment-fears-bernie-sanders/2016/02/19/2323482e-d70c-11e5-be55-2cc3c1e4b76b_story.html.

Miller, Carolyn R., and Amy J. Devitt, Eds. *Landmark Essays on Rhetorical Genre Studies* (2018). https://www.routledge.com/Landmark-Essays-on-Rhetorical-Genre-Studies/Miller-Devitt/p/book/9781138047709.

Miller, Daniel. "Andrew Jackson: The American Franchise." UMiller Center (2021). https://millercenter.org/president/jackson/the-american-franchise.

Miller, Jared T. "The Psychology of Tribalism." *New York Magazine* (September 26, 2017). https://nymag.com/intelligencer/2017/09/the-psychology-of-tribalism.html?fbclid=IwAR2uDXeBbNM2Hzvc_PffEwx0TkMBONY15TCjH6JkQo525YK-CPAWx-aL920.

Mitchem, Stephanie Y. *Race, Religion and Politics: Toward Human Rights in the United States.* Lanham, MD: Rowman and Littlefield, 2019.

Mitsotakis, Kyriakos. "Interview with Kyriaskos Mitsotakis." By Fareed Zakaria. *Fareed Zakaria GPS*, CNN (July 21, 2019). http://transcripts.cnn.com/TRANSCRIPTS/1907/21/fzgps.01.html.

Mondschein, Jared. "Biden's Job Gets Easier After Senate Wins in Georgia—But Don't Expect a Progressive Revolution." *The Conversation* (January 7, 2021). https://theconversation.com/bidens-job-gets-easier-after-senate-wins-in-georgia-but-dont-expect-a-progressive-revolution-152176.

Montanaro, Domenico. "5 Takeaways From Super Tuesday and Joe Biden's Big Night." NPR (March 4, 2020a). https://www.npr.org/2020/03/04/811868704/5-takeaways-from-super-tuesday-and-joe-bidens-big-night.

———. "The 2020 Election Was A Good One For Republicans Not Named Trump." NPR (November 11, 2020b). https://www.npr.org/2020/11/11/933435840/the-2020-election-was-a-good-one-for-republicans-not-named-trump.

Mounk, Yascha. "America Is Not a Democracy." *The Atlantic* (March 2018a). https://amp.theatlantic.com/amp/article/550931/?fbclid=IwAR0_jcKU0cic3iy8FtMXxrE0QfglcFaKk_3u4-RQc0-rhyWkUuxM7LR7P2k.

———. "The Red and the Brown." *Slate* (May 11, 2018b). https://slate.com/news-and-politics/2018/05/the-far-left-and-far-right-find-it-astonishingly-easy-to-unite.html?fbclid=IwAR2YSr-fBhhuJyG69c3QbRbJf0-8CQybNbgB6lqvem-fRslncaxj7e3MYyv4.

Muller, Alana, Lindsey A. Sirianni, and Richard J. Addante. "Neural Correlates of the Dunning-Kruger Effect." *The European Journal of Neuroscience* (August 6, 2020). https://doi.org/10.1111/ejn.14935.

Mungai, Christine. "Pundits Who Decry 'Tribalism' Know Nothing About Real Tribes." *The Washington Post* (January 30, 2019). https://www.washingtonpost.com/outlook/pundits-who-decry-tribalism-know-nothing-about-real-tribes/2019/01/29/8d14eb44-232f-11e9-90cd-dedb0c92dc17_story.html.

Murdock, Deroy. "Joe Biden: Centrist?" *The National Review* (May 17, 2019). https://www.nationalreview.com/2019/05/joe-biden-centrist/.

Murphy, Mark. "The Dunning-Kruger Effect Shows Why Some People Think They're Great Even When Their Work Is Terrible." *Forbes* (January 24, 2017). https://www.forbes.com/sites/markmurphy/2017/01/24/the-dunning-kruger-effect-shows-why-some-people-think-theyre-great-even-when-their-work-is-terrible/?sh=6959c0315d7c.

Murray, Stephanie. "AOC Stars in Markey's New TV Ad." *Politico* (July 30, 2020a). https://www.politico.com/newsletters/massachusetts-playbook/2020/07/30/ocasio-cortez-featured-in-markes-new-tv-ad-beacon-hill-to-extend-lawmaking-calendar-officials-dont-plant-mystery-seeds-489924.

———. "Why Joe Kennedy's Senate Campaign Flopped." *Politico* (September 2, 2020b). https://www.politico.com/news/2020/09/02/joe-kennedy-senate-campaign-failed-408033.

Mutnick, Ally. "The House Members Already Facing the Redistricting Chopping Block." *Politico* (November 30, 2020). https://www.politico.com/news/2020/11/30/house-congressional-redistricting-danger-441313.

Nagle, Molly. "Joe Biden Says He's 'Not a Fan' of 'Court Packing' as SCOTUS Hearings Continue." ABC News (October 13, 2020). https://abcnews.go.com/Politics/joe-biden-fan-court-packing-scotus-hearings-continue/story?id=73585081.

National Election Pool 2020 Election Day Coverage. Edison Research (November 3, 2020). https://www.edisonresearch.com/election-polling/.

"National Exit Polls: How Different Groups Voted." *The New York Times* (November 3, 2020). https://www.nytimes.com/interactive/2020/11/03/us/elections/exit-polls-president.html.

NBC News Exit Poll. "Latino Voters in Florida Shift Toward Trump." NBC News (November 3, 2020). https://www.nbcnews.com/politics/2020-election/blog/election-day-2020-live-updates-n1245892/ncrd1246223#blogHeader.

"Nearly Half of Republicans and Democrats Say 'Too Extreme' Describes Own Party Very or Somewhat Well." Pew Research Center (October 10, 2019). https://www.people-press.org/2019/10/10/the-partisan-landscape-and-views-of-the-parties/pp_2019-10-10_state-of-parties_1-08/.

Needleman, Sarah E., and Georgia Wells. "Twitter, Facebook and Others Silenced Trump. Now They Learn What's Next." *The Wall Street Journal* (January 14, 2021). https://www.wsj.com/articles/twitter-facebook-and-others-silenced-trump-now-they-learn-whats-next-11610320064.

Nesse, Randolph M., ed. *Evolution and the Capacity for Commitment.* New York, NY: Russell Sage Foundation, 2001.

Neumann, Peter R. "Options and Strategies for Countering Online Radicalization in the United States." *Studies in Conflict and Terrorism* 36, no. 6 (2013): 431–459. https://doi.org/10.1080/1057610X.2013.784568.

Newman, Elizabeth. "Far-right Extremists Went Mainstream Under Trump: The Capitol Attack Cements His Legacy." *USA Today* (February 15, 2021). https://www.usatoday.com/story/opinion/2021/02/15/capitol-riots-have-lasting-impact-domestic-terrorism-column/6709778002.

Newport, Frank. "Democrats More Positive About Socialism Than Capitalism." *Gallop* (August 13, 2018). https://news.gallup.com/poll/240725/democrats-positive-socialism-capitalism.aspx.

Nguyen, Tina, and Mark Scott. "Right-wing Extremist Chatter Spreads on New Platforms as Threat of Political Violence Ramps Up." *Politico* (January 6, 2021). https://www.politico.com/news/2021/01/12/right-wing-extremist-social-media-458387.

Nichols, John. "Republicans Won't Stop Screaming 'Socialism' Until Democrats Stop Cowering." *The Nation* (August 28, 2020). https://www.thenation.com/article/politics/republican-convention-socialism/.

———. "The Alexandria Ocasio-Cortez Effect." *The Nation* (August 15, 2018). https://www.thenation.com/article/archive/the-alexandria-ocasio-cortez-effect/.

Nickerson, Raymond. "Confirmation Bias: A Ubiquitous Phenomenon in Many Guises." *Review of General Psychology* 2, no. 2 (1998): 175–220.

Nilsen, Ella. "A New Generation of Black Progressives Has Been Elected to Congress." *VOX* (November 4, 2020). https://www.vox.com/2020/11/4/21538719/cori-bush-ritchie-torres-jamaal-bowman-election-results.

Nwanevu, Osita. "Joe Biden's Cabinet Is a Lost Cause for the Left." *The New Republic* (November 13, 2020). https://newrepublic.com/article/160432/biden-cabinet-progressive-defeat-2020.

"Ocasio-Cortez Says Biden Picking Rahm Emanuel for His Cabinet Would Be 'Hostile' to Progressives." *Haaretz* (November 23, 2020). https://www.haaretz.com/world-news/ocasio-cortez-calls-biden-putting-rahm-emanuel-in-cabinet-hostile-to-progressives-1.9304444.

"Official 2016 Presidential General Election Results." Federal Election Commission (January 30, 2017). https://transition.fec.gov/pubrec/fe2016/2016presgeresults.pdf.

Oliphant, J. Baxter. "6 facts about Democrats in 2019." Pew Research Center (June 27, 2019). https://www.pewresearch.org/fact-tank/.

———. "The Iraq War Continues to Divide the U.S. Public, 15 Years After It Began." Pew Research Center (March 19, 2018). https://www.pewresearch.org/fact-tank/2018/03/19/iraq-war-continues-to-divide-u-s-public-15-years-after-it-began/.

Olsen, Henry. "Ilhan Omar is the Steve Kind of the Left." *The Washington Post* (March 4, 2019). https://www.washingtonpost.com/opinions/2019/03/04/ilhan-omar-is-steve-king-left/?fbclid=IwAR27giX1vktBe544FsXOqJpDLjGG-1j6a395d1IciQMTUIh6H-9MYAyFgOk.

———. "Opinion: Democrats Are Trying to Appease Left-Wing Revolutionaries." *The Washington Post* (August 11, 2020). https://www.washingtonpost.com/opinions/2020/08/11/democrats-are-trying-appease-left-wing-revolutionaries-it-wont-work/?fbclid=IwAR1roBzrgJv-w9ouYKUloP74GmGELYMJ6lw-0WX71Waee3_mSwtR_xsU_OPM.

"On This Day, the First Democratic Party Convention." Constitution Daily (May 21, 2020). https://constitutioncenter.org/blog/on-this-day-the-first-democratic-party-convention.

Orr, Gabby. "Inside Donald Trump's Reelection Campaign, Joe Biden is a Shadow of the Past." *Politico* (February 1, 2020). https://www.politico.com/amp/news/2020/02/10/trump-dream-scenario-dem-disarray-2020-112946?fbclid=IwAR0k7uhjxwdNdQGCtNtLvh7EQXItQPEm-wrH7Zme7jMg1Jl4noIWtnVp-6k.

Osnos, Evan. "Can Biden's Center Hold?" *The New Yorker* (August 23, 2020a). https://www.newyorker.com/magazine/2020/08/31/can-bidens-center-hold?fbclid=IwAR2gqDzDLvDAzlwdY8-r7y4gC9fTOnh2khJJmGqy7eI11Vd4547LsNDcOzQ.

———. *Joe Biden: American Dreamer*. New York, NY: Scribner, 2020b.

Ott, Brian L. "The Age of Twitter: Donald J. Trump and the Politics of Debasement." *Critical Studies in Media Communication* 34 no.1 (2016): 59–68.

Ott, Brian L., and Greg Dickinson. *The Twitter Presidency: Donald J. Trump and the Politics of White Rage*. New York, NY: Routledge, 2019.

Otterbein, Holly. "Schumer Quietly Nails Down the Left Amid AOC Primary Chatter." *Politico* (February 1, 2021). https://www.politico.com/news/2021/02/01/chuch-schumer-aoc-senate-464255.

Pace, Julie. "Analysis: Democrats Strain For Civility, Contrasts Burst Through." *Associated Press News* (January 15, 2020). https://apnews.com/209a67424383f5

628171c46519497644?fbclid=IwAR3B6FhXwNKXir4sm8Pmxhz8zTrqb23O61NQO4K929loK3R1leUsEtdrm5k.

Packer, George. "A New Report Offers Insight Into Tribalism in the Age of Trump." *The New Yorker* (October 13, 2018). https://www.newyorker.com/news/daily-comment/a-new-report-offers-insights-into-tribalism-in-the-age-of-trump/amp?fbclid=IwAR1AY9Eo3bnoOib5W2__e6IN8j-tLlUZHevM8JwmO-liXryFpzwmy-OEUjc.

Parker, Ashley, and Robert Costa. "The Once-mocked 'Never Trump' Movement Becomes a Sudden Campaign Force." *The Washington Post* (July 11, 2020). https://www.washingtonpost.com/politics/the-once-mocked-never-trump-movement-becomes-a-sudden-campaign-force/2020/07/11/8683c14c-c1f3-11ea-b178-bb7b-05b94af1_story.html.

Parker, Kathleen. "If We're to Unite as a Country Again, we Need the Media's Cooperation." (November 27, 2020). https://www.washingtonpost.com/opinions/if-were-to-unite-as-a-country-again-we-need-the-medias-cooperation/2020/11/27/0d34828a-30e9-11eb-bae0-50bb17126614_story.html.

Parsons, Christi, and Lisa Mascaro. "Obama, Who Sought to Ease Partisanship, Saw it Worsen Instead." *Los Angeles Times* (January 14, 2017). https://www.latimes.com/projects/la-na-pol-obama-partisan/.

"Partisan Apathy: More Intense, More Personal." *Pew Research Report* (October 10, 2019). https://www.people-press.org/2019/10/10/partisan-antipathy-more-intense-more-personal/.

"Party Platform: The 2020 Democratic Platform." The Democratic National Committee (August 2020). https://democrats.org/where-we-stand/party-platform/.

Pasley, Jeffrey L. "The Two National 'Gazettes': Newspapers and the Embodiment of American Political Parties." *Early American Literature* 35, no. 1 (2000): 51–86.

Pateman, Carole. *Participation and Democratic Theory*. Cambridge, UK: Cambridge University Press, 1970.

Pedersen, Eric. "Cognitive Linguistics and Linguistic Relativity." *Oxford Handbooks Online* (September 2012). doi: 10.1093/oxfordhb/9780199738632.013.0038.

Peoples, Steve. 'Way Too Extreme': Some Democrats Warn Against Moving Left." *AP News* (September 24, 2019). https://apnews.com/55dddb1f5a7f428f9cc6354fea43e67e?fbclid=IwAR0MeNj_p52X3FB-1tGnv54DROfWawsuhdM71N-08Gz0sAwLUvBMCoLgFAk.

Peoples, Steve, and Alan Fram. "One Thing Unites Establishment Democrats: Fear of Sanders." *AP News* (February 17, 2020). https://apnews.com/4788e8a658d7934e38a389746a7c58c5?fbclid=IwAR2-38xzcYtbYk6A6PGix5orALcjfDS1AfSVrNQ9oyDUzQ7Ru6oiJuL7Qto.

Peoples, Steve, and Thomas Beaumont. "The Critical Fight Inside Democrats' Establishment Primary." *AP News* (February 2, 2020). https://apnews.com/683bb0205ef54eb29ace10917f26a177?fbclid=IwAR2gGD1AIx5dxPwtRzux4dXEpQRC5nN36s8Uu8dBeu_w8Va06t0waEmqL4A.

Peoples, Steve, Will Weissert, and Kevin Freking. "Biden, Trump Snipe From Road and Rails After Debate Chaos." *The New York Times* (September 30, 2020). https://apnews.com/article/450b2b1198279867938ff70b8ccfc0b1.

Perrrett, Connor. "Candidates Who've Dropped Out of the Presidential Race Are Endorsing Either Biden or Sanders." *Business Insider* (March 11, 2020). https://www.businessinsider.com/harris-endorsed-biden-heres-who-the-other-candidates-have-picked-2020-3.

Peters, Jeremy. "In Free-Range Trump, Many See Potential for a Third Party." *The New York Times* (September 11, 2017). https://www.nytimes.com/2017/09/11/us/politics/trump-third-party-republican.html.

———. "The Tea Party Didn't Get What It Wanted, but It Did Unleash the Politics of Anger." *The New York Times* (August 30, 2019). https://www.nytimes.com/2019/08/28/us/politics/tea-party-trump.html.

Peters, Jeremy, and Annie Karni. "Republicans Watch Fractious Democratic Debates and Like What They See." *The New York Times* (August 1, 2019). https://www.nytimes.com/2019/08/01/us/politics/debates-republican-reaction.html?smid=nytcore-ios-share&fbclid=IwAR23cfcqZ8hV2k_KKfgHI6ViF1WZG6f4I03Te9-x0yqljYnsVfyx7g6wxuI.

Pettypiece, Shannon. "Trump Advisers Say Their Ideal Democratic Primary Scenario is Taking Shape." *NBC News* (February 11, 2020). https://www.nbcnews.com/news/amp/ncna1133276?fbclid=IwAR37l-5623bjY9r2gmhZWkaa8Klp5-4_5zfNtxS_HqoqKRbESB-fG4k-zKA.

Phillips, Amber. "Four Reasons Bernie Sanders Waited So Long to Endorse Hillary Clinton." *The Washington Post* (July 15, 2016). https://www.washingtonpost.com/news/the-fix/wp/2016/07/12/four-reasons-bernie-sanders-waited-so-long-to-endorse-hillary-clinton/.

———. "Is Kamala Harris Really the Most Liberal Senator, as Trump Claims?" *The Washington Post* (August 13, 2020).

Pindell, James, and Victoria Graham. "Alexandria Ocasio-Cortez Endorse Markey for Relection." *The Boston Globe* (September 13, 2019). https://www.bostonglobe.com/metro/2019/09/13/aoc-endorses-markey-for-election/WT32VASrDLneIqIG24caeO/story.htlm.

"Political Polarization in the American Public." *Pew Research Center* (June 12, 2014). https://www.people-press.org/2014/06/12/political-polarization-in-the-american-public/.

"Political Typology Reveals Deep Fissures on the Right and Left." *Pew Research Center* (October 24, 2017). https://www.pewresearch.org/politics/2017/10/24/political-typology-reveals-deep-fissures-on-the-right-and-left/.

Porterfield, Carlie. "Trump's Popularity Rebounds Among Republicans After Impeachment Trial, Poll Suggests." *Forbes* (February 16, 2021). https://www.forbes.com/sites/carlieporterfield/2021/02/16/trumps-popularity-rebounds-among-republicans-after-impeachment-trial-poll-suggests/?sh=1acd91b6237e.

Pullum, Amanda. "Social Movement Theory and the 'Modern Day Tea Party'." *Sociology Compass* 8, no. 2 (2014): 1377–1387, 10.1111/soc4.12231.

Rampell, Catherine. "Trump Has Shifted the Country to the Left— Or At Least Away From His Own Views." *The Washington Post* (October 19. 2020). https://www.washingtonpost.com/opinions/2020/10/19/

trump-has-shifted-country-left-or-least-away-his-own-views/?fbclid=IwAR2_c33syyd-DfoxSF4o_UPmWAHkJSmr-u25d1L3fkJsz_-Ngt63moBWfro.
Rauch, Jonathan. "Rethinking Polarization." *National Affairs* 42 (Winter 2020). https://www.nationalaffairs.com/publications/detail/rethinking-polarization.
Regner, Elizabeth, and Thomas Rywick. "Left-and Right-Wing Perceptions of Presidential Candidates: Similarities and Differences Between French and American Voters." *International Review of Social Psychology* 19, no. 2 (2006): 103–125.
Reid, Ronald F., and James K. Klumpp, eds. *American Rhetorical Discourse.* 3rd ed. Long Grove, IL: Waveland, 2005.
Reid, Tim, James Oliphant, David Morgan, and Joseph Ax. "Prominent Anti-Trump Republicans Reject Third Party." *Reuters* (February 11, 2021). https://www.reuters.com/article/us-usa-trump-third-party-insight/prominent-anti-trump-republicans-reject-third-party-idUSKBN2AC053.
Relman, Eliza, and Walt Hickey. "Here's How Americans Rank the 2020 Presidential Candidates on the Political Spectrum." *Business Insider* (May 19, 2019). https://www.businessinsider.com/2020-democratic-presidential-candidates-political-spectrum-ranking-2019-5.
Remnick, David. "The Tribalism of American Politics." Transcript of Political Discussion Series with the Public Theater, *The New Yorker Videos,* May 4, 2017. https://video.newyorker.com/watch/the-tribalism-of-american-politics-2017-05-04.
Rendell, Ed, and Larry Platt. "On the Debate Stage, Let It Rip, Joe." *The Hill* (July 29, 2019). https://thehill.com/opinion/campaign/453914-on-the-debate-stage-let-it-rip-joe?amp&fbclid=IwAR0sTSWfzYew6DSrR-3iSE9PjfELix1ASUbXyZZ5g-rYzOW16BnOZ8FYV7M.
Resnik, Brian. "An Expert On Human Blind Spots Give Advice On How To Think." *VOX* (June 26, 2019). https://www.vox.com/science-and-health/2019/1/31/18200497/dunning-kruger-effect-explained-trump.
"Resolution Regarding the Republican Party Platform." The Republican National Committee (August 2020). https://prod-cdn-static.gop.com/docs/Resolution_Platform_2020.pdf.
Reston, Maeve. "Democrats Fear a 2016 Repeat in 2020." CNN (March 4, 2020). https://www.cnn.com/2020/03/04/politics/2020-vs-2016-democrats/index.html.
"Revealed: The Social Media Platforms That Make the Most Revenue Off Their Users." *Digital Information World* (December 1, 2019). https://www.digitalinformationworld.com/2019/12/revenue-per-social-media-user.html#.
Reynolds, Glenn Harlan. "Democrats Just Might Reelect Trump, and They'll Have No One to Blame But Themselves." *USA Today* (November 27, 2019). https://amp.usatoday.com/amp/4292960002?fbclid=IwAR3HAHAFqJvzJeTWnxwIbIj037CXy3pScdVN0t4-WMcYxSLjO9lK3flbGeA.
Riccardi, Nicholas, and Angeliki Kastanis. "Trump's Election Day Surge Powered By Small-Town America." AP News (November 4, 2020). https://apnews.com/article/election-2020-donald-trump-elections-e915054734d4914d8f1f3c27b369c8af.
Rieger, Jon. "Republicans Have Been Tying Democrats to Socialism for 90 Years. Trump is Going All in On the Tradition." *The Washington Post* (June 20, 2019). https://www.washingtonpost.com/politics/2019/06/20/

republicans-have-been-tying-democrats-socialism-years-trump-is-going-all-tradition/.

Roarty, Alex. "2020 Democrats Keep Shifting Left. Moderates Fret They'll Shift Even Further at the Next Debate." *McClatchy* (July 29, 2019). https://www.mcclatchydc.com/news/politics-government/election/campaigns/article233177051.html.

Robillard, Kevin. "Ed Markey Wins Massachusetts Senate Primary in Show Of Progressive Force." *The Huffington Post* (September 1, 2020). https://pa.caesarsonline.com/?btag=a_987657043b_1422c_0&utm_source=BG&utm_medium=display&utm_campaign=Brand&utm_content=728x90.

Robillard, Kevin, and Igor Bobic. "Democratic Senators Split On Wiping Out Student Loan Debt." *HuffPost* (November 19, 2020). https://www.aol.com/democratic-senators-split-wiping-student-182720156.html?fbclid=IwAR2ZsRHXF33V_7d4iMCDc_AWSkzkPkVLgl8Zpg5uzwE8S1ei4mfdTCe8eLg.

Robinson, Eugene. "Democratic Candidates Are Doing Trump's Job For Him." *The Washington Post* (February 17, 2020). https://www.washingtonpost.com/opinions/democratic-candidates-are-doing-trumps-job-for-him/2020/02/17/a4f563aa-51bf-11ea-929a-64efa7482a77_story.html?fbclid=IwAR1eXJzw3oSOA8G6GgyZd9ISr9YCVDyS." FY4hN6PZ73WGF1MyQ1fN7Hj2wRo.

Robinson, Nathan. "The Difference Between Liberalism and Leftism." Current Affairs (June 7, 2017). https://www.currentaffairs.org/2017/06/the-difference-between-liberalism-and-leftism.

Rogers, Alex. "Sen. Ed Markey Defeats a Kennedy in Massachusetts." CNN (September 2, 2020). https://www.cbs58.com/news/sen-ed-markey-defeats-a-kennedy-in-massachusetts.

Rogers, Katie, and Maggie Haberman. "Trump's 2020 Campaign Announcement Had a Very Trumpian Rollout." *The New York Times* (February 27, 2018). https://www.nytimes.com/2018/02/27/us/politics/trump-2020-brad-parscale.html.

Romm, Tony, and Isaac Stanley-Becker. "Facebook Takedowns Show New Russian Activity Targeted Biden, Praised Trump." *The Washington Post* (October 21, 2019). washingtonpost.com/technology/2019/10/21/facebook-fine-tunes-disinformation-defenses-but-leaves-controversial-political-ad-rules-intact/?fbclid=IwAR2aMQHDmBaxjiSMKxHaX4s8ZxERd3El_h_y2xgKoIIcuU7u5Q-JrgmqYG4.

Rosen, Jeffrey. "America Is Living James Madison's Nightmare." *The Atlantic* (October 2018a). https://www.theatlantic.com/magazine/archive/2018/10/james-madison-mob-rule/568351/.

———. "James Madison Would Be Horrified by a Tweeting President. *The Atlantic* (June 2018b). https://www.theatlantic.com/technology/archive/2018/06/james-madison-jeffrey-rosen-national-constitution-center/563675/.

Rosen, Lawrence. "A Liberal Defense of Tribalism: There's Nothing Wrong With Political Tribes That Can't Be Fixed By What's Right With Them." *Foreign Policy*, (January 2018), https://foreignpolicy.com/2018/01/16/a-liberal-defense-of-tribalism-american-politics/.

Rosenbluth, Frances, and Ian Shapiro. *Responsible Parties: Saving Democracy from Itself*. New Haven CT: Yale University Press, 2019.

Rosenthal, Joel. "Narrowing Hearts and Minds: Diagnosing the Global Rise of Illiberal Democracy." Carnegie Council for Ethics In International Affairs (June 2, 2021). https://www.carnegiecouncil.org/publications/articles_papers_reports/narrowing-hearts-minds-global-rise-illiberal-democracy.

Rosentiel, Tom. "Midterm Match-Up: Partisan Tide vs. Safe Seats." *Pew Research Center* (February 12, 2006). https://www.pewresearch.org/2006/02/12/midterm-matchup-partisan-tide-vs-safe-seats/.

———. "The Millennials." *Pew Research Center* (December 10, 2009). https://www.pewresearch.org/2009/12/10/the-millennials/.

Rossi, Rosemary. "Kamala Harris Laughs When Norah O'Donnell Asked If She Presents a 'Socialist or Progressive Perspective'" [video transcript]. *The Wrap* (October 25, 2020). https://www.thewrap.com/kamala-harris-60-minutes-socialist-perspective.

Rothman, Noah. "Democrats Caught in a Civil War." *THE WEEK* (April 19, 2019): 12.

Rubin, Gabriel T. "Moderate Democrats Fear Suburban Backlash to a Bernie Sanders Nomination." *The Wall Street Journal* (January 31, 2020). https://www.wsj.com/amp/articles/moderate-democrats-fear-suburban-backlash-to-a-bernie-sanders-nomination-11580466601?fbclid=IwAR2oapfp7foMd32iIEgtJURWfDAzB8gCabHUEnx9jh55cugaCex-A_CIB5c.

Rubin, Jennifer. "Bernie Sanders's Trump-like Campaign is a Disaster for Democrats. *The Washington Post* (January 27, 2020a). https://www.washingtonpost.com/opinions/2020/01/27/bernie-sanderss-trump-like-campaign-is-disaster-democrats/?fbclid=IwAR2WozB54cBXf_HhwbxgFTZH1k0Vi16fAwrtr1vGtW6V8xllkUK6PcjuEMw.

———. "'Electability' and 'Bernie' Don't Belong in the Same Sentence." *The Washington Post* (April 31, 2019a). https://www.washingtonpost.com/opinions/2019/03/31/electability-bernie-dont-belong-same-sentence/?fbclid=IwAR2gG0VeXkKTslMczlhRrGDzP2lIWll60IvgVr_ZKZNHUFbwXcQzLCqRrMA.

———. "Opinion: It's Over. Biden is the Presumptive Nominee." *The Washington Post* (March 17, 2020c). https://www.washingtonpost.com/opinions/2020/03/17/its-over-biden-is-presumptive-nominee/.

———. "Opinion: The Republican Party Has Split in Two. Let's Keep it That Way." *The Washington Post*(November 23, 2020b). https://www.washingtonpost.com/opinions/2020/11/23/republican-party-split-two-lets-keep-it-that-way/.

———. "The Mistakes Biden's Opponents Made Will Haunt Them." *The Washington Post* (August 1, 2019b). https://www.washingtonpost.com/opinions/2019/08/01/mistakes-bidens-opponents-made-will-haunt-them/?fbclid=IwAR2ECrNXAyTbMzfjVygMjM5vQfomOjpQRzz13x3yPJryiZAvVS5bG3MZbb8.

———. "We Must End the Post-Truth Society." *The Washington Post* (January 12, 2021). https://www.washingtonpost.com/opinions/2021/01/12/we-must-end-post-truth-society/ _.

Rubin, Ruth Bloch. *Building the Bloc: Intraparty Organization in the U.S.* Cambridge, UK: Cambridge University Press, 2017.

Rutland, Robert A., and Thomas A. Mason, eds. *The Papers of James Madison, vol. 14, 6 April 1791 – 16 March 1793*. Charlottesville VA: University Press of Virginia, 1983.

Saad, Lydia. "Americans' Political Ideology Held Steady in 2020." *Gallup* (January 11, 2021). https://news.gallup.com/poll/328367/americans-political-ideology-held-steady-2020.aspx.

Sach, Maddie, and Yutong Yuan. "Why The Democrats Have Shifted Left Over The Last 30 Years." *FiveThirtyEight* (December 10, 2019). https://fivethirtyeight.com/features/why-the-democrats-have-shifted-left-over-the-last-30-years/.

Sanger, David. "Same Goal, Different Playbook: Why Russia Would Support Trump and Sanders." *The New York Times* (February 22, 2020). https://www.nytimes.com/2020/02/22/us/politics/russia-election-meddling-trump-sanders.html?referringSource=articleShare&fbclid=IwAR2Pig_wN89X1Qh0Z0RM2y8btkONh0mxwuIpt-MrAVpJoi3RxXAJ1inL8yI.

Sargent, Greg. "Opinion: A Damning Senate Report on Jan. 6 Shows What Republicans Want to Keep Buried." *The Washington Post* (June 8, 2021a). https://www.washingtonpost.com/opinions/2021/06/08/damning-senate-report-jan-6-shows-what-republicans-want-keep-buried/.

———. "Opinion: Stop Saying Republicans are Cowards Who Fear Trump. The Truth is Far Worse." *The Washington Post* (May 20, 2021b). https://www.washingtonpost.com/opinions/2021/05/10/republicans-cowards-fear-trump-mccarthy/.

Schaul, Kevin, Kate Rabinowitz, and Ted Mellink. "2020 Turnout is the Highest in Over a Century." *The Washington Post,* (November 5, 2020). https://www.washingtonpost.com/graphics/2020/elections/voter-turnout/.

Scherer, Michael, and David Weigel. "'Blue Wave' or 'Left-Wing Mob'? Anti-Trump Fervor Fuels a New Movement Aimed Squarely at Winning Elections." *The Washington Post* (October 15, 2018). https://www.washingtonpost.com/politics/blue-wave-or-left-wing-mob-anti-trump-fervor-fuels-a-new-movement-aimed-squarely-at-winning-elections/2018/10/15/ed184146-bd1b-11e8-be70-52bd11fe18af_story.html?fbclid=IwAR1AlBKwsJ5acAsheksitn8l72AoyPvlDhReQ-zEPwDF1XgjzsUmW8kKdfc.

Scherer, Michael, and Mike DeBonis. "Centrist Democrats Push Back Against Party's Liberal Surge." *The Washington Post* (March 1, 2019). https://www.washingtonpost.com/politics/centrist-democrats-push-back-against-partys-liberal-surge/2019/03/01/a6674430-3c38-11e9-a2cd-307b06d0257b_story.html.

Scherer, Michael, and Sean Sullivan. "Top Democrats Turn On Each Other After Iowa, Complicating the Party's Chance Against Trump." *The Washington Post*, (February 9, 2020). https://www.washingtonpost.com/politics/top-democrats-turn-on-each-other-after-iowa-threatening-the-partys-chances-against-trump/2020/02/09/e2838386-4aae-11ea-b4d9-29cc419287eb_story.html?fbclid=IwAR1iNWsvMtgyaRlbbao5AmBGT5eMtwY5DZjVbXu-07npSVURDhB9gV6RtBM.

Schoen, Douglas. "The Progressive Takeover of Democratic Party Continues." *The Hill* (March 21, 2021). https://thehill.com/opinion/white-house/544222-the-progressive-takeover-of-democratic-party-continues.

Schoon, Eric, and Corey Peck. "Why is American Democracy in Danger? To Understand, Look No Further Than Other Collapsed Democracies." *The Washington Post* (March 5, 2019). https://beta.washingtonpost.com/outlook/2019/03/05/why-is-american-democracy-danger/?outputType=amp&fbclid=IwAR0XYMRebVTW4SyoQUBZPyZe0O21x7R7NQP3xhYJ2Jix3ydCsOT_RWEC8SQ.

Schmitt, Mark. "Yes, Democrats Are the Party of Fiscal Responsibility. But That Will (and Should) Change." *VOX* (April 20, 2018). https://www.vox.com/polyarchy/2018/4/20/17262944/democrats-fiscal-responsibility-budget-deficits.

Schumacher, Shannon. "Brexit Divides the UK, But Partisanship and Ideology are Still Key Factors." *Pew Research Center* (October 28, 2019). https://www.pewresearch.org/fact-tank/2019/10/28/brexit-divides-the-uk-but-partisanship-and-ideology-are-still-key-factors/.

Schutz, Alfred. *On Phenomenology and Social Relations*. Chicago IL: University of Chicago Press, 1970.

Scott, Eugene. "Casio-Cortez Puts a Spotlight on the Optics of Pelosi vs. the 'Newly Elected Women of Color.'" *The Washington Post* (July 11, 2019a). https://www.washingtonpost.com/politics/2019/07/11/demoralizing-disrespectful-ocasio-cortez-pressley-pelosi-singling-out-women-color/?fbclid=IwAR0IOQZilYStTYRXPu6o-laSCzaKYkx-18y-1ddw7UVwMKmRkSBtzJE4x9Y.

———. "When Are Age and Acuity Fair Game? Castro's Biden Attack Means Democrats Are Now Going to Have to Decide. *The Washington Post* (September 13, 2019b). https://www.washingtonpost.com/politics/2019/09/13/when-is-age-acuity-fair-game-castros-biden-attack-means-democrats-are-now-going-have-decide.

Searing, Donald, Frederick Solt, Pamela Johnston Conover, and Ivor Crewe. "Public Discussion in the Deliberative System: Does It Make Better Citizens?" *British Journal of Political Science* 37, no. 4 (October 2007): 587–618. https://doi.org/10.1017/S0007123407000336.

"Section 230 of the Communications Decency Act." Electronic Frontier Foundation (2021). https://www.eff.org/issues/cda230#:~:text=47%20U.S.C.,of%20the%20Communication%20Decency%20Act&text=Section%20230%20says%20that%20%22No,%C2%A7%20230).

Seib, Gerald F. "A New Tribalism Spreads in Donald Trump's Washington." *The Wall Street Journal* (April 3, 2017). https://www.wsj.com/articles/a-new-tribalism-spreads-in-donald-trumps-washington-1491229525.

———. "Democrats Built a Big Tent; Can They Keep It?" *The Wall Street Journal* (November 12, 2018). https://www.wsj.com/articles/democrats-built-a-big-tent-can-they-keep-it-1542037487.

"Senate Democrats Who Voted for Gorsuch Meet with Trump." CBS News (June 29, 2018). https://www.cbsnews.com/news/senate-democrats-who-voted-for-gorsuch-meet-with-trump/.

Seneca, Christopher. "How to Break Out of Your Social Media Echo Chamber." *Wired* (September 17, 2020). https://www.wired.com/story/facebook-twitter-echo-chamber-confirmation-bias/.

Shapiro, Daniel, and Mikhaila Fogel. "Tribalism in the Trump Era: The Societal Resilience Index." *Negotiation Journal* [Oxford] 35, no. 1, (January 2019): 235–241.

Shear, Michael D., and Jonathan Martin. "Top Contenders for Biden's Cabinet Draw Fire From All Sides." *The New York Times* (December 3, 2020). https://www.nytimes.com/2020/11/28/us/politics/biden-cabinet.html.

Shear, Michael D., and Michael Crowley. "Biden Cabinet Leans Centrist, Leaving Some Liberals Frustrated." *The New York Times* (December 19, 2020). https://www.nytimes.com/2020/12/19/us/politics/biden-cabinet.html.

Sheard, Cynthia Miecznikowski. "Kairos and Kenneth Burke's Psychology of Political and Social Communication." *College English* 55, 3, (March 1993): 291–310.

Sherman, Amy. "Trump's False Claim that Biden is a Socialist." *POLITICO* (October 15, 2020). https://www.politifact.com/factchecks/2020/oct/15/donald-trump/trumps-false-claim-biden-socialist/.

Shermer, Michael. "Evolution Explains Why Politics Is So Tribal." *Scientific American* (June 1, 2012).

Shieber, Jonathan. "Parler Jumps to No. 1 on App Store after Facebook and Twitter Ban Trump." *yahoo finance*! (January 9, 2021). https://au.finance.yahoo.com/news/parler-jumps-no-1-app-184525125.html.

Sides, John. "Did Enough Sanders Supporters Vote For Trump to Cost Clinton the Election?" *The Washington Post* (August 24, 2017). https://www.washingtonpost.com/news/monkey-cage/wp/2017/08/24/did-enough-bernie-sanders-supporters-vote-for-trump-to-cost-clinton-the-election/.

"S.I. Hayakawa: Language in Thought and Action." *Université Libre de Bruxelles, Homepages Membres Corps Académique* (April 4, 2008). http://homepages.ulb.ac.be/~jpvannop/HAYA.html.

Sillars, Malcolm, and Bruce E. Gronbeck, eds., *Communication Criticism: Rhetoric, Social Codes and Cultural Studies*. Long Grove, IL: Waveland, 2001.

Skelley, Geoffrey. "America Isn't Really Set Up For Third-Party Presidential Bids." *FiveThirtyEight* (January 31, 2019). https://fivethirtyeight.com/features/america-isnt-really-set-up-for-third-party-presidential-bids/.

Smith, Allan, "How Lincoln Project Anti-Trump Republicans Got Into His Head. Spoiler Alert: It Was Easy." NBC News (July 6, 2020). https://www.nbcnews.com/politics/donald-trump/how-lincoln-project-anti-trump-republicans-got-his-head-spoiler-n1232669.

Smith, Craig Allen. *Presidential Campaign Communication*. Cambridge: Polity Press, 2015.

———. *Rhetoric and Human Consciousness: A History*. Long Grove, Illinois: Waveland Press, 2003.

Smith, David. "Trump's 2020 Strategy: Paint Joe Biden as a Puppet for the 'Radical Left.'" *The Guardian* (July 19, 2020). https://www.theguardian.com/us-news/2020/jul/19/trump-2020-joe-biden-extreme-left?fbclid=IwAR2erhjV5hLJo8alb2Zp7M0qdYKdj1BpdeAk2eK-5m-k5cEIVIW-Z7h5RJg.

Somin, Ilya. "Opinion: Is the Overthrow of a Democratically Elected Government Ever Justified?" *The Washington Post* (July 18, 2016). https://www.washingtonpost.com/news/volokh-conspiracy/wp/2016/07/18/is-the-overthrow-of-a-democratically-elected-government-ever-justified/.

Songalia, Ryan, and Christian Murray. "Tiffany Cabán Holds Insurmountable Lead in Astoria Primary, Declares Victory." *Sunnyside Post* (June 22, 2021). https://sunnysidepost.com/tiffany-caban-holds-insurmountable-lead-in-astoria-primary-declares-victory.

Spaeth, Ryu. "The Strange Liberal Backlash to Woke Culture." *The New Republic* (November 25, 2019). https://newrepublic.com/article/155681/strange-liberal-backlash-woke-cult.

Sprunt, Barbara. "Biden Says He's 'Not A Fan' Of Expanding The Supreme Court." NPR (October 13, 2020). https://www.npr.org/2020/10/13/923213582/biden-says-hes-not-a-fan-of-expanding-the-supreme-court.

Srikrishnan, Maya, Jared Pliner, Jennifer Schlesinger, Joshua Goldstein, and Huma Khan. "Which Tea Party Candidates Won?" ABC News (September 24, 2010). https://abcnews.go.com/Politics/2010_Elections/vote-2010-elections-tea-party-winners-losers/story?id=12023076.

Stafford, Joe. "Profound Divisions in the UK Revealed by Brexit Study." *Manchester* (February 1, 2018). https://www.manchester.ac.uk/discover/news/profound-divisions-brexit/.

Stalder, Daniel. "Tribalism Politics." *Psychology Today* (June 18, 2018). https://www.psychologytoday.com/us/blog/bias-fundamentals/201806/tribalism-in-politics?amp&fbclid=IwAR0e7uNWBiLzU3piwTrzZ2O70IZ_PApTS8IVjVMB1N41t7IDyQgp2rO4Dwk.

Stanyer, James. *Intimate Politics: Publicity, Privacy and the Personal Lives of Politicians in Media Saturated Democracies.* Cambridge: Polity Press, 2012.

Stein, Jeff. "The Bernie Voters Who Defected to Trump, Explained By a Political Scientist." *VOX* (August 24, 2017). https://www.vox.com/policy-and-politics/2017/8/24/16194086/bernie-trump-voters-study.

Stelter, Brian. "The Pro-Trump Media Part Of The Equation." *Reliable Sources* (January 10, 2021). Transcript. http://transcripts.cnn.com/TRANSCRIPTS/2101/10/rs.01.html.

Stephens, Bret. "How Trump Wins Next Year: What Happened in India and Australia is a Warning to the Left." *The New York Times* (May 24, 2019). https://www.nytimes.com/2019/05/24/opinion/trump-elections-india-australia.html?smid=nytcore-ios-share&fbclid=IwAR1YwN26UB3fZy853BxqlfVuAeq6n2868jntOmhYNgiMIOi71Q59S_2CpXI.

Stevens, Matt. "Joe Biden Accepts Presidential Nomination: Full Transcript." *The New York Times* (August 20, 2020). https://www.nytimes.com/2020/08/20/us/politics/biden-presidential-nomination-dnc.html.

Stokols, Eli. "The Day the Republican Party Ruptured." *POLITICO* (March 2, 2016). https://www.politico.com/story/2016/03/the-day-the-republican-party-ruptured-220108.

Suhadolnik, Alexandria. "Essay II: Long Term Cultural Effects of the Printing Press." English 360: Principles of Rhetoric (blog), Washington State University (October 31, 2011). https://asuhadolnik360.blogspot.com/2011/10/essay-ii-long-term-cultural-effects-of.html.

Sullivan, Sean. "Bernie Sanders Expresses Concerns About Biden Campaign." *The Washington Post*(September 12, 2020). https://www.washingtonpost.com/politics/bernie-sanders-expresses-concerns-about-biden-campaign/2020/09/12/a0ccc4fa-f4a1-11ea-b796-2dd09962649c_story.html?fbclid=IwAR3_L1njiSGpaBdz4XQ-KIgvL1eYye9UT29umx1sGgmM2dDXbn2DeL9C-WI.

———. "For Bernie Sanders, 2016 Gets in the Way of 2020." *The Washington Post* (April 20, 2019a). https://www.washingtonpost.com/politics/for-bernie-sanders-2016-gets-in-the-way-of-2020/2019/04/20/8746f8ac-621c-11e9-9412-daf3d-2e67c6d_story.html?fbclid=IwAR3GmzEOV3GpPb3Z4vq4rqHCEf2fB9XgAXFbXPBqvM4JT32qWB8OeYUykDk.

———. "Obama Tells Democratic Candidates to Ease Off Talk of Revolution." *The Washington Post* (November 15, 2019b). https://www.washingtonpost.com/politics/obama-tells-democratic-candidates-to-ease-off-talk-of-revolution/2019/11/15/93569ddc-07fd-11ea-924a-28d87132c7ec_story.html?fbclid=IwAR2MdjemWmpSSKBoVr3cTJ4jmEDx10_FQJ1egTf2coY9QqQtJRU8X4LfQD.

———. "'Tribalism is Ruining Us:' Flake Uses Kavanaugh Fight to Plead for Civility and Cooperation." *The Washington Post* (October 1, 2018). https://www.washingtonpost.com/powerpost/tribalism-is-ruining-us-flake-uses-kavanaugh-fight-to-plead-for-civility-and-cooperation/2018/10/01/d80eaf7a-c5ad-11e8-b2b5-79270f9cce17_story.html?fbclid=IwAR3kla9Ma2rmnFD17f8F-PB5c3uM8FCcySkcSqkiRIi5eNjAsN19MrVXeu8.

Sullivan, Sean, and Robert Costa. "Sanders Toughens His Critique of Biden, Signaling More Clashes Ahead." *The Washington Post* (July 16, 2019). https://beta.washingtonpost.com/politics/bernie-sanders-targets-trump-biden-in-interview-with-the-post/2019/07/16/c75cc10a-a7c3-11e9-a3a6-ab670962db05_story.html?outputType=amp&fbclid=IwAR2RmmgPCHQ7XMqCaiq3ujjHZkFUcewiIcYB-iFoqjyFgUkjq15t8rvlEuU.

Sullivan, Sean, and Matt Viser. "Joe Biden's Strong Debut Puts Pressure on Other Candidates Vying to Challenge Trump." *The Washington Post* (May 4, 2019). https://www.washingtonpost.com/politics/joe-bidens-strong-debut-puts-pressure-on-other-candidates-vying-to-challenge-trump/2019/05/04/f20a40c6-6d08-11e9-be3a-33217240a539_story.html?fbclid=IwAR3c2nasARZE2I9LZrT_8yx_.

Sullivan, Sean, and Rachael Bade. "Criticized By Moderates and Pressured By Their Base, Liberals Fight For a Voice in the Democratic Party." *The Washington Post* (November 29, 2020). https://www.washingtonpost.com/politics/democratic-party-future-liberals/2020/11/29/3da05bfe-2ba5-11eb-92b7-6ef17b3fe3b4_story.html.

Swasey, Benjamin. "Bernie Sanders Endorses Joe Biden For President." NPR (April 13, 2020). https://www.npr.org/2020/04/13/833528203/bernie-sanders-endorses-joe-biden-for-president.

Swearingen, C. Jan, and and Dave Pruett, Eds. *Rhetoric, The Polis and the Global Village*. Mahwah, NJ: Lawrence Erlbaum Associates, 1999.

Sykes, Charles. "Dear Democrats, Here's How to Guarantee Trump's Reelection." *Politico* (June 25, 2019). https://www.politico.com/magazine/story/2019/06/25/democrats-trump-election-2020-227215?fbclid=IwAR3I2WjYzm4A-Jp_Bks0_uGNIDiGk9TuldOHswhFh8KzEQA-_7mWG5LXEYs.

Taibbi, Matt. *Hate, Inc.* New York, NY: OR Books, 2019.

Tankersley, Jim. "Why Trump's Efforts to Paint Biden as a Socialist Are Not Working." *The New York Times*,(October 14, 2020). https://www.nytimes.com/2020/10/14/business/socialist-biden-trump.html.

Tate, Kristin. *The Liberal Invasion of Red State America*. Washington, D.C.: Regnery Publishing, 2020.

Tau, Byron. "Democrats Have Votes to Block Neil Gorsuch, Sparking Rule-Change Fight." *The Wall Street Journal* (March 3, 2017). https://www.wsj.com/articles/democrats-have-votes-to-block-neil-gorsuch-sparking-rule-change-fight-1491241190.

Taub, Amanda. "It Wasn't Strictly a Coup Attempt. But It's Not Over, Either." *The New York Times* (January 7, 2021). https://www.nytimes.com/2021/01/07/world/americas/what-is-a-coup-attempt.html.

Tavernese, Sabrina, and Nate Cohn. "The America That Isn't Polarized." *The New York Times* (September 24, 2019). https://www.nytimes.com/2019/09/24/upshot/many-americans-not-polarized.html.

Taylor, Jessica. "Republicans and Democrats Don't Agree or Like Each Other—And It's Worse Than Ever." NPR (October 5, 2017), https://www.npr.org/2017/10/05/555685136/republicans-and-democrats-dont-agree-dont-like-each-other-and-its-worst-than-eve?fbclid=IwAR0ZPcEgfi1_vlef3qX6Nl-NfH9gw-MckU557MxdozW2mZV9BrVh7qcdVgY.

Taylor, Jessica, and Renee Klahr. "Debate May Be Last-Ditch Effort For Struggling Democrats To Stay Alive." NPR (July 29, 2019). https://www.npr.org/2019/07/29/745606868/debate-may-be-last-ditch-effort-for-struggling-democrats-to-stay-alive?fbclid=IwAR3POZj5yyIZrytx8bJmzvkBmmD_FpgSPF2R1DsVYuwLa9MdVjvhUrS53Zc.

Teles, Steven M., and Robert P. Saldin. "The Future is Faction." *National Affairs* 47 (Spring 2021). https://nationalaffairs.com/publications/detail/the-future-is-faction.

Tepperman, Jonathan. "Why Biden Will Lose the Left—and How That Could Help Him." *Forbes* (December 11, 2020). https://foreignpolicy.com/2020/12/11/why-biden-will-lose-the-left-and-thats-ok/?utm_source=PostUp&utm_medium=email&utm_campaign=28308&utm_term=Editors%20Picks%20OC&?tpcc=28308.

"The Generation Gap in American Politics." *Pew Research Center* (March 1, 2018). https://www.pewresearch.org/politics/2018/03/01/the-generation-gap-in-american-politics/.

"The Latest: Trump Urges Backers to 'Take Revenge' By Voting." *The Washington Post* (December 5, 2020). https://www.washingtonpost.com/politics/the-latest-trump-falsely-claims-he-won-georgia/2020/12/05/c84bb7f0-375b-11eb-9699-00d311f13d2d_story.html.

"The People, the Press & Politics." *Pew Research Center* (September 21, 1994). https://www.pewresearch.org/politics/1994/09/21/the-people-the-press-politics-2/.

Theye, Kirsten, and Steven Melling. "Total Losers and Bad Hombres: The Political Incorrectness and Perceived Authenticity of Donald J. Trump." *Southern Communication Journal* 83, no. 5 (2018): 322–337. https://www.tandfonline.com/doi/full/10.1080/1041794X.2018.1511747.

Thibodeau, Paul. "How to Talk About People Disengaging from Violent Extremism: The Power of Strategic Language." Panel Discussion, United States Institute of Peace (August 6, 2019). https://www.usip.org/events/how-talk-about-people-disengaging-violent-extremism.

Thiessen, Marc A. "Forget Moderates vs. Radicals. The Debate Was a Left vs. Far Left Brawl." *The Washington Post* (August 1, 2019). https://www.washingtonpost.com/opinions/2019/08/01/forget-moderates-vs-radicals-debate-was-left-vs-far-left-brawl/?fbclid=IwAR0sTSWfzYew6DSrR-3iSE9PjfELix1ASUbXyZZ5g-rYzOW16BnOZ8FYV7M.

Thomas, Ken, and Eliza Collins. "Joe Biden United the Democrats—It's Not Likely to Last." *The Wall Street Journal* (August 19, 2020). https://www.wsj.com/articles/biden-united-the-democratsits-not-likely-to-last-11597847147?fbclid=IwAR0NiShqDruoNPq8IsjNHVuKnBDD_ILZLNZb3goWKwX6R5n8jQChd8GTmaY.

Thompson, Derek. "The Deep Story of Trumpism." *The Atlantic* (December 29, 2020). https://www.theatlantic.com/ideas/archive/2020/12/deep-story-trumpism/617498/.

Thrush, Glen. "Obama Moves Off Political Sidelines, Earlier Than He Expected." *The New York Times* (November 20, 2019a). https://www.nytimes.com/2019/11/20/us/politics/obama-2020-candidates.html?smid=nytcore-ios-share&fbclid=IwAR0GIgEDzwP6Cv0FAdPcY-eqOJYVCbNCNBClGZpQI5Q8umXj68VBOHdKzcE.

———. "Pelosi Warns Democrats: Stay in the Center or Trump May Contest Election Results." *The New York Times* (May 4, 2019b). https://www.nytimes.com/2019/05/04/us/politics/nancy-pelosi.html?smid=nytcore-ios-share&fbclid=IwAR28p9SjzFDVhT-O5ZL7DeSWrkYlF69O4MI6ToVR9R0g-SZlwrQvbYac6T4w.

Tindale, Christopher W. *Rhetorical Argumentation: Principles of Theory and Practice*. Thousand Oaks, CA: Sage Publications, 2004.

Toner, Ralph, and Jim Rutenberg. "Partisan Divide on Iraq Exceeds Split on Vietnam." *The New York Times* (July 30, 2006). https://www.nytimes.com/2006/07/30/washington/30war.html.

Touchberry, Ramsey. "Tulsi Gabbord, With Only Two Delegates, Isn't the First Candidate to Stay in a Race This Long." *Newsweek* (March 9, 2020). https://www.newsweek.com/tulsi-gabbard-only-two-delegates-isnt-first-candidate-stay-race-this-long-1491334.

"Tracking the United States Congress." GovTracks.us, (2021). https://www.govtrack.us/.

Truax, Chris. "Republican: I'm Telling Democrats How to Beat Trump in 2020. It's Job One So Get Over It." *USA Today* (July 13, 2019). https://www.usatoday.com/story/opinion/2019/07/12/beat-trump-with-mainstream-ideas-not-far-left-fantasies-column/1703543001/.

Trump, Donald. "Donald Trump: Democrats 'Medicare for All' Plan Will Demolish Promises to Seniors." *USA Today,* (October 20, 2018). https://www.usatoday.com/story/opinion/2018/10/10/donald-trump-democrats-open-borders-medicare-all-single-payer-column/1560533002/

Trump, Jr., Donald. "Donald Trump Jr. Says Democrats Lost Control of Radical Left, Media Doing Whatever They Can To Protect Biden." Fox News (September 31, 2020). https://www.foxnews.com/transcript/donald-trump-jr-says-democrats-lost-control-of-radical-left-media-doing-whatever-they-can-to-protect-biden?fbclid=IwAR2Th6g3Av5ujV4sJ93CqcFHMXZt-c4bj_KIAye2DRiOxsvtxtqnQJqmYFY.

Tucker, Cynthia. "Trumpism: The Movement That Will Outlast Its Leader." *Literary Hub* (December 17, 2020). https://lithub.com/trumpism-the-movement-that-will-outlast-its-leader/.

Tuttle, Ian. "On the Alt-Right and the 'Alt-Left.'" *National Review* (August 16, 2017). https://www.nationalreview.com/corner/alt-left-alt-right-ideologies/.

Tyler, Andrea, Mari Takada, Yiyoung Kim, and Diana Marinova. *Language in Use: Cognitive and Discourse Perspectives on Language and Language Learning.* Washington, DC: Georgetown University Press, 2005.

"2016 Electoral College Results." *National Archives and Records Administration* (2016). https://www.archives.gov/federal-register/electoral-college/2016/election-results.html.

"2016 Presidential Primaries, Caucuses, and Conventions." *The Green Papers* (February 22, 2019). https://www.thegreenpapers.com/P16/events.phtml?s=c&f=m.

"2020 Democratic National Convention (DNC) Transcripts." *REV* (2020). https://www.rev.com/blog/transcript-tag/democratic-national-convention.

"2020 Democratic Party Platform." *The Democratic National Committee* (August 2020). https://democrats.org/wp-content/uploads/sites/2/2020/08/2020-Democratic-Party-Platform.pdf.

"2020 Election Transcripts." *REV* (2020). https://www.rev.com/blog/transcript-category/2020-election-transcripts.

"2021 New York City Primary Results." *The Washington Post* (July 10, 2021). https://www.washingtonpost.com/elections/election-results/new-york/nyc-primary/.

"U.S. Election Results By States." *Reuters* (February 8, 2021). https://graphics.reuters.com/USA-ELECTION/RESULTS-LIVE/qzjpqadqapx/index.html?st=N.

vanden Heuvel, Katrina. "Progressives, Get Ready to Push Biden and Harris." *The Washington Post* (August 18, 2020). https://www.washingtonpost.com/opinions/2020/08/18/progressives-get-ready-push-biden-harris/?fbclid=IwAR0uVlXVf1GQ2Qhnw8QjWHLWRf6kzKJ7btus3rcF4kkHhnXlwoPEmrFDPnU.

Verhovek, John. "Biden Builds On Moderate Coalition, Collecting Endorsements From Former 2020 Candidates." ABC News (March 20, 2020). https://abcnews.go.com/Politics/biden-builds-moderate-coalition-collecting-endorsements-2020-candidates/story?id=69442331.

Viser, Matt. "As Candidates Fight, Democrats Fear a Rupture That Will Help President Trump." *The Washington Post* (January 21, 2020a). https://www.washingtonpost.com/politics/as-candidates-fight-democrats-fear-a-rupture-that-will-help-president-trump/2020/01/21/a6f5848c-3c7a-11ea-8872-5df698785a4e_story.html?outputType=amp&fbclid=IwAR23JFejRFuuvAmfJzsnW78fSMzkrZ6S-HDqMqbVMmRN95cDFNsxYf1S_qk.

———. "Initially Spurned By His Own Party, Mocked By His Opponent, Joe Biden Has Emerged More Popular As He Closes In On a Job He Has Wanted For Decades." *The Washington Post* (October 24, 2020b). https://www.washingtonpost.com/politics/biden-campaign-optimism/2020/10/24/c793947a-1548-11eb-ad6f-36c93e6e94fb_story.html?fbclid=IwAR3mXcTjaklYbpcj3iKOQkduGOHOj6EcZzBX_eWs-mJ-9IzH5Y73Q_pGrOc.

Viser, Matt, and Chelsea Janes. "As Biden Defends Himself on Civil Rights, Other Democratic Candidates Go After Him." *The Washington Post* (June 28, 2019). https://www.washingtonpost.com/politics/four-hours-of-debate-scrambles-the-democratic-presidential-field-exposing-joe-bidens-vulnerabilities/2019/06/28/91ec1b78-995f-11e9-830a-21b9b36b64ad_story.html.

Voght, Kara. "Biden Was MIA for Black Lives Matter During the Primary. They're Hoping That'll Change Now." *Mother Jones* (June 5, 2020). https://www.motherjones.com/politics/2020/06/joe-biden-black-lives-matter/.

Volz, Dustin, Warren P. Strobel, and Tarini Parti. "Democrats' Unease Mounts as Biden Considers a CIA Director." *The Wall Street Journal,* (December 2, 2020). https://www.wsj.com/articles/democrats-unease-mounts-as-biden-considers-a-cia-director-11606949863.

Von Drehle, David. "The Party is Over." *The Washington Post*, (October 20, 2017). https://www.washingtonpost.com/opinions/both-political-parties-may-be-doomed/2017/10/20/4c6cf8b2-b5ca-11e7-be94-fabb0f1e9ffb_story.html?fbclid=IwAR3pZMOJSsBDA4_AYFebjREuCLFAlAwvSeurJtVAQnSezOTdIfVx6gJS6UM.

Von Rennenkampff, Mark. "Another Reason to Celebrate: The Implosion of 'Woke' Identity Politics." *The Hill* (November 20, 2020.) https://thehill.com/opinion/campaign/525227-another-reason-to-celebrate-the-implosion-of-woke-identity-politics.

———. "Warren and Sanders Turn Billionaire Steyer Into a Foil as They Seek Campaign Donations." *The Washington Post* (July 11, 2019b). https://www.washingtonpost.com/politics/warren-and-sanders-turn-billionaire-steyer-into-a-foil-as-they-seek-campaign-donations/2019/07/11/000bd0ac-a3e3-11e9-b8c8-75dae2607e60_story.html?fbclid=IwAR1obtlc3QKWfbOuAVwqoYQ6VQjOGijVmWndWcRIMr9cYMRJiJA_Xit8SdY\.

Von Rennenkampff, Mark, and Felicia Sanmez." Election Live Updates: Buttigieg, Klobuchar and Harry Reid Endorse Beiden." *The Washington Post* (March 2, 2020). https://www.washingtonpost.com/politics/2020/03/02/campaign-live-updates/?fbclid=IwAR2KO7pP58Y6xNxqd7R7dLQkrb4ukIBOAtQQv141ZDdySXbEhOuCwUBCziY.

Wahl-Jorgensen, Karin. *Emotions, Media and Politics.* Cambridge: Polity Press, 2019.

Waldman, Paul. "How Joe Biden is Moving Left While Still Being Seen as a Moderate." *The Washington Post* (July 16, 2020). https://www.washingtonpost.com/opinions/2020/07/16/how-joe-biden-is-moving-left-while-still-being-seen-moderate

/?fbclid=IwAR3w2DAV5OvKs95bgqO4wKL4JDnQ02yXXo3MnX5ZqtkVC9ZUpkjtNR5bd5U.

———. "In Trump's America, Tribalism Reigns." *The New York Times* (June 26, 2018a). https://beta.washingtonpost.com/blogs/plum-line/wp/2018/06/26/in-trumps-america-tribalism-reigns/?outputType=amp&fbclid=IwAR2LjYIUQoamOCRRQHjmYo3s4I6wryx4EjN1cwKDx3R6ViVFID2VC01vVWQ.

———. "Stop Trying to Be 'Responsible' on the Budget, Democrat." *The Washington Post* (June 7, 2018b). https://www.washingtonpost.com/blogs/plum-line/wp/2018/06/07/stop-trying-to-be-responsible-on-the-budget-democrats/.

Wallach, Phillip A. "Prospects For Partisan Realignment: Lessons From the Demise of the Whigs." *Brookings* (March 6, 2017). https://www.brookings.edu/author/philip-a-wallach/?type=opinions.

Wang, Vivian. "House Democrats Prepare For Civil War as Challengers Plot Primary Battles." *The New York Times* (July 19, 2019a). https://www.nytimes.com/2019/07/19/nyregion/ny-democrat-house-challengers.html?smid=nytcore-ios-share&fbclid=IwAR30DYtimZ0sLN4TxjDlmRLDR8R4j_nrUC3FuJaNjALRkqQOe6MGPeRgMCQ.

Warnick, Barbara, and David Heineman. *Rhetoric Online: The Politics of New Media*. New York, NY: Peter Lang Publishing, 2012.

Warren, Michael. "The Republican Party is at War With Itself as it Charts Its Post-Trump Future." CNN (January 26, 2021). https://www.cnn.com/2021/01/26/politics/republican-party-future/index.html.

Watson, Kathyn, Camilo Montoya-Galvez, Grace Segers, and Caitlyn Huey-Burns. "All the Democratic Candidates Who Ran for President in 2020." CBS News (June 22, 2020). https://www.cbsnews.com/media/2020-democratic-presidential-candidates/.

Watzlawick, Paul. *Pragmatics of Human Communication: A Study of Interactional Patterns, Pathologies, and Paradoxes*. New York, NY: Norton, 1967.

Weaver, Richard M. *The Ethics of Rhetoric*. New York, NY: Routledge, 1953, 1985.

Wehner, Peter. "Have Democrats Pulled Too Far Left?" *The New York Times* (May 27, 2015). https://www.nytimes.com/2015/05/27/opinion/have-democrats-pulled-too-far-left.html.

———. "Trump's Most Malicious Legacy." *The Atlantic* (December 17, 2020). https://www.theatlantic.com/ideas/archive/2020/12/trumps-most-malicious-legacy/617319/.

Weigel, David. "Sanders Steps Up Attacks on Bloomberg at Candidates Event in Nevada." *The Washington Post* (February 16, 2020a). https://www.washingtonpost.com/politics/2020/02/16/sanders-steps-up-attacks-bloomberg-candidates-event-nevada/?fbclid=IwAR0NS9f60AHTUAtUlbYadbQtutHATeucoXEpBgUt51YCt30F8MGaWGwefLY.

———. "Sen. Coons Turns Back Left-Wing Challenge, Wins Democratic Nomination in Delaware." *The Washington Post* (September 15, 2020b). https://www.washingtonpost.com/politics/primary-delaware-senate-coons/2020/09/14/8e193d76-f6e9-11ea-be57-d00bb9bc632d_story.html.

Weiyi, Cai, Annie Daniel, Jon Huang, Jasmine C. Lee, and Alicia Parlapiano. "Trump's Second Impeachment: How the Senate Voted." *The New York Times*

(February 13, 2021). https://www.nytimes.com/interactive/2021/02/13/us/politics/senate-impeachment-live-vote.html.

Weissert, Will. "Sanders Calls For Unity, But His Supporters Have Other Ideas." *Associated Press News* (February 1, 2020a). https://apnews.com/03e9dff1a43ef-7b6789e357f9f19cbe9?fbclid=IwAR0uYixSgteyaLy-Ev1m08kyxwgdjHGpgcrebbXH119pcqjKQopA0IlKj6U.

———. "Sanders Calls For Party Unity to Prevent 'Authoritarianism'." *AP* (August 18, 2020b). https://apnews.com/article/virus-outbreak-election-2020-health-politics-joe-biden-b9e26befa1f3e0bec61426163893faed.

"What is the Connection Between Influenza and Pneumonia?" *American Lung Association* (2021). https://www.lung.org/lung-health-diseases/lung-disease-lookup/pneumonia/what-is-the-connection.

"What is Democratic Socialism?" Democratic Socialist of America [website] (March 13, 2021). https://www.dsausa.org/about-us/what-is-democratic-socialism/.

Wheeler, Tom. Philip Verveer, Gene Kimmelman, and Dipayan Ghosh. "Digital Platforms and Democracy." Harvard Kennedy School Shorenstein Center on Media, Politics and Public Policy (2020). https://shorensteincenter.org/programs/digital-platforms-democracy/.

Wichens, Herbert A. "The Literary Criticism of Oratory" in *The Rhetorical Idiom*. Ed. Donald C. Bryant. Ithaca: Cornell University Press, 1958, 5–42.

Williamson, Vanessa, Theda Skocpol, and John Coggin. "The Tea Party and the Remaking of Republican Conservatism." *Perspectives on Politics* 9, no. 2 (March 2011): 25–43 https://scholar.harvard.edu/files/williamson/files/tea_party_pop_0.pdf.

Wilson, Reid. "Democrats Fear 2016 Repeat Despite Biden's Lead in the Polls." *The Hill* (September 8, 2020). https://thehill.com/homenews/campaign/515575-democrats-fear-2016-repeat-despite-bidens-lead-in-polls.

Wolf, Zachary. "America is Going From an Outsider President to the Ultimate Insider." CNN (December 5, 2020). https://www.cnn.com/2020/12/05/politics/president-in-waiting-joe-biden/index.html.

Wolkenstein, Fabio. "Intra-party Democracy Beyond Aggregation." *Party Politics*, 24, no. 5 (June 2016). doi: 10.1177/1354068816655563https://www.researchgate.net/publication/304339782_Intra-party_democracy_beyond_aggregation.

Woodward, Calvin. "Trump's 'Big Lie' Imperils Republicans Who Don't Embrace It." *Associated Press* (May 9, 2021). https://apnews.com/article/michael-pence-donald-trump-election-2020-government-and-politics-0c07947f9fd2b9911b3006f0fc128ffd.

Yglesias, Matthew. "Democrats Are Learning The Wrong Lesson From Donald Trump." *VOX* (July 2, 2019). https://www.vox.com/2019/7/2/20677656/donald-trump-moderate-extremism-penalty.

———. "The Price Progressives Paid For Getting Rid of Trump." *The Washington Post* (November 25, 2020). https://www.washingtonpost.com/outlook/trump-obama-biden-clinton-progressive-moderate/2020/11/25/9bb8263c-2ea1-11eb-96c2-aac3f162215d_story.html.

Yoo, Christopher. "Common Carriage's Domain." *Yale Journal on Regulation*. 35 (2018): 991–1026.

Younis, Mohamed. "Four in 10 Americans Embrace Some Form of Socialism." *Gallup* (May 20, 2019). https://news.gallup.com/poll/257639/four-americans-embrace-form-socialism.aspx.

Zakaria, Fareed. "Interview With Colin Powell About Capitol Hill Riot: Republicans Face Backlash for Challenging Biden Win." *GPS* (January 10, 2021). Transcript. http://transcripts.cnn.com/TRANSCRIPTS/2101/10/fzgps.01.html.

———. "How the Story of Impeachment Tells the Story of Polarization." *The Washington Post* (January 30, 2020). https://www.washingtonpost.com/opinions/how-the-story-of-impeachment-tells-the-story-of-polarization/2020/01/30/cdf1ad28-43a4-11ea-b5fc-eefa848cde99_story.html.

———. "The Rise of Illiberal Democracy." *Foreign Affairs* 76, no. 6 (1997): 22–43. https://www.foreignaffairs.com/articles/1997-11-01/rise-illiberal-democracy.

Zhao, Christina. "As Michigan Votes, #DemExit Trends With Sanders Supporters Threatening to Leave Dem Party If Biden Wins Nomination." *Newsweek* (March 10, 2020). https://www.newsweek.com/michigan-votes-demexit-trends-sanders-supporters-threatening-leave-dem-party-if-biden-wins-1491569.

Zinn, James D. *Supremely Partisan*. Lanham, MD: Rowman and Littlefield Publishers, 2016.

Zitner, Aaron. "The National Republican and Democratic Parties Have Far Less Sway Now in Anointing Candidates and Enforcing Discipline." *The Wall Street Journal* (February 16, 2020). https://www.wsj.com/articles/rise-of-sanders-trump-shows-decline-in-party-power-11581742860?fbclid=IwAR2TcwiugUU3M-vJRwJbCB9oDhBFMvrO2a42Otg-o0l6ZwmjbZ8LtJpfyfs.

Zitser, Joshua. "Following Trump's YouTube Ban, It is Feared His Supporters are Migrating to a 'Wild West' of Video-sharing, Mingling With Far-Right and Neo-Nazis Terror Groups." *Business Insider* (January 17, 2021). https://www.businessinsider.com/trump-supporters-migrating-to-a-wild-west-of-youtube-alternatives-2021-1.

Zompetti, Joseph. *Divisive Discourse: The Extreme Rhetoric of Contemporary American Politics*. 2nd Ed. San Diego: Cognella, 2018.

Zurcher, Anthony. "US Election: How Left-Wing is the Democratic Field?" *BBC News* (February 2, 2020). https://www.bbc.com/news/world-us-canada-51470131.

Index

ABC News, 72–73
Abrams, Stacey (congressperson, Georgia), 84
Adams, Eric, 140
Adams, John (president), 8, 35
Affordable Care Act, 54–55. *See also* Obamacare
Airbnb, 130
Alexander, Lamar (senator), 53
alienation, 10, 16
Amazon Web Services, 130
anti-establishment, 1, 9, 83, 85, 92
Arab spring, 78
arbitration, rhetorical, 65, 152, 155
audience, 2–3, 27–28, 74, 82, 140, 149, 152
Austin, Lloyd (secretary of defense), 122
authoritarianism, 8, 10, 26

Baby Boomers, 42
Becerra, Xavier (secretary of health and human services), 122
Bacon, Don (congressperson), 130
Bacon, Perry, 83, 103
Barrett, Amy Coney (associate justice of the supreme court), 62, 115–116
Bass, Karen (congressperson), 99
BBC, 72
Bennett, Matt, 122
Bennet, Michael (congressperson), 86–87
Bernie Bros, 11, 92
bias, 39, 111, 145–46, 150; cognitive, 145; media, 71–74; social media, 81. *See also* confirmation bias
Biden, Jr., Joseph R. (president), 5, 15, 19, 33, 37–38, 40, 43–49, 54–55, 61–63, 70–72, 75, 85–105, 107–20, 122–33, 136–39, 141–42, 147–48, 155–59, 162
Big Lie (conspiracy theory), 140, 147
bigotry, 15, 96
bipartisanship, 33, 62, 112, 127
Bitzer, Lloyd, 2–3, 149
Black Lives Matter, 14, 44, 63, 86
Blinken, Antony (secretary of state), 131
Bloomberg, Michael (mayor), 19, 87–90, 92
blue wall, 138
Booker, Charles (congressperson, Kentucky), 98
Booker, Cory (senator), 19, 84, 86, 91
Boston Globe, 71
Boushey, Heather, 123, 159
Bowman, Jamaal (congressperson), 55, 61, 63, 124–25, 137, 159–60
Brady, Kevin (congressperson), 108

brain, 12
Bravery Project, 46
Brexit, 37
Brisport, Jabari (senator, New York), 158
Brookings Institution, 93
Brown, Edmund "Pat" (governor), 136
Brown, Lara, 49
Burke, Kenneth, 2, 27–28, 103, 151
Burns, William (director of CIA), 133
Bush, Cori (congressperson), 55, 57, 61, 63, 124–27, 137
Bush, George W. (president), 24, 36
Buttigieg, Peter "Mayor Pete" (secretary of transportation), 15, 19, 84, 86–88, 91–92, 99

capitalism, 83, 106–7
Capuano, Michael (congressperson), 56
Carlucci, David (senator, New York), 156
Carter, James "Jimmy" (president), 59
Castro, Fidel, 110
Castro, Julian (secretary of housing and urban development), 84, 86
CBS News, 72–73, 112
censoring, 10
Center for Popular Democracy Action, 95
centrist, 16, 33, 41, 46, 50, 53–55, 60, 63–64, 83, 86–88, 91–95, 98–101, 105, 108, 112, 115, 120, 122, 124, 127, 130, 136–38, 149, 158, 161–62
charismatic populist, 142
Chavez, Hugo, 110
Christians Against Trumpism and Political Extremism, 46
civic engagement, 137, 149, 153, 161
civility, 26, 29, 141, 153, 163
Civil War, 30
class divide, 35
Clay, William Lacy Jr. (congressperson), 63
Clinton, William "Bill" (president), 11, 136

Clinton, Hillary Rodham (secretary of state and senator), 71, 91–92, 96, 98, 108, 113, 116, 121, 129–30, 143
Clyburn, James E. (congressperson), 54, 132, 137
CNN, 56, 69, 72–74, 78
cognitive bias, 145
Cohen, Larry, 131
Cole, Thomas "Tom" (congressperson), 52
common ground, 144
Communications Decency Act, 80
communicative action, 1
communism, 110
compromise, 6, 9–11, 16, 19, 22, 24, 36, 43, 48, 62, 102, 110, 124–25, 130, 137, 147, 152–54, 156, 159, 164, 166
confirmation bias, 76, 145, 150
conflict, 5, 10–13, 20, 26, 30, 37, 54, 68, 122, 124, 153, 162; intraparty, 23, 63, 107, 151; intratribal, 54
consensus, 3, 8, 13, 20, 100, 113, 124, 145
conservatives, 50; core, 31; country first, 31; market skeptic, 31; new era enterprisers, 31
conspiracy theory, 69–70, 80
Constitution, 7–9, 13–14, 35–36, 41, 49, 68, 153–54
constraints, 3, 8, 20–21, 75, 81, 107, 147–49, 154, 156, 163
consubstantiality, 28
Coons, Christopher (senator), 61, 118
Corker, Robert "Bob" Jr. (senator), 53
COVID-19 pandemic, 24, 37–38, 45, 49, 56, 78, 110, 1157, 126–27, 159
Crowley, Joseph "Joe" (congressperson), 61, 64, 158
Cuellar, Henry, 33
cult of personality, 142
culture wars, 24
cyberspace, 69, 81

Data for Progress (think tank), 92
de Blasio, Bill (mayor), 84

defund the police, 75, 101, 108, 137, 138, 148
Delaney, John (congressperson), 19, 86–87
deliberation, 3, 6, 81, 122, 151–52
democracy, 1, 3, 5–6, 8–9, 11, 19, 25–26, 35, 68, 74, 77, 79–82, 93, 95–97, 114, 136, 140–41, 143, 150, 153–55, 158–61, 163; constitutional, 26, 163; deliberative, 26, 158; direct, 1, 8; illiberal, 1, 25; mass, 8; participatory, 20, 77; pluralistic, 26; representative, 3, 20, 35, 67; rhetorical, 26; strong, 79; thin, 79
Democracy for America, 43, 56
Democratic National Committee (DNC), 88, 94
Democratic Party, 1, 4–5, 8, 11, 14–18, 20, 29, 32, 38–44, 47–48, 51, 53–54, 57, 59, 75–76, 78, 80, 83, 91–96, 100–1, 103, 105, 107–09, 111, 114–19, 121, 124, 128, 131, 133–37, 140, 142–43, 146–49, 152–53, 155–57, 159–60, 163. *See also* Democrats
democratic republic, 1, 147
Democratic-Republican Party, 51
Democratic Socialists of America, 42, 61, 107, 139
Democrats: bystanders, 33; conservative, 36, 39, 42, 47–48, 53, 55, 58, 83, 85, 89, 91, 103, 132, 159, 162; devoted and diverse, 32; disaffected, 32; establishment, 51; liberal, 11, 16–17, 42, 47, 63, 76, 100, 121, 127, 156; moderate, 51; opportunity, 32; progressive, 5, 45, 51, 55, 63, 65, 86, 114, 129, 136, 155; resist Trump, 36; solid liberals, 31–32, 61. *See also* Democratic Party
devil-terms, 108, 120
Devoted Conservatives, 22
digital curator(s), 80
discourse: persuasion, 2; public, 3, 6, 13, 21, 68, 152; rhetorical, 2, 4, 154, 158

division, 4, 9, 11–12, 27–28, 30, 35, 52, 72, 100, 103, 109, 116, 118, 144, 146, 150–51, 155, 157, 162
domestic terrorism, 50
Donnelly, Joseph "Joe" (senator), 53
Donovan, Joan, 76–77
Dorsey, Jack, 77
Dunn, Anita, 89
Dunning-Kruger Effect, 145, 146

Eastman, Kara, 130
echo chamber(s), 79, 81, 150
Edwards, John Bel (governor), 85
electoral college, 114, 123
embattled majority, 54
empathy deficit, 43
End Citizens United, 14
Engel, Eliot (congressperson), 63, 158
equality, 5, 29, 79
Erdogan, Recep Tayyip (president), 27
errors of omission, 146
exceptionalism, 37
Exhausted Majority, 23
exigence, 2–3, 5, 9, 12, 20, 50, 110, 141, 149
extremism, 23, 46, 138

Facebook, 74, 77–78, 82, 125, 128
fake news, 69, 72, 74, 76, 81, 140
Fallon, Brian, 62
Federal Communications Corporation (FCC), 77
Federalists, 67
Federal Reserve, 43
Feinstein, Dianne (senator), 62, 85
filibuster, 61, 114–115
filter bubble(s), 81
Fisher, Patrick, 42
FiveThirtyEight (website), 103
fossil fuel, 98, 111
four-party system, 36–37
Fox News, 69, 71–75, 78, 108, 140
fracking, 102, 111, 119, 129
FreedomWorks, 141
Freedom Caucus, 53, 64–65, 98

Fudge, Marcia (secretary of housing and urban development), 122, 132

Gabbard, Tulsi (congressperson), 19, 87
Galston, William, 93
Garcia, Kathryn, 140
Geevarghese, Joseph, 98
Generation "Gen-" X, 42, 58
gerontocracy, 41
gerrymandering, 114
Ginsberg, Ruth Bader "RBG" (associate justice of the supreme court), 114
Goehl, George, 101
Goldwater, Barry (senator), 9
GOP, 1, 31, 36–37, 40, 52, 61, 65, 691–70, 73, 123. *See also* Republican Party
Gorsuch, Neil (associate justice of the supreme court), 52
Gottheimer, Joshua "Josh" (congressperson), 85
Governing Republicans, 53
Graham, Lindsey (senator), 62
Green New Deal, 42, 54–55, 57–58, 61, 84, 89, 91, 94–95, 101–2, 111–12, 124, 135
Greene, Marjorie Taylor (congressperson), 49, 65
gun control, 15, 91

Haley, Nikki (united nations ambassador and governor), 141
Hannity, Sean, 71, 108–9
Harris, Kamala Devi (vice-president and senator), 5, 19, 84, 86, 91, 93, 95, 97–102, 105, 107–9, 111–12, 116, 119–20, 128
hashtag #DemExit, 15
Hatcher-Mays, Meagan, 62
hate groups, 80
Hauser, Jeff, 130–31
Haynes, Bruce, 36
Heinrich, Martin (senator), 133
Heitkamp, Heidi (senator), 36, 132

Herrera Beutler, Jaime (congressperson), 49, 65
Hoover, Herbert, 132
Humphrey, Hubert (vice president), 9
Hurricane Katrina, 41

identification, 4–5, 27–28, 42, 115, 149, 151–52. *See also* discourse, persuasion
identity politics, 5, 13–14, 41
ideology (-ies), 4, 9–10, 38–39, 41–42, 50, 54, 76, 82–83, 86–87, 128, 130, 155, 157, 163
immanent value, 5, 29
immigrant(s), 31, 121, 128
Immigration and Customs Enforcement (ICE), 85, 105
impeachment, 47, 49, 65
inclusion, 45, 123, 125, 155
independent blues, 143–44
Indivisible (organization), 43
Inslee, Jay (governor), 43
Instagram, 68, 82
insurgents, 140
insurrection, 48–49, 64–65, 72, 76–78, 140, 142–43, 150
intergroup violence, 151
internet intermediary, 80
intraparty discord, 96
intratribal hostility, 1, 33, 155. *See also* tribalism
Iraq, 24
isolation, 27; partisan, 10

Jackson, Andrew (president), 51
Jayapal, Pramila, 124
Jealous, Ben, 106
Jefferson, Thomas (president), 14, 17, 41
Jeffries, Hakeem (congressperson), 139
Johnson, Ronald "Ron" (senator), 141
Jones, Daniel J., 133
Jones, Mondaire (congressperson, New York), 101, 124, 156

Justice Democrats (political action committee), 55

Kasich, John (governor), 94, 128
Kavanaugh, Brett (associate justice of the supreme court), 62
Kelton, Stephanie, 159
Kennedy, Joseph "Joe" III (congressperson), 56–61, 71
Kennedy, Ted (senator), 24
Kerry, John (secretary of state), 60, 101–2
Khanna, Ro (congressperson), 98
Kibbe, Matt, 141
Klein, Ezra, 33, 68, 81, 135, 140
Klobuchar, Amy (senator), 19, 86–88, 91–92, 99
Knock Down the House (documentary), 55

Lamb, Conor (congressperson), 85, 124, 128–29, 139, 156
language, 2, 4–6, 25–28, 78, 135, 137, 144, 149–52, 161
leadership, 4, 24, 45, 46, 54, 62, 121, 126, 140, 142, 146, 153
Leahy, Patrick (senator), 133
liberals, 8, 11, 17, 35, 41, 44, 48, 55, 60, 86, 94, 98, 101, 108, 114, 121, 123, 126, 131, 133, 144, 157–59; democratic, 55; passive, 21; solid, 31–32, 61; traditional, 21, 135; white, 18, 39–40
liberalism, 84; constitutional, 25; hegemonic, 8
Libertarian, 51
Limbaugh, Rush, 72
Lincoln Project, 46
Linden, Michael, 159
Lipinski, Daniel "Dan" (congressperson), 55
Loeffler, Kelly (senator), 135
Lyft, 130

Madison, James (president), 7, 67–68

mainstream, 54, 64, 96, 114, 130; political, 1, 12, 40
majority: embattled, 55; exhausted, 134–135; mob, 8; partisan, 7; political power, 163; voters, 16
Make America Great Again (MAGA), 47, 143
Manchin, Joseph "Joe" (senator), 53, 58, 61, 85, 159
Markey, Edward "Ed" (senator), 55–60, 71
mass media, 5, 67–68, 72, 74, 77, 79
Maybe-Sometimes-Trump Democrats, 53
Mayorkas, Alejandro (secretary of homeland security), 122
McCain, John (senator), 53
McCarthy, Kevin (congressperson), 49, 65
McCaskill, Claire (senator), 36
McChesney, Robert, 77, 81
McConnell, Mitch (senator), 42, 61, 126, 159
McElwee, Sean, 92
McGovern, George (senator), 9
McGrath, Amy (senator), 98
McLuhan, Marshall, 68
mediation, 79, 150, 153; rhetorical, 1, 2
Medicare for all, 55, 57, 61, 89, 91, 94, 98, 101–3, 106, 112, 124–25, 130–31, 139
Melton-Meaux, Antone, 55
Menino, Thomas, (mayor), 60
Merkley, Jeffery "Jeff" (senator), 84
Middle East, 78
millennials, 41, 58, 84, 89, 107
Mitchell, Maurice, 33, 86–87, 95
mobilization politics, 147
Moderate, 22
moderates, 11, 14–16, 19, 22, 39–40, 48, 54, 57–58, 60–61, 71, 89, 91, 97, 103, 106, 122–23, 125–27, 131–35, 138, 142, 146–48, 154, 156–59, 161; Democratic, 16–17, 40, 85–86, 146, 159

More in Common (organization), 21, 134
Morell, Michael (senator), 133
Moulton, Seth (congressperson), 86
MSNBC, 7, 72–73

National Public Radio (NPR), 72–74
NBC News, 72–74, 109
Never-Trump Democrats, 53, 137
New Deal, 42, 45
The New York Times, 70, 72–74
Newman, Marie (congressperson), 55
news media, 69–70, 81, 143
newspaper(s), 67, 72
Nixon, Cynthia, 139
Nixon, Richard (president), 136, 157

Obama, Barack (president), 11, 24, 42–48, 84–85, 89, 98, 100, 113, 127, 131, 133, 156
Obamacare, 53, 89, 95, 110, 116, 118
O'Brien, Drew, 60
Ocasio-Cortez, Alexandria "AOC" (congressperson), 16–17, 54–55, 57–60, 63–64, 75, 84, 89, 93–95, 96, 101–2, 107, 111, 114, 122, 124–29, 133–34, 137, 158–59
O'Donnell, Norah, 112
oligarchy, 96
Omar, Ilhan (congressperson), 16, 55, 84, 126
One America News, 72
online radicalization, 78
O'Rourke, Beto (congressperson), 19, 84, 91, 99
Ossoff, Jon, (senator), 135
othering, 12, 35, 82, 135, 148, 152, 154
Our Revolution, 98

Parker, Kathleen, 71–72
partisanship, 6, 8–9, 12–13, 21, 23, 52, 69, 73, 75, 119, 127, 150, 157–58, 163
Passive Liberals, 21
Patrick, Deval (governor), 19, 87

patriotism, 107, 144, 153
Pelosi, Nancy (congressperson), 16–17, 42, 56–57, 60–61, 85, 103, 124, 136
Pence, Michael "Mike" (vice president), 111–12
People's Action, 101
Perdue, David (senator), 135
Perez, Tom, 53
Pew Research Center, 11, 30, 32–33, 37, 41–42, 48, 52, 69, 72, 90
Pocan, Mark (congressperson), 17, 84, 116
polarization, 5, 9–10, 12–13, 19, 23, 41, 48, 52, 64, 70, 81, 118, 122, 130, 136, 140, 144, 150, 163
Politically Disengaged, 22, 134
political parties, 1, 3–11, 13, 19, 21, 24–28, 30, 35, 38, 47, 50–52, 64, 69, 78, 81–82, 136, 140, 144–46, 148–49, 151–52, 155, 160–63
politics, 4, 6, 9, 19–22, 25–26, 30, 32–33, 36–39, 43, 47, 52, 67–68, 81, 83, 87, 99, 106, 122, 127, 135, 142–43, 151, 153, 155, 160–63
populism, 1, 7, 9, 21, 82, 91, 129, 142–43, 156, 165
populist alliance, 7, 47
populist ethos. *See* populism
populist insurgencies, 7
populist parties, 37
populist partisanship, 20
populist revolt, 51
Portman, Robert "Rob" (senator), 53
Prakash, Varshini, 102
presidential debate(s), 115–19, 129
President's Tribe, 52
Pressley, Ayanna (congressperson), 16, 18, 61, 84, 125–26
primarying (-ied), 5, 54–55, 60, 95
priming, 161
probabilities, 162
Progressive Activists, 21–22
progressive new guard, 84
progressive old guard, 84–85, 89
propaganda, 69, 82, 109

propagandists, 143
purity tests, 18

QAnon, 70

Rand, Paul (senator), 141
Raskin, Sarah Bloom (deputy secretary of the treasury), 131
Reagan, Ronald (president), 136, 157
RealClear Opinion Research, 143
Reclaim Our Party (political action committee), 46
red baiting, 110
Republican Party, 5, 8, 11, 19–20, 36–37, 40, 46–47, 50, 52–53, 64–65, 78, 105, 123, 129, 134–36, 140–43, 147, 149, 156–57. *See also* GOP
Republican Political Alliance for Integrity and Reform "Repair," 46
Republican Voters Against Trump, 46
resentment, 75
resist Trump, 151–153
resistance camp, 143
revenge, 75
revenge voting, 15, 108
Revolving Door Project, 130
rhetoric, 2–4, 10, 25–28, 45, 74, 82, 90, 93, 101, 113, 121, 148, 150–53, 161, 163; bipartisan, 53; invitational, 29, 152–153; political, 10, 39, 150
rhetorical analysis, 4
rhetorical discourse/persuasion, 1–2, 4, 154. *See* strategic discourse
rhetorical mediation. *See* strategic discourse
Rhodes, Ben, 44
Ricchetti, Steve, 131
Richmond, Cedric (congressperson), 131
Rockefeller, Nelson (vice president), 9
Rojas, Alexandra, 55
Roosevelt, Franklin "FDR" (president), 45, 100, 132
Rouse, Cecilia (Council of economic advisors, chair), 123
Ryan, Tim (congressperson), 19, 86

Sanders, Bernard "Bernie" (senator), 1, 7, 9, 11, 14–15, 19, 33, 43–45, 47–48, 52–53, 57, 61, 63–65, 75, 84, 86–102, 106–8, 111, 117–19, 121, 127, 130–32, 139, 157–58
Sasse, Benjamin "Ben" (senator), 49
Scarane, Jessica, 61
Schlesinger, Arthur Jr., 47
Schumer, Charles "Chuck" (senator), 60–61, 85, 114, 127, 158–59
scorched earth, 17, 41
self-determination, 5, 29
Senate Judiciary Committee, 63
Shaheen, Jeanne (senator), 59
Shahid, Waleed, 59, 159
Shakir, Faiz, 99
Shalala, Donna (congressperson and health and human services secretary), 54
Shorenstein Center on Media, Politics and Public Policy, 76–77
Silent Generation, 42
Sinema, Krysten (senator), 159
single-payer health care, 110, 118, 135
slanting, 27
social media, 5, 11, 17, 38, 54, 68, 72, 74, 77–78, 80–81, 86, 144, 150, 159, 161
social mobility, 35
socialism, 40, 42, 45, 54, 105–10, 112, 116, 119, 124
Spanberger, Abigail (congressperson), 40, 54, 85, 122, 124
Sroka, Neil, 43
Stand Up Republic, 46
stereotyping, 27
Steyer, Thomas "Tom," 87, 91
strategic discourse, 3
Strother, Colin, 33
student debt, 97, 101–2, 107, 126–27, 159
Sunrise Movement, 56, 58–60, 99–100, 102, 131
super progressives, 83
Super Tuesday, 18–19, 86, 99

Supreme Court, 52–53, 113–16, 135
Swalwell, Eric (congressperson), 86
symbolic interaction, 2, 25. *See also* discourse; discourse, rhetorical
systemic racism, 139

Tai, Katherine (trade representative), 122
Tea Party Republicans, 5, 47, 51–52, 64–65, 142
Team Trump, 54
the detached, 143–44
The Donald Base, 46
The Squad, 16–18, 54–57, 60, 126
Third Way (think tank), 122
Thomas-Greenfield, Linda, 122
Thunberg, Greta, 42
Tlaib, Rashida (congressperson), 16, 55, 84, 128
Torres, Ritchie (congressperson), 102
Traditional Conservatives, 22
Traditional Liberals, 21, 135
transition candidate, 44
treaties, 160
Trent, Corbin, 94
tribal membership, 22
tribalism, 3, 5, 9, 12–14, 21–22, 27, 30, 35–36, 47, 50, 78, 122–23, 135–37, 139, 142–44, 148–52, 154–56; amoral, 21; congressional, 51; dysfunctional, 5; generational, 41; identity, 13; interparty, 30; intraparty, 3–7, 12, 20, 23–24, 27, 30, 49, 65, 90, 120–22, 136, 141, 147, 150, 154, 160; mediated, 67; partisan, 1, 23, 75, 81, 129, 159, 162; political, 30, 50, 148–49; rhetorical, 5–6, 21, 26, 90, 154–55, 160, 162
tribalistic political communication, 149
tribe of Trump, 50, 104, 110, 141–42
tribe(s), 10, 12, 20–23, 29, 33, 38–41, 43–50, 53–54, 57, 60–61, 64, 69, 76, 78, 95, 108, 110, 120, 123, 129, 138, 142–44, 146, 151, 152,
156–57, 159–60, 162; Democratic, 43, 121, 126, 154; liberal, 60, 157; political, 14, 23, 30, 40–41, 46, 81, 118, 121, 129, 134–35, 141–43, 151, 162; progressive, 61, 152, 157; Republican, 43, 53, 64; rhetorical, 35, 108, 120; woke(-en)(-ness), 39–40, 84
Trotsky, Leon, 47
Truman, Harry (president), 136
Trump, Donald J. (president), 1, 7, 9, 13–16, 18–19, 21, 24, 31–33, 36–38, 45–50, 52–55, 60–63, 65, 69–72, 75–77, 88–100, 103, 105, 107–10, 113, 115–19, 121, 123, 125, 127, 129–30, 132–33, 135, 138, 140–42, 147, 150, 155–57; campaign, 76; fatigue, 128
Trump, Jr., Donald, 71, 109
Trumpism, 40, 42–43, 46, 75, 142. *See also* tribe of Trump
Twitter, 11, 15, 17, 68, 72, 75–77, 82, 90, 159
two-valued orientation, 27

United Nations, 42
University of Missouri, 14
University of Virginia, 14
Urbina, Maria, 43
US Capitol, 47, 49, 65, 76, 78, 140–41, 150

very progressives, 84–85
victimization, 75
Vilsack, Thomas "Tom" (secretary of agriculture), 132
violence, 7, 19, 24, 49–50, 67, 77–78, 108–9, 117, 134, 140, 151–53
Vox (website), 33

Waleed, Shahid, 131, 159
Wallace, Chris, 116–17
Walton, India B. (mayor), 157
Warnock, Raphael (senator), 135

Warren, Elizabeth (senator), 11, 15, 43, 56–59, 84, 86–87, 89–93, 95, 99, 101, 106, 114, 127, 130–32, 139
Washington, George (president), 8, 41
Washington Post, 70–72
Watts riot, 136
Ways and Means Committee, 108
Weber, Evan, 58, 99–100
Weber, Steven, 141
Wehner, Pete, 36
Weiss, Antonio, 159
WestExec Advisors, 130
Whig party, 30
Whitehouse, Sheldon (senator), 62, 127
Williams, Brian, 92
Wily, Maya, 140

woke(-en)(-ness), 156
Wong, Felicia, 159
Working Families Party, 33, 86, 95, 159
Wyden, Ronald "Ron" (senator), 133

Yang, Andrew, 19, 87
Yellen, Janet (secretary of the treasury), 123, 131
Young Delegates Coalition, 94
Young Turks, 72
YouTube, 58

Zuckerberg, Mark, 77

About the Author

Colleen Elizabeth Kelley is an associate professor of rhetorical communication at Penn State Erie, The Behrend College. Dr. Kelley holds a Ph.D. in rhetorical theory and criticism from the University of Oregon. Her previous books include *A Rhetoric of Divisive Partisanship: The 2016 American Presidential Campaign Discourse of Bernie Sanders and Donald Trump*; *Post-911 American Presidential Rhetoric: A Study of Protofascist Discourse*; and *The Rhetoric of First Lady Hillary Rodham Clinton: Crisis Management Discourse.*